Praise for
The Faith of Fifty
Baseball, Religion, and A........

◇ ◇ ◇

◇ "This book is a unique and deeply felt study of the game so close to the dreams and emotions of many generations. Through its compelling insights *The Faith of Fifty Million* helps bring further understanding to baseball's mystique, clarifying why this beautifully balanced game can be enjoyed at so many different levels." —Donald Honig, novelist, baseball historian, and author of *Baseball America*

◇ "A gem in every way. *The Faith of Fifty Million* is a wonderful and never boring addition to the serious study of the role that baseball has played in American culture and society. These essays make a distinctive contribution to the growing awareness that baseball had, and still has, a deep hold on the nation's psyche." —John Rossi, LaSalle University, author of *The National Game: Baseball and American Culture*

◇ "For those who think American baseball is just a game, think again. In stunning detail this collection of essays presents baseball as America's Civil Religion. The concept is fascinating and the scholarship rich in detail and imagination. Through all of the essays the reader gains a profound respect for America's love for the game, and with it, Americans' love of the 'American Way of Life.' Sports fans and students of religion and American culture will both find much to take from this superb collection. I know of no other book that treats the cultural phenomenon of baseball with such intelligence and dexterity." —Harry S. Stout, Jonathan Edwards Professor of American Christianity, Yale University

◇ "*The Faith of Fifty Million* is a lively, stimulating, and orig~~~ lection of essays presenting America's National Pastim~ religion and a cultural institution of conside~ not a work that sees the hand of God in the (ing individual performances but rather bring. to our continuing effort to understand the maj. and our culture." —Richard C. Crepeau, Unive   ..orida, author of *Baseball: America's Diamond Mind*

◇ "An incredible book, *The Faith of Fifty Million* scores in each inning— or essay. Captivating like a World Series game and illuminating like fresh exegesis, the essays consistently stimulate one's imagination and enlarge one's understanding of baseball, religion, and American culture. While acknowledging the imperfections of baseball and the inequalities in the economics of the game, the essays celebrate the contributions of baseball to the pursuit of racial justice in America, and they point to the unifying possibilities that the national pastime affords." —Joseph L. Price, Whittier College, author of *From Season to Season: Sports as American Religion*

◇ "Lively essays on American baseball by diamond-minded theologians whose artful blendings of insights from religion and the national game afford unique perspectives into our heritage. Like a sprightly nine-inning game, these nine essays will delight thoughtful fans." —David Q. Voigt, Albright College, author of *Baseball: An Illustrated History*

◇ "Graced by some wonderful photographs, this collection of essays will grip everyone interested in the "metaphysics" of baseball. The book will be especially appealing to those fans who think that the game has a religious significance. But they should remember a lesson from the theologian Horace Bushnell: sacralizing the secular can lead to the secularization of the sacred!" —Bruce Kuklick, University of Pennsylvania, author of *To Every Thing a Season: Shibe Park and Urban Philadelphia 1909-1976*

◇ "Saying 'baseball is a religion' has been, until now, nothing but a cliché. The singular accomplishment of *The Faith of Fifty Million* is to fill those words with meaning—specific, varied, and constantly surprising. For all those whose relationship to the greatest game is emotional, familial, inexplicable, or reverent, this book contains at least one essay that will provoke a response of deep recognition and satisfaction. Baseball has taught generations of intellectuals and scholars what it means to be connected to something bigger than one's self, something with origins shrouded in legend, a sacred history, saints and villains, and a future bright with hope but constantly threatened by the forces of modernity. In short, baseball has taught us, churched or unchurched, what it means to be religious. These connections, long mythologized, have finally been brought to light and subjected to scholarly scrutiny in these provocative and diverse essays." —Donna Bowman, Honors College, University of Central Arkansas

◇ "This important book offers exactly what the title promises; a look at American religious practices, the American civil religion, American culture, and American baseball and how each of these streams interact with the others to influence 'the American mind.' One might say that the connection between baseball and such lofty concerns has been over-stated in the past—but it can be understated as well, as this books shows.

We live in secular times, and so as we go about our lives, the myths, the legends and articles of belief that define life in America can easily escape us. Then, when a September 11 intervenes, Americans grasp the essential truth of this book; whether at work or play, whether going about our routines or when facing common dangers, and when facing defining moments in our lives, Americans recall the tenets of their distinct way of life, tenets expressed in and reinforced by their popular culture, their modes of worship and by their sports, particularly baseball." – David Eisenhower, Public Policy Fellow, Annenberg School of Communications, University of Pennsylvania, author of *Eisenhower: At War, 1943-1945*

◇ "This thoughtful collection of essays, which explores the symbiotic connection between baseball and American culture, deflates a few myths and burnishes a few others. It includes a meditation on statistics, a story of redemption, a morality tale, and paeans to diversity and opportunity. If that sounds like the script for a good ballgame, it's also the description of a lively and illuminating book." –Randall Balmer, Ann Whitney Olin Professor of American Religion, Barnard College, Columbia University

◇ "If *Bull Durham* celebrated "the church of baseball," this book demythologizes it. This diverse collection of essays probes the multiple ways that baseball reflects and symbolizes America's aspirations and dysfunctions. Yet, like the demythologizers of the Bible, the essayists retain a wistful hope that somehow, even though demythologized, baseball can retain its power to save us. For all who love baseball, this book will provide a provocative starting place for reflection about the religious meanings with which we have invested the game." –Richard B. Hays, George Washington Ivey Professor of New Testament, Duke Divinity School

◇ "Sport historians have long written about baseball and religion, but here is a most welcome examination of religion and baseball by students of religion. In treating such diverse topics as civil religion, sin and virtue, innocence, moral example and means of grace from a Protestant theological perspective, this unique collection of essays is an important addition to the literature on the historical role of baseball and Christianity in American culture." –Larry R. Gerlach, University of Utah, author of *Men in Blue: Conversations with Umpires*

The Faith
of Fifty Million

"It never occurred to me that one man could start to play with the faith of fifty million people . . ."

—F. Scott Fitzgerald, *The Great Gatsby*

THE FAITH
OF FIFTY MILLION

Baseball, Religion, and American Culture

Edited by
Christopher H. Evans and William R. Herzog II

Foreword by Stanley Hauerwas

Westminster John Knox Press
LOUISVILLE • LONDON

Book design by Sharon Adams
Cover design by Mark Abrams
Cover photo: Courtesy of The Sporting News. *All-Star Game at Candlestick Park with Huey Lewis and the News singing the national anthem, July 10, 1984.*

First edition
Published by Westminster John Knox Press
Louisville, Kentucky

This book is printed on acid-free paper that meets the American National Standards Institute Z39.48 standard. ∞

PRINTED IN THE UNITED STATES OF AMERICA

02 03 04 05 06 07 08 09 10 11 — 10 9 8 7 6 5 4 3 2 1

Library of Congress Cataloging-in-Publication Data

The faith of fifty million : baseball, religion, and American culture / edited by Christopher H. Evans and William R. Herzog II.—1st ed.
    p. cm.
    Includes bibliographical references and index.
    ISBN 0-664-22305-2
    1. Baseball—Social aspects—United States. 2. Sports—United States—Religious aspects. 3. Civil religion—United States. I. Evans, Christopher Hodge, 1959- II. Herzog, William R. II, 1944-

  GV867.6 j.F35 2002
  796.357'0973—dc21

                  2001046685

In Memory and Honor of David Nelson Duke (1950–2000)
Husband, Father, Teacher, Scholar, and Lover of the Elysian Fields

Contents

◇ ◇ ◇

Foreword

The Faith of Fifty Million has turned my world upside down. I was unprepared to face the personal and intellectual challenge this book demands of the reader. I suddenly felt sympathy for those who in 1919 read Karl Barth's *Commentary on Romans* and realized that life would never be the same again. I had heard rumors, of course, that all may not be as it seems. I had even read suggestions that the history may suffer from ideological distortions. But I was not prepared to face the ugly reality that reading *The Faith of Fifty Million* makes unavoidable. I am finally forced to acknowledge, to confess, that baseball, like life itself, has been and continues to be distorted by sin. I have lost my innocence.

Because I have suggested that the church best serves the world in which it finds itself through faithful worship, I am alleged to believe that Christians cannot be responsible citizens in democratic societies. I have often tried to counter these criticisms by pointing out that, of course, Christians can participate in American society and political life. For example, I have recommended that there are few things better that Christians can do in and for America than play and watch baseball. No matter how bad things get, I have always thought, at least we have baseball, the exemplary and crucial practice necessary for the creation of a politics shaped by the love of truth. Even though I refuse to sing, I do stand for the "Star-Spangled Banner" at baseball games.

Yet the essays in this wonderful book make clear that baseball is part of our fallen world. Indeed it seems that baseball, like the Congress of the United States, is the mirror into which we must look if we are to see ourselves—a sobering thought this book emphasizes. Therefore, if I am a critic of American civil religion, I must recognize that baseball, for better or worse, is the great exemplification of that religion. If I am a critic of American exceptionalism, American individualism, the American inability to face the racism of our past and present, I must be the critic of baseball. Indeed, if Christopher Evans is right—and I think he is—baseball is *the* outworking of the liberal Protestant hope for the kingdom of God to be realized in America.

All of which is an indication that this book is not only a serious book, but an important book for anyone trying to understand America and/or the continuing place of Christianity in America. A book about the relation of baseball, Christianity, and America risks not being taken seriously. The whole project seems too whimsical to be appropriately "academic." Yet this is a deadly serious book that profoundly probes the fears and the hopes shaped by the American love affair with baseball. I may not have wanted to know that Abner Doubleday did not create the game; I would have just as soon not known how Albert Goodwill Spalding transformed the game into the business it was and is; I really did not want to acknowledge that baseball exemplifies the Victorian male commitment to vim, vigor, and virility; I could have lived without the recognition that Shoeless Joe Jackson is a Girardian scapegoat; because I am a pacifist I would have rather not faced knowing that baseball was not only born in war, but has served the ends of war; yet the authors of these essays unrelentingly force a recognition of the truth about baseball and ourselves.

Nevertheless, these essays, hard and truthful though they may be, are not mean-spirited. The exact opposite is the case. These essays are hard and truthful because they are essays by lovers of the game. They love the beauty of the game. They love the intricacy and the details of the game that constitute its beauty. They love the time it takes to play the game. They love the history that the time it takes to play the game creates. They love the memories of the games as well as the memories baseball makes possible. They love the hard times of a losing season as well as the good times of winning. They know baseball is as much a game of failure as it is of success, and they would not have it otherwise. In short, these essays are written by fans—a status that comes only through perseverance and training.

I am also a lover of the game. I am also, in spite of what my critics may think, a lover of America. That I am intent on helping Christians rightly order our love of America to our love of God does not entail a rejection of America or baseball. Rather it means we must become, as this book insists we must be, truthful lovers. I believe, moreover, that learning to play or to be a fan of baseball can be one of the means through which we develop some of the skills commensurate with being a Christian. Christianity and baseball are, after all, sets of practices set in time to make time possible.

For me time began with the Dallas Eagles—Texas League, Double A baseball. I no longer remember the year but it was in the early fifties, when Red Murphy (who was already in his thirties) won twenty-eight games for the Eagles. Because of Red I learned there was something called the major leagues. It seems teams in the majors wanted to buy Red's contract. At that time the Dallas Eagles were an independent, so Red could have signed with a number of different teams. I vaguely remember he went to Milwaukee, where he pitched for the Braves. Suddenly Red made me part of a wider world. I began to read the newspaper religiously to see how Red was doing up in the "North." I understood that the "North" was where people lived who were called "Yankees" and whom I was told not to trust. It did turn out that you could not trust them—the Braves turned Red into a rather ineffective reliever.

I had identified with Red because I loved to listen to my father talk about his playing days. My bricklaying father had played at a semi-pro level. He was like Red—a thin-as-a-rail pitcher who relied on his fastball. Dad had even been on a team that had faced a young fastballer named Dizzy Dean. This was particularly important for me because I discovered that I could get the St. Louis Cardinals radio broadcast so I knew who Dizzy Dean was. That my Daddy had actually been in a game with Dizzy Dean made me proud to be his son. I fantasized that my Dad would have been a major leaguer if the war and needing to make a living had not gotten in the way. I loved to sit with him at Eagles games and have him explain the fine points of the game to me.

Like most Southerners, I believe I was playing ball before I learned to walk or talk. I desperately wanted to be as good as my father, but I was not blessed with natural coordination. For some reason I thought I should be a first baseman. I spent hours throwing a ball against the garage so I could learn to catch the damned thing in my oversized mitt, a mitt I had bought by growing and selling okra and black-eyed peas. In Little League I ended up being a catcher, but I was never the ballplayer I wanted to be. By college, however, I had become a pretty good left fielder in intramural softball. But the truth of the matter is I could never hit at any level. Yet like most avid fans, I played enough to learn that what appears to be a simple game requires the acquisition of extraordinary skills.

My history as a fan, I confess, is mixed. I admire those fans who never change their loyalty, but so often that depends on proximity. Growing up in Texas in the fifties meant no major-league team was close. I began following the Cardinals, then discovered the Cubs, but in graduate school in New Haven I became a Red Sox fan. I suffered through several seasons of futility until that magical year, 1967, when they won the pennant. That was the year Jim Lonborg won twenty-two, Carl Yastrzemski ("Yaz") was playing left, Tony Conigliaro was in center, Rico Petrocelli was at shortstop, and George Scott on first. Of course the next season was a nightmare, but what a season 1967 was. I no longer pretend to be a Red Sox fan—American League after all—but at least I remain a determined Yankee-hater.

Moving back to the Midwest meant, however, I accepted my destiny, returned to my roots, and again became a Cubs fan. This commitment came at the same time I was convinced by reading John Howard Yoder that I had to become a pacifist. I like to think being a Cubs fan and a pacifist are closely linked—namely, both commitments teach you that life is not about winning. Yet if life is not about winning, how do I explain I am now a Braves fan? The answer, of course, is the Durham Bulls, who were the Single A affiliate of the Braves when I came to Durham in 1984. Even before the movie *Bull Durham* (a movie I love), my son Adam and I were avid fans. Struggling to survive a troubled home life, we probably saw sixty games a season during our first years in Durham. The beautiful "Historic Durham Athletic Park" became our home away from home. We knew all the other faithful fans at the games. Adam even became a grandstand vendor selling drinks and hot dogs while also becoming a connoisseur of the game. I was extremely proud of him.

One season we almost won the Southern Division of the Carolina League because we had Jeff Blauser playing short, Ronnie Gant was on second, and David Justice came through on his way up. That is how I began to follow the Braves who, because of Ted Turner, were also on television in Durham. For whatever you say about Ted Turner, he learned the hard way to let Bobby Cox manage and thereby he became a better owner and person. Turner Television made it possible for me to follow the kids who had come through Durham. In the process I became a Braves fan. Of course I continued to pull for the Bulls. After all, that is where you find players like the thirty-two-year-old second baseman who will never make it to the majors but keeps at it even if it means playing Single A. Such players are the heart of baseball.

My love of baseball is inseparable from other loves in my life. Paula, now my wife, was not at all sure she wanted to marry me. When we began dating, she was only nominally interested in baseball. Of course our first date consisted of watching the Bulls play a Sunday afternoon game. Before long Paula found herself watching the Braves with great interest. One night as we were eating at the Flying Burrito, our favorite restaurant (which also sold burritos at the Historic Durham Athletic Park), Paula looked lovingly into my eyes, paused—indicating what she was about to say was serious—and said, "We are only three back." That was the moment I knew this was going to work.

I sometimes now think that Paula is more knowledgeable about the game than I am. I can never remember our pitching rotation, but she never forgets. She is even able to think ahead about which relief pitcher Bobby might use as a spot starter. Her attention to pitching may be due to her abiding attraction for Tommy Glavine. I could get jealous, but I like to think that at least one of the reasons she is so taken with Glavine is that Glavine reminds her of me. Glavine never gives in to a hitter. It does not matter whether the umpire is giving him the outside corner or not, he is not going to throw it down the middle. I would like to think Glavine's refusal to give in is not unlike the way I do theology—I refuse to give in to critics who think I am constantly off the plate.

My own love for the game makes it clear to me that the authors of these wonderful critical essays about baseball love the game. They know not all is well. Why do the Yankees keep winning? Why did anyone ever think round ballparks were a good idea? We all know that the designated hitter is not baseball. It is clear that the world has been ontologically off kilter ever since baseball has been played in Florida during the season (after all, Florida is for spring training). We are not quite sure what to make of the new ballparks that look good but turn out to be food courts with a field. Yet knowing all this, we eagerly await the start of each season with the unending surprises we know are in store. At this writing the Phillies are leading the Eastern Division by five games. Life is weird.

We also know learning to be a fan is at least analogous to learning to be a Christian. To be and survive Christianity requires the willingness to live by the ever new surprises of God. So it is not surprising that we will learn much about ourselves as Christians—what it means for us to survive as well as flourish as God's people—by attending to the relationship among our faith, baseball, and God. There is no better place to start those reflections than the essays that make up this book. So step up to the plate, dig in, and start reading.

STANLEY M. HAUERWAS

Acknowledgments

This book emerged from the editors' love for baseball, as a sport and out of our belief that the game illuminates significant patterns of faith and meaning in American culture. We are grateful to numerous people at Westminster John Knox Press who shared our vision and gave us the freedom to create this volume. To Nick Street we extend our gratitude for helping us flesh out this project in its embryonic stages and for enabling us to turn disparate ideas into a coherent book outline. To Ella Brazley, our project editor, we are thankful for her work in moving the book through its preparation for publication. We are especially grateful to our editor, Don McKim. Don's encouragement, critical suggestions, and friendship were indispensable throughout the process of compiling and writing this book. We could not ask for a better editor and partner in this endeavor.

Our love of baseball as a sport and as a topic for serious study has been supported by numerous people. We honor the memory of our parents, Arthur W. Evans, C. Chester Herzog, and Helen M. Herzog, for instilling in us a love for the game. To our spouses and children, Mary Herzog, Robin Olson, Dan and Catherine Herzog, Peter and Andrew Olson Evans, we give thanks for indulging our love of baseball—as a sport to be played and as a topic to be studied. We acknowledge the invaluable research assistance offered to us by the staff of the National Baseball Hall of Fame Library in Cooperstown, New York, under the direction of Timothy Wiles. Maribelle Reiss at Colgate Rochester Crozer Divinity School provided lifesaving word processing assistance, and Naomi Annandale, a student at the Divinity School, provided invaluable aid by compiling the book's index. Special thanks to Colin Kerr-Carpenter, whose excursion with one of us several years ago to the Baseball Hall of Fame served as a catalyst for one of the essays in this volume and helped spawn the idea for this book.

Also, we acknowledge the assistance of Bill Burdick at the Hall of Fame Library and Bob Mayhall of *The Sporting News* for many of the photographs that appear in this volume.

This book is dedicated to the memory of David Nelson Duke, who until his death in December 2000 served as a professor of religion at William Jewell College in Liberty, Missouri. David had planned to contribute an essay for this book. That task, however, could not be completed due to his courageous, but losing, battle against cancer. Although David could not make a "printed" contribution to this volume, his love for the Elysian Fields serves as the bond that ties each chapter together. Like David, we believe that baseball, like good scholarship, ties together passion and critical judgment that can feed our hearts and minds. We hope our readers will concur.

CHRISTOPHER H. EVANS
WILLIAM R. HERZOG II

1	2	3	4	5	6	7	8	9	R	H	E

Introduction: More than a Game:
The Faith of Fifty Million

Christopher H. Evans   *William R. Herzog II*

Baseball was born in the Elysian Fields of Hoboken, New Jersey, during the 1840s and, from its earliest days, has conveyed a sense of the mythical magic of its origins to generations of Americans. Baseball was always more than a game. In a mysterious and unexpected way, it captured the imagination of nineteenth-century Americans and rapidly became "the national pastime." This impulse explains, in part, the obsessive concern to keep baseball clean and above reproach, in spite of a good deal of evidence that it was a "no holds barred" brawl susceptible to the lure of gamblers' money. The public display of shock and disbelief that accompanied the revelation of the so-called Black Sox scandal witnesses to the faith of Americans in their national game. This wonderment is depicted in a scene from *The Great Gatsby* in which Jay Gatsby introduces Nick Carraway (the narrator) to Meyer Wolfsheim, a luncheon companion unknown to Nick. (Wolfsheim is a fictional version of the gambler Arnold Rothstein, who fixed the 1919 World Series.) After their lunch, Nick asks Gatsby about the man with whom they have just broken bread.

> "Who is he, anyhow, an actor?"
> "No."
> "A dentist?"
> "Meyer Wolfsheim? No, he's a gambler." Gatsby hesitated, then added coolly: "He's the man who fixed the World Series back in 1919."

"Fixed the World Series," I repeated.

The idea staggered me. I remembered, of course, that the World Series had been fixed in 1919, but if I had thought of it at all I would have thought of it as a thing that merely *happened,* the end of some inevitable chain. It never occurred to me that one man could start to play with the faith of fifty million people—with the single-mindedness of a burglar blowing a safe.

"How did he happen to do that?" I asked after a minute.

"He just saw the opportunity."[1]

The immensely popular game attracted gamblers from its very beginning. They were always the snakes in the idyllic garden threatening the Edenic innocence of the game and, in time, when they saw their opportunity, would precipitate its fall.

Like the cosmos of which it is a part, baseball was not created in a day. The Genesis account of creation puts it nicely: "In the beginning when God created the heavens and the earth, the earth was a formless void and darkness covered the face of the deep, while a wind from God swept over the face of the waters" (Gen. 1:1–2). From a biblical point of view, creation is as much a process as an accomplished fact, and the history of baseball reveals the same truth about the national pastime. Its fall at the hands of gamblers did not lead to its demise but to its transformation with the coming of another "babe"[2] who would redeem the game from its fallen past. At least, that is the orthodox version of the history of the game. Whether true or not, it points to the indisputable fact that baseball has survived more than one near-death experience and has been reborn many times during its history.

Baseball's enduring stature as a sacred symbol of American identity highlights how the sport occupies a unique crossroads between historical realities and popular myth. Baseball flourished because of its ability to convince Americans that to participate in the game, as a player or a fan, was to engage in the quintessential American experience. Although contemporary arguments abound that baseball is no longer the undisputed American sport, "the national pastime" continues to be perceived as an enduring symbol of America's unique past—and among some people a sign of hope for a better future.

In the context of American history, baseball was indeed more than a game. It was a sport that came to symbolize national virtues of freedom, justice, and equality. Within the popular imagination of Americans, baseball embodied the soul of the nation, distinctively historical yet uniquely transcendent. The repeated "resurrection" of baseball in American history reflects the faith of many that the game was a symbol of our national identity—that we are "one nation under God." This sacred mythology that baseball has created for itself within American history, one that Nick Carraway from *The Great Gatsby* evokes when he ponders the Black Sox scandal, serves as a way of uniting the disparate topics contained within this book.

This book reflects an attempt to understand the "sacred" meaning of baseball in American culture. Through historical analysis, ethical inquiry, and theological reflection, we seek to explore not only how baseball serves as a distinctive symbol of American identity, but how that identity reflects on personal and communal dimensions of religious faith in American life. From the outset we acknowledge the limitations of our effort. First, all of the authors are practicing Christians from different Protestant traditions. We do not say this apologetically, but to underscore that the themes represented by the authors reflect but one perspective on gauging the larger topic of religion, baseball, and American culture: "the faith of fifty million."

At the same time, the American Protestant experience seems an important lens by which to examine baseball. Protestant faith communions were responsible for shaping many of the dominant ideological suppositions that defined America historically as an intensely religious society.[3] Indeed, many of these Protestant suppositions, spawned since the days of New England Puritanism, live on in America today. Even though we speak of contemporary American religion in terms of its plurality, the term "Protestant work ethic" still resonates among those who know only vaguely the names of John Calvin or Max Weber. Historically speaking, the American Protestant experience was fraught with paradox. On one hand, faith communions as theologically distinct as Presbyterians, Methodists, and Baptists affirmed the importance of being part of a covenant community, citing how fidelity to one's neighbor symbolized fidelity to God. At the same time, the covenant idea was superceded by an appeal to the individual's conscience, in which the Reformation doctrine of "faith alone" served for many Americans as a "Bill of Rights" to defend individual liberty. To infringe on a person's ability to worship God in a manner consistent with one's beliefs represented a violation both of American democratic presuppositions and a violation of the Protestant belief that God's grace was sufficient to save even the lowliest sinner. This paradox between the individual and the community has led to numerous theological schisms in American religious history. Yet this paradox also has crafted a cohesive legacy among the faith traditions associated with so-called mainline Protestantism. Today the descendants of Cotton Mather, Roger Williams, Jonathan Edwards, Francis Asbury, Phoebe Palmer, Walter Rauschenbusch, and Martin Luther King Jr. struggle with how best to define the role of the community (often expressed in the United States through the language of denominationalism), while allowing individual members a diverse leeway of belief.

In a similar fashion, baseball as a sport has struggled throughout its history with the same paradoxical tension between the needs of the individual and the community. Although a team sport, baseball's persistent appeal relates partly to how the game elevates individual virtue. Even though professional baseball players, no less than other professional athletes, reflect equal amounts of greed when it comes to matters of salary, the American popular imagination has elevated baseball players to a quasi-mythical stature unmatched in other sports. In part, the fascination with baseball players reflects their deeds on the playing diamond. But it also reflects the deep-seated belief that baseball players are accountable to a standard of moral virtue that doesn't apply to other professional athletes. Baseball romanticized the ideal in American professional sports that one's fulfillment came not through individual achievement, but in helping your team win. No less a figure than former Governor of New York Mario Cuomo (a practicing Roman Catholic) made the theological observation that baseball's transcendent role in America related to how the individual found his fulfilment in service to the team (the community).

> The idea of coming together—We're still not good at that in this country. . . . In moments of crisis we're magnificent at it. . . . At those moments we understand community—helping one another. In baseball, you do that all the time. You can't win it alone. . . . You need all nine people helping one another. I love the idea of the bunt. I love the idea of the sacrifice. . . . Giving yourself up for the good of the whole. . . . You find your individual fulfillment in the success of the community—the Bible tried to teach you that and didn't teach you. Baseball did.[4]

Cuomo's assertion illustrates how baseball's mythology has been able to cast the game's history in ways that are strongly egalitarian. Baseball lore certainly valued natural talent. But it put even greater emphasis on a ballplayer's work ethic as a measure of his success (and character). The sport popularized the idea that even the lowliest utility player with a .170 batting average could be a "hero" if he performs his job well in a given situation and helps his team win. At the core of Cuomo's assertion rests the popular belief that baseball's uniqueness is predicated upon an inherent social equality—an equality shared by players as diverse in skill as Cal Ripkin Jr. and Crash Davis (the fictitious catcher in the film *Bull Durham* who was destined to spend the majority of his career in the minor leagues).

As much as baseball has promoted itself as a sport where all men are created equal, the realities of history have tested America's faith in that supposition. In part, what made the 1994 players strike so devastating for the public was that people had a difficult time comprehending that players could be so greedy as to betray the core values of the national pastime. If baseball embodies the virtues of sacrificing your own interests for the good of the team, as Mario Cuomo suggests, then why were so many players demanding more money? For the average baseball fan, many of whom have still not forgiven the players for the strike, the sense of betrayal was enormous. The players had not only betrayed the core values of the game, they had betrayed, in some unquantifiable sense, the nation itself. Few Americans at the time wanted to face up to the fact that professional ballplayers, like all athletes, perceived individual fulfillment not through a love of the game and a love for their team, but through a love of money.

As many of this book's essays reveal, however, often baseball's sacred mythology of individual and group fulfillment has been used to serve the interests of the rich and powerful, while at the same time claiming that the game's purpose was to serve the masses. And sadly, as many Americans continue to scapegoat ballplayers for their greed, few focus on the way that the contemporary baseball establishment, as was the case over a hundred years ago, has evoked baseball's sacred language as a way of preserving its own privileged economic status. Perhaps the most egalitarian aspect of baseball's history was the way club owners treated both superstar and utility player with an equal amount of contempt.

Similarly baseball's unique rise in American history was interconnected with distinctive popular mythologies associated with nineteenth- and twentieth-century masculinity. Although commentators like Ken Burns have argued with metaphorical grace that baseball is a sport for all Americans, historically baseball was a male sport, whose iconic cultural status was achieved by associating the game with "male virtues" of intelligence, athletic acumen, and technical skill. Despite the fact that women have played the game (and played it well) since its inception, baseball's uniqueness as "a game invented by boys and played by men" has been hard to reconcile with issues of gender equality. It might be true, as Ken Burns and others have noted, that baseball historically was played by all Americans regardless of race, gender, and class. Yet much of the history of professional baseball reflects how the game's economic interests were tied around the goal of keeping professional baseball a sport that would be played only by white men. Baseball has always promoted itself as a "fair game," where the only thing that mattered was talent. But the ideal of fairness often has been superceded by racial and gender discrimination.

However, this book also argues that the faith that Americans have put in baseball as their national pastime has at times been justified. Jackie Robinson's integration of the major leagues in 1947 is arguably the most significant event in the history of modern American sport. However, Robinson was not the only African American to integrate an "all-white" sport in the middle of the twentieth century, nor was he the first.[5] At the same time, his achievement is remembered, and continues to have powerful social ramifications today, because no other American sport has the symbolic meaning of baseball. Although in our era baseball has struggled to keep pace with the popularity of sports like football and basketball (and in many markets, ice hockey), Jackie Robinson's integration still represents a major event that transcends the realm of sports.

As it did a hundred years ago, the popular language of baseball continues to affect the social outlook of twenty-first-century America. Contemporary Americans may watch a variety of sports on a given weekday or weekend. Yet most would likely find it hard to find personal, communal, and transcendent meaning with terms like "blitz," "coffin corner," or "zone defense." However, they would likely find both a personal and social connection to words from the lexicon of baseball like "sacrifice," "safe," and "home." Mario Cuomo is ultimately right when he argues that baseball connects us to larger biblical-ethical morals related to how Americans ought to live together in community. To honor the individual, as you honor the community, represents an American virtue that is embodied historically, metaphorically, and theologically in baseball. Even though baseball has often fallen short of that ideal, the power of that mythology throughout American history needs to be taken seriously.

Like all arguments of a highly abstract nature, a case can be made that we have written something that cannot be quantified by scholarly analysis, and that what we are doing is merely another means of romanticizing sport beyond what can be proven through historical evidence. But at the same time, the authors of this volume, like many Americans, believe that baseball is more than a game. It is a mirror of our experiences as a nation, reflecting both our successes as well as our failures. Baseball is also a transcendent symbol, a sport that in its own way emerged out of its own mythical Garden of Eden. Today the national pastime continues to appeal to many who hope that the lure of the Elysian Fields will turn our hearts away from the world's despair, in order that we may glimpse a vision of a world better than our current one.

Part I of this volume includes two essays by Christopher Evans, both of which explore the relationship of baseball to civil religion and national identity. As an increasingly important part of the national mythology and civil religion, baseball confirmed what Americans wanted to believe about themselves and their common life. It did not mirror American life so much as it served as a projection for what was best in our national identity and most noble in our democratic ideology, and as an exercise in wish fulfillment, baseball captured the imagination and loyalty of Americans even as it was being captured by the dysfunctions of the culture that idolized it. As it became larger than life, baseball came to express something like an eschatological vision of American history and culture. The kingdom of God came to resemble, in significant ways, the kingdom of baseball. At its best, baseball served as a metaphor for the highest hopes and best dreams of America. The game itself was a meritocracy (so the theory went) in which a man could go as far as his ability could take him. On the baseball diamond, a man was not measured by his pedigree, his job, his wealth or poverty, his social status, or his education. Nothing mattered but the skill with which he played the game. Baseball was the people's game, as available to all as the freedom of America itself, a living embodiment of the promise of "life, liberty, and the pursuit of happiness." Of course, the popular view masked the hard realities of the game. The reserve clause prevented players from earning what their abilities could command on the open market. They were more akin to slaves whose labor was controlled by a powerful "plantation class" of owners who used and abused their players before discarding them when their skills began to fade or they were injured. In effect, baseball reproduced the relations of production already dominant in late-nineteenth-century and early-twentieth-century American life. The two essays by Evans in part I develop these themes more fully.

If the essays in part I deal with baseball as an American institution, the essays in part II focus on individual baseball players who came to be viewed either as saints or sinners, icons of our human potential or fallen humanity. In the early years of this century, Christy Mathewson served just such a role as the incarnation of "the Christian gentleman." He was contrasted with another pitcher of equal skill, "Ol' Pete," Grover Cleveland Alexander, whose life resembled the flawed hero of a Greek tragedy. In his essay, Donald McKim analyzes the theological themes embodied in their lives. In time, baseball players began to figure prominently in American fiction. Exploring the narrative potential of the baseball player as icon, Ernest Hemingway turned to the figure of Joe DiMaggio, whose fading years provide Santiago, the aging protagonist of *The Old Man and the Sea,* with a hero whose intimations of mortality resemble his own and comfort him in his long, futile struggle to bring home the big catch. The brilliance of a baseball career, even the great DiMaggio's, cannot disguise its evanescence or mask the great loss that accompanies aging, as bit by bit, we lose the vitality of our youth. All human achievement ultimately must come to terms with this inevitable loss. Harold Hurley analyzes Hemingway's use of Joe DiMaggio in his famous novel. In all three cases, baseball players' lives have served to illustrate what Donald McKim calls "the struggle for redemption, tragedy, loss, suffering, virtue, and character" common to our humanity. The lives of baseball players illustrate some major themes of Christian anthropology, as the chapters by Hurley and McKim indicate.

The difficulty with icons is that they may be more ambiguous than they seem. No one illustrates this ambiguity better than Shoeless Joe Jackson, who was, during his lifetime, vilified by the baseball establishment for his presumed role in the Black Sox scandal but has, in more recent times, been exonerated and seen as a scapegoat sacrificed to protect the interests of the owners and gamblers. Joe Jackson's strange journey stands as a reminder that, in baseball as in every other area of life, there is often a "cover story" and a "real story" underneath it. The story of Joe Jackson illustrates well the scapegoating theory developed by René Girard. It can help the inquirer comprehend the journey from scapegoat to icon illustrated by Jackson's life and his life beyond death. The essay by William R. Herzog II focuses on the journey of Shoeless Joe Jackson.

Almost from the first day of its creation, baseball has been associated with the "American dream" and believed to offer an embodiment of it. The history of baseball has served as one expression of Americans' search for the American dream. Part III explores how baseball has both fulfilled and frustrated that quest. Nowhere was the fulfillment of that quest more clearly visible than in 1947, when Jackie Robinson broke the modern color barrier, ending the long period of exile for African American baseball players. From 1947 forward, they would cross the Jordan and enter the promised land of major-league baseball in record numbers, fulfilling the vision of baseball's Moses, Moses Fleetwood Walker, the black player whose banishment from the game in the 1890s had led to the long exile of African Americans until another Joshua named Jackie appeared to lead them home. With the coming of Jackie Robinson, baseball fulfilled its prophetic promise by leading the way into a new future rather than colluding with America's racist past. The essay by Fred Glennon explores the prophetic moment precipitated by Jackie Robinson and Branch Rickey. The experience of women with baseball has been different. Although women participated in "a league of their own" during World War II and attracted an enthusiastic following, they were discarded as soon as the war was over. Even today, they remain largely ostracized from the game they helped to preserve during the national crisis caused by the war. Their banishment raises questions about the relationships between gender and power, often masked in the history of the game. The essay by Eleanor Stebner and Tracy Trothen explores this ambiguous legacy and fleshes out how women's experience might challenge the predominant masculine cultural values that have historically surrounded the game.

For all of the vicissitudes of its history, baseball has retained its distinctive place in American culture. The two essays in part IV explore the continuing lure of the Elysian Fields. Baseball continues to inspire generations of Americans because it remains a part of the spiritual journey of so many people. In an essay consisting of whimsy, fantasy, and history, William R. Herzog II examines how the power of a baseball memory from the past can evoke a biblical theme (the coming of Elijah) and disclose an eschatological vision. The concluding essay, by Tex Sample, explores a lifetime entwined with baseball and assesses its role in his spiritual autobiography. Both essays suggest why baseball will retain its privileged role in American life and culture and why its religious characteristics continue to inspire loyalty and devotion from generation to generation.

Many who cite the uniqueness of baseball's place in American culture frequently appeal to the words of the French scholar Jacques Barzun, who wrote, "Whoever wants to know the heart and mind of America had better learn baseball."[6] Recent scholars have critiqued Barzun's assertion, noting how his remarks often did not relate to the historical realities of twentieth-century American sports. Yet this book takes Barzun's words seriously. Indeed we believe that the sacred place of baseball goes beyond matters dealing with "the heart and mind of America." In a very personal and communal sense, we believe that baseball deals with matters of the soul.

Part I

Baseball and American Religion:
The Theological Quest for a National Identity

1	2	3	4	5	6	7	8	9	R	H	E

Chapter 1

Baseball as Civil Religion:
The Genesis of an American Creation Story

Christopher H. Evans

Why have countless Americans throughout the twentieth century zealously identified baseball as the country's national pastime? For A. Bartlett Giamatti, the former commissioner of major-league baseball, the game symbolized an intrinsic uniqueness that reflected on the character of America itself. Not long before his death in 1989, he wrote these words relating baseball to the core values of American culture:

> To know baseball is to continue to aspire to the condition of freedom, individually and as a people, for baseball is grounded in America in a way unique to our games. Baseball is part of America's plot, part of America's mysterious, underlying design—the plot in which we all conspire and collude, the plot of the story of our national life. Our national plot is to be free enough to consent to an order that will enhance and compound—as it constrains—our freedom. That is our grounding, our national story, the tale America tells the world.[1]

Many persons have debunked Giamatti's sentiments, seeing in his words a banal sentimentality that obscures more complicated historical realities. Baseball's coronation as the so-called national pastime was the product of a distinctive historical era and its future success, many have argued, had more to do with the zeal for economic profits on the part of a handful of baseball moguls, as opposed to any intrinsic grace inherent within the game. In fact, G. Edward White argues that there was nothing intrinsically "American" about baseball. Baseball "became the national pastime because those at the upper echelons of the sport as an enterprise consciously, and unconsciously, transformed it from a working class, 'rough,' urban sport to a game that simultaneously embodied America's urbanizing commercializing future and the memory of its rural, pastoral past."[2] The result of this paradox was the synthesis of an appealing baseball mythology, whereby "the game, instead of reflecting the historical and cultural context in which it came to prominence, was a timeless, even magical, phenomenon, insulated from the rest of life."[3]

At the same time, one cannot simply dismiss as whimsical sentimentality this statement of Giamatti, a man who gave up a career as a distinguished Renaissance scholar and Ivy League university president for a career in the establishment of organized baseball.[4] When one examines his words closely it is apparent that he is extolling the virtues of not just baseball, but America itself. Although he is vague in defining the specific contours contained in the storyline of "America's plot," he is very clear in articulating his faith that baseball accentuates such uniquely American virtues as personal liberty and collective freedom. For Giamatti, baseball is an embodiment of what scholars have defined as "civil religion."

Very generally, civil religion describes how Americans throughout the nation's history have created a collective national identity through bestowing sacred meaning on a variety of secular symbols, rituals, and institutions. Civil religion, in its many guises, seeks to relate how God bestows on America a unique place among the family of nations. Robert Bellah observed that the ethos of American civil religion was a desire to show how Americans had an individual and collective responsibility to carry out God's will on earth.

> Behind the civil religion at every point lie Biblical archetypes: Exodus, Chosen People, Promised Land, New Jerusalem, Sacrificial Death and Rebirth. . . . *It has its own prophets and its own martyrs, its own sacred events and sacred places, its own solemn rituals and symbols.* It is concerned that America be a society as perfectly in accord with the will of God as men can make it, and a light to all the nations (emphasis mine).[5]

Bellah's understanding of civil religion focused on the political dimensions of American history, especially looking at the rhetoric of

American presidents like John F. Kennedy and Abraham Lincoln. At the same time, one can apply Bellah's attributes of civil religion—consisting of sacred people, events, places, rituals, and symbols—to numerous institutions in American life, including recreational sports like baseball. Bart Giamatti's association of baseball to larger qualities of being American is more than an anomaly. It reflects a powerful historical sentiment that sees baseball as a quasi-sacred sign and symbol for all that is noble, virtuous, and unique about the American experience. One can argue that Giamatti, and others of lesser stature, go overboard in praising the virtues of baseball as a uniquely American game. Yet one would be remiss to dismiss this sentiment without wondering why so many Americans since the mid-nineteenth century proclaim baseball as the great arbiter of all that is exceptional about the American experience.

To understand baseball's appeal, one must come to terms with how the sport embodies a powerful symbolic hold on the lives of many Americans. At the center of baseball's symbolic power there resides a unique language of civil religion, proclaiming that the game can redeem America and serve as a light to all nations. It has been argued that baseball has lost popular ground in recent years to other professional sports in the United States, particularly basketball and football. At the same time, baseball continues to serve as the historical paradigm by which other professional sports in America are judged.[6] The very fact that so many commentators raise the question of whether baseball still deserves the national pastime moniker reveals that the game's hold on the American public is, to a degree, intrinsic.

That intrinsic quality, however, is not simply metaphorical or narrative, in the sense that Giamatti argues. The tendency to speak of baseball in such sweepingly nostalgic ways reflects the fact that baseball as an American institution arose from concrete historical circumstances. Edward White is correct in asserting that baseball's rise was a product of a number of distinctive factors emerging from the late nineteenth and early twentieth centuries. However, baseball's ascendency to its status as the national game depended on the ability of the sport's prognosticators to negate the factual realities surrounding the game's origins (or to rewrite the facts to suit their own purposes). Baseball became the national game because it succeeded in creating its own narrative tradition. At the core of that narrative tradition was a faith that the game was as pure as America itself.

Understanding baseball as a manifestation of civil religion is to marvel at a number of historical paradoxes that emerged in the nineteenth century. We see a game that was promoted for its virtues related to health and recreation, a game that women and children could play for fun. Yet it was also a "manly" game that required skill, muscle, and a zealous will to win. In its professional guise, baseball, in its early years, was a sport played mainly by poor immigrants who saw in the game a way to escape lives of poverty. Yet baseball was also an egalitarian game, whose prognosticators preached a gospel that everyone through hard work and perseverance had a chance to play and excel.

These paradoxes, however, point to one grand paradox: Baseball was a game for the world, yet its origin and genius were unequivocally American. Such a fervent faith in the inherent greatness of baseball not only enables us to see how the game served as an embodiment of a distinct civil religion. As we come to understand the historical paradoxes at work in baseball's emergence as the national pastime, we also confront a paradox among contemporary faith communities in twenty-first-century America. That paradox centers on the historical struggle of faith communions in America to continually redefine sacred meaning in ways that are perceived as transcendent, timeless, *and* intrinsically inherent within the American experience.

In the Beginning:
Baseball's Promise to America

Despite a professed love of tradition, Americans have been relatively selective in their appeals to the past. Unlike their counterparts in Western European nations, Americans have been fond of valuing historical rootlessness, often seeing virtue only in events that take place in the here and now. When tradition is evoked, it often appeals to a primordial past—a time of alleged purity and simplicity—that serves as a measuring stick to condemn all that is seen as impure and corrupt in the present. This tendency has been true in American politics and in religion—and it has certainly been true in baseball.

Such historical rootlessness tells us something about the chaotic state of religion in the United States during the nineteenth and twentieth centuries, which spawned thousands of movements that appealed to the heritage of primitive Christianity, while at the same time claiming a distinct uniqueness from all other historical antecedents. When Philip Schaff, considered the father of American church history, came to America from his native Germany, he was shocked by the historical mindset of his adopted homeland. Schaff drew the ire of many of his contemporaries by suggesting that the Protestant Reformation was not just a matter of God's divine revelation upon the lives of Luther, Calvin, and other reformers, but centered on how developments within the sixteenth-century Roman Catholic Church shaped the thought of these Protestant divines. For many church leaders in Schaff's time, it was arrogant to suggest that something as "pure" as the Reformation bore any theological relationship whatsoever to the corrupt vices of medieval Catholicism.[7] Yet the same historical shortsightedness that Schaff spent much of his career combating was evident in the nineteenth-century rise of baseball to its status as national pastime.

Baseball's nineteenth-century coronation as the national pastime demonstrates how a cadre of men ignored historical realities to create a timeless portrait of baseball as eternally American. This portrait became the centerpiece of baseball's role as civil religion that extends into our time.

Since colonial days, Americans played a variety of games of "ball." It was, however, the English game of rounders (as well as cricket) that holds the closest relationship to the modern game of baseball. Rounders was essentially a children's game, in which two sides played on a field marked by four posts (or bases). The feeder (pitcher) threw the ball to a striker (batter) who could reach base by hitting the ball in just about any direction on the playing field (there were no uniform foul lines in rounders so, in essence, a hit within the circumference of the entire field was considered a "fair" ball). The only way for the striker to be called out was to have the ball caught on a fly, or to be "soaked," whereby a fielder hit the runner with the ball. Americans in the early nineteenth century played a variety of games such as "old cat" and "town ball" that used variations of rules derived from rounders. The specific rules for these various games of "ball" reflected the proclivities of the regions, towns, and villages in the northeastern United States and New England.

Most historians consider the New York Knickerbockers, a team composed of up-and-coming New York City merchants, to have played the first "authentic" baseball games in the 1840s. However, it was through the efforts of an English-born journalist, Henry Chadwick (1824–1908), that baseball derived much of its current form. Born in Exeter, England, Chadwick emigrated to the United States with his family when he was a boy. A resident of Brooklyn, New York, he became one of the first professional sport journalists in the country. Originally a cricket player, Chadwick came of age at a time when a nascent baseball league was being spawned in and around New York City, with over twenty "base ball" clubs by 1860.[8] While baseball was being referred to as the "national game" by the beginning of the Civil War, it was largely through Chadwick's efforts that baseball was "united" around a common set of rules that set the parameters for the rise of professional baseball in the late 1860s.

Chadwick did more than just become a pioneer in the evolution of baseball's rules, including devising the "box score" for keeping track of individual and team performances in a game. He became baseball's first great evangelist, who devoted his writings to promote baseball as a morally pure and uniquely American enterprise. One of Chadwick's obituaries observed reverently that he devoted his life to the single-minded purpose "in keeping the game he loved pure and free from evil, . . . "[9] Not surprisingly, Chadwick was referred to by the baseball establishment as "the father of baseball."

A great emphasis in Chadwick's early writings was to differentiate baseball from team sports from his native England, especially rounders and cricket. While acknowledging that baseball derived from rounders, he was quick to argue that baseball, unlike rounders, was a "serious" game played by strong, athletic men. More than a children's game, baseball "requires the possession of muscular strength, great agility, quickness of eye, readiness of hand, and many other faculties of mind and body that mark a man of nerve."[10] Chadwick cited the superiority of baseball over rounders (and other sports) because baseball was, quite simply, a man's game. "But from this little English acorn of Rounders has the giant American oak of Base Ball grown, and just as much difference exists between the British schoolboy sport and our American National game as between the seedling and the full grown king of the forest."[11] From the beginning of its history, baseball's virtues were inextricably tied to the American male.

This focus on the virtues of an emerging American middle-class masculine identity can also be seen in terms of how baseball quickly supplanted cricket in popularity. In the early nineteenth century, the British national game of cricket enjoyed wide popularity in America, especially on the East Coast. However, the rise of baseball in the 1850s and 1860s was synonymous with the virtual disappearance of cricket in America.

The Faith of Fifty Million

In part, the growing popularity of baseball was associated with the fact that the game was time efficient, in that a ball game could easily be completed in a few hours (unlike cricket, where matches could go on for days). In an era where American middle-class men were drawing a separation between public vocational and private family identities, baseball's rise fit a growing American obsession with time management. "Americans had become an extraordinarily time-conscious people, impatient with delay, more and more regulating their lives by the clock at both work and play."[12] Although baseball, unlike later team sports in the United States, was not dependent on a time clock, the game, in actuality, became popular because one could find the leisure time to play. (This historical reality is ironic given that many commentators later praised baseball because it was one of the few sports not dependent on a time clock.)

Cricket's decline not only related to the complexity of that game, but to the perception that the British pastime, compared to baseball, was anti-democratic. Despite the fact that Americans from a variety of social classes played cricket in the early nineteenth century, it could not shake the label that it was a game for the aristocracy—not the masses. Baseball, on the other hand, quickly became associated as a sport for the masses, even as it identified itself with the virtues of middle-class life. As Charles Alexander observes, cricket seemed "incompatible" with the democratic ethos of America. "Thus the strident American nationalism of the period, in combination with the complexity and sophistication of cricket, meant that the British game would continue to find its followers mainly among a shrinking number of Americans with close ties to Britain."[13] In blunt terms, cricket was a feminine game for the gentile aristocracy. Baseball, on the other hand, was a game for hardworking men, regardless of one's social class.

Coupled with this masculine ethos, the rise of baseball, particularly as a professional sport, was connected to a belief that the game fostered intense, but healthy, competition. As historian Warren Goldstein observed, baseball's rise was built on a sense of geographical and psychological localism.[14] In an era when basketball did not exist and football was still an evolving game to be played primarily on college campuses, baseball was perceived as a sport that any man could play (at least in theory). Part of this perception related to the fact that the game could be played cheaply. All you needed was some sort of ball, bat, and a field to construct a diamond (the ability to turn outdoor space into a playing field was seen in itself as a sign of American ingenuity). Further, at a time when urban growth was changing America demographically, baseball turned competition into a matter of civic pride, creating intense rivalries between players from different communities. In Goldstein's words, "in a baseball game, offense and defense were not abstractions: they were the home club and the visitors, or our boys and the out-of-towners, or us and them."[15] Coupled by the growing rise of urbanization, baseball offered both the potential for economic gain for players and exciting entertainment for fans eager to show pride in their home team.

The rise of professional baseball in the 1870s and 1880s was centered on a belief, in theory, that it was one of the few sports in America that could be enjoyed by everyone—including women and children. Other professional sports existed at the time of baseball's ascendency (boxing, billiards, and horse racing were very popular). But these sports also had association with the basest features of American life, in particular, intemperance and gambling. What fueled the zeal of men like Henry Chadwick and early proponents of professional baseball was not only a desire that the sport be profitable financially. They were driven by the zeal to make sure that their beloved game did not fall victim to the evil vices lurking throughout America. Professional ball games drew on an urban fan base that frequently came from the same immigrant classes who graced the playing field. At the same time, baseball club owners and their public supporters, like Chadwick, were determined that the game balance both brawn *and* brain in a way acceptable to an emerging segment of late-nineteenth-century middle-class Americans.

By the 1880s, two independent journals, *Sporting Life,* published in Philadelphia, and *The Sporting News,* published in St. Louis, covered organized baseball on every level; from the major leagues to semi-pro clubs (the exception to this coverage was the network of African American baseball clubs that emerged by the 1880s). Although these journals covered other popular professional sports of that era, the majority of their printed space was devoted to the propagation of baseball. These journals not only provided their readership with substantial individual and team statistics. They also provided an ongoing series of editorials and articles designed to promote the sanctity and virtues of the game in a fashion that could be easily digested by a middle-class audience. A key feature in the language of these periodicals was the driving theme that baseball needed to be kept "morally pure" from all elements of intemperance and vice that existed in America.[16]

Such a task was difficult, as organized baseball was beset by "evils" on all fronts. Some of the problems did originate from gamblers themselves, and almost from the time that the National League was established in 1876, the game had to deal with the very real possibility that players would be tempted to throw games. Professional baseball dealt with other "moral" issues in its early years, such as whether or not ball games could be played on Sunday, or whether alcoholic beverages should be sold at games. But the greatest challenge to the game, one that struck at the heart of baseball's role as the national game, was the question of who would control the game's affairs: players or owners. From the standpoint of our time, it is easy to view the history of professional baseball in neo-Marxist terms, whereby a separate class of workers (players) has struggled to free itself from the oppressive yoke of ruthless owners (the bourgeois class). Yet for many baseball prognosticators living at the end of the nineteenth century, the issues were seen far differently. Although the ascendency of professional baseball owners virtually reduced ballplayers to a class of serfdom (culminating with the instigation of the so-called "reserve clause," which left a ballplayer's future squarely in the owner's hands), the control of the game by owners was seen as a necessary act to keep baseball safe from the vile grip of those elements in American society who sought to destroy the game. Both *The Sporting News* and *Sporting Life* became de facto supporters of baseball's owner establishment, seeing any move toward greater player independence as a threat to the sanctity of baseball as an organized team sport. Henry Chadwick, along with other writers, not only attacked the efforts of gamblers to soil the game (and the players who associated with them), but disdained players who complained that the owners violated their personal rights.

By the end of the 1880s, the organized baseball establishment propagated a consistent and powerful ideology about the game that was very much in step with the times. Baseball became the undisputed national game largely because it presented itself as a sport that reflected popular sentiments of Victorian middle-class maleness. In the eyes of its prognosticators, the game balanced rugged manliness and athletic acumen with social acceptability. The next step was to equate the game's origins with the ethos of America's national destiny.

Christopher H. Evans

Let There Be Baseball!
Baseball and American Exceptionalism

Despite the fact that Henry Chadwick pioneered a view that saw baseball as "the" American game, he never questioned the fact that baseball largely derived from the English game of rounders. By 1880, however, a new generation, while reverent toward Chadwick's stature as "the father of baseball," took the argument for baseball's uniqueness a step further. For this younger generation, baseball was not just America's game because it embodied qualities of manliness, teamwork, hard work, and fair competition. Baseball, it was argued, became America's game because these same virtues that made baseball a unique game were *the sole domain* of America itself. Baseball advocates were no longer willing to accept the fact that the game had its origins from rounders, not just because it was a child's game, but because rounders originated outside the United States. John Montgomery Ward, one of the most popular players of the 1880s (and leader in 1889 of a players' revolt that led to the creation of a short-lived "players' league") published a popular guide book in 1888 that reflected the heart and soul of this new ethos. In his book, *Base-Ball: How to Become a Player,* Ward not only discussed how to physically condition one's self as a baseball athlete, he also opened his book with a discussion concerning baseball's origins and ascendency as the national pastime. For Ward, baseball's early inception did not depend on rounders; it rested on the initiative of American youth. "I believe it to be the fruit of the inventive genius of the American boy. Like our system of government, it is an American evolution, and while, like that, it has doubtless been affected by foreign associations, it is none the less distinctively our own. Place in the hands of youth a ball, and they will invent games of ball . . ."[17]

Ward's explanation accentuated the paradox between the importance of baseball as manly labor with the virtues of child's play. While stressing the skill needed to compete in the game, he amplified the sentiment that baseball was a game that arose from the inherent genius of the American boy. "In the field of out-door sports the American boy is easily capable of devising his own amusements, and until some proof is adduced that base-ball is not his invention I protest against this systematic effort to rob him of his dues."[18] For Ward, baseball was not simply a game for youth; it was a game that reflected the inherent uniqueness of American male youth.

The twin virtues of baseball, as a rural "pastoral" game played by young boys and as a manly professional sport, came together around the remarkable career of one man, Albert Goodwill Spalding. Almost single-handedly, Spalding manufactured one of the great myths that remains to this day the centerpiece for understanding the civil religion of baseball: the belief that the game was "invented" in 1839 by the future Civil War hero General Abner Doubleday in Cooperstown, New York. The alleged invention of baseball by Doubleday not only gave to baseball a compelling creation story, it also gave the sport a sacred place of origin that corroborated claims that the sport was uniquely American. As Benjamin Rader notes, "As Jews and Christians have their Jerusalem and Moslems their Mecca, baseball fans now had their special place, the pastoral village of Cooperstown."[19]

Spalding traveled an unlikely road on his way to becoming the greatest baseball impresario of the late nineteenth century. Born in Illinois in 1850, he learned his baseball from a returning Civil War veteran in 1863. As a teenager Spalding was apprenticed to a grocery store in Rockford, Illinois, although his passion soon was diverted into playing baseball fulltime. By the early 1870s, he was a star pitcher for the Boston Red Stockings and later the Chicago White Stockings, until he stopped playing at the end of the 1876 season. But Spalding was destined for far greater things off the field than on the field. At the end of his playing career, he launched the Spalding Brothers Sporting Goods Company, which soon became one of the dominant sporting-goods enterprises in the world (not to mention the sole supplier of equipment for all of organized baseball). In 1876, Spalding became a part owner of the Chicago franchise, and by 1882, he not only had assumed complete ownership of the club, but had emerged as the dominant club owner in the major leagues. In 1901, amidst threats of player unrest, Spalding became president of the National League, holding that post until his retirement in 1905. As his biographer, Peter Levine, noted, Spalding had the ability "to recognize the possibilities for a personal gain and social purpose inherent in the promotion of sport, [he] acted on them in a manner that encouraged the commercialization of sport and its transformation into a significant social institution in America."[20]

Spalding's career as a baseball mogul was characterized by two interconnected traits: a desire to make money and a desire to promote baseball. One of the highlights of his career came after the 1888 baseball season, when he assembled a group of major-league all-stars to play a series of exhibition games against his Chicago White Stockings on a six-month world tour. Despite the fact that Spalding lost money on the tour, the enterprise received a great deal of attention in the pages of *Sporting Life* and *The Sporting News*. Referred to as "baseball missionaries," Spalding's teams literally circled the globe, playing in Australia, Egypt (in the shadow of the Great Pyramids), Italy, and France, and concluding with a series of exhibition games in Great Britain. While the touring party was treated with respect by their host countries, the game received a largely mixed reception. Upon the tour's return to the United States in April 1889, however, a gala celebration was organized in a New York City restaurant, attended by figures such as Mark Twain and Theodore Roosevelt. The highlight of the evening occurred when National League President A. G. Mills rose to speak. Reacting to the British critique that baseball was no more challenging than rounders, Mills extolled the virtues of baseball as an American game to which the audience responded enthusiastically, "No rounders! No rounders!"[21]

Spalding's grand finale in the promotion of baseball, however, was still to come. In his retirement, he became obsessed with the idea of having an "official" history of baseball published, one that would clearly show that baseball's origins were solely American. His initial choice to write the book was Henry Chadwick, now an octogenarian but still highly revered throughout the baseball establishment and a close friend of Spalding's. Although Chadwick agreed to take on the project, Spalding made it clear that he wanted to have a say in the book's content. He reminded Chadwick of the need to complete the book in an expeditious fashion, commenting a bit tersely, "You are not going to live forever."[22] As much as Chadwick may have wanted to heed Spalding's admonition to avoid aging, it proved impossible. After Chadwick's death in April 1908, Spalding did not bother to look for another author; he took it upon himself to write the history.

The book, *America's National Game,* published in 1911, is as much the biography of Spalding's rise to power as it is a story of nineteenth-century baseball. Emerging as an archetype hero in a Horatio Alger novel, Spalding's rags-to-riches story parallels the emergence of baseball as an honest, clean, and completely American game. As Benjamin Rader notes, the book reads as a "morality play in which the forces of good repeatedly triumphed over the forces of evil."[23] The book presents Spalding's account of baseball's wars against gamblers and players in a highly moralistic tone, taking a patronizing tone toward players' uprising and asserting over and over again that baseball was not just a "clean," corruption-free sport, but that baseball's cleanliness related to larger American virtues of hard work, temperance, and missionary zeal. The book is filled with much dubious history (including Spalding's assertion that during the presidential election of 1860, Abraham Lincoln found out about his electoral victory while playing a game of baseball). The cornerstone of Spalding's history of baseball, however, was the now famous assertion that Abner Doubleday "invented" baseball, while a boy growing up in Cooperstown, New York, in 1839.

Baseball's great creation story reflects Spalding's unflinching zeal to prove the Americanness of baseball's origin. At the time he conceived of his baseball history in 1905, Spalding hatched the idea of forming a commission that would have the responsibility of investigating the origins of the national game. Made up mostly of his friends and associates in the National League, the committee did no research but used the sporting media to issue a "call" for letters from persons still living to provide firsthand accounts that could clarify baseball's origins (ironically, Henry Chadwick was not a member of the committee, even though he was probably the best living source concerning the early history of baseball). Instead the committee followed a series of arcane leads from persons all over the country, claiming to know the true story behind baseball's authentic origins (including one story that baseball originated as a drinking game). Even *The Sporting News,* a periodical that gave uncritical support to Spalding and other baseball moguls in the past, questioned the authenticity of the claims being considered by the commission. "Any Tom, Dick, or Harry with a possible bull and con story can make a 10-strike with this alleged commission," the magazine complained in December 1905.[24]

Nevertheless, in the summer of 1907, Spalding found the golden nugget he was looking for. His attention was called to a letter written by a mining engineer in Denver, Colorado, who claimed that Abner Doubleday interrupted a marble game with a group of boys to draw a diagram of a baseball diamond and then gave an explanation of the game's rules to the young boys. Not only did the letter say that Doubleday drew the design for the baseball diamond, but the writer also claimed that the original drawing was in the possession of a "Mr. Wadsworth," an elderly gentlemen living in New York City. From the moment he learned of the letter, Spalding pushed the commission to pursue the Doubleday theory. "Reminding its members of Doubleday's exploits as a northern officer during the Civil War, he added that 'it certainly appeals to an American's pride to have had the great national game of Baseball created and named by a Major-General in the United States Army.'"[25] To make matters even more interesting, the commission's chair, former National League President A. G. Mills, a man who felt just as passionately about proving baseball's American origins as did Spalding, not only had served with Doubleday in the Civil War, but was part of the general's honor guard at his funeral in 1893. Although the commission never received any confirmation on the story from the mysterious Mr. Wadsworth, the commission issued its report anyway in December 1907, stating as its first and primary point that "Base Ball had its origin in the United States," and second, that "the first scheme for playing it, according to the best evidence obtainable to date, was devised by Abner Doubleday, at Cooperstown, New York, in 1839."[26] Even though most people close to the baseball establishment were highly dubious of this assertion (Henry Chadwick, who died only a few months after the report was issued, had reportedly viewed it as a joke between himself and Spalding), the Doubleday claim went largely unchallenged for several years.

Even when conclusive proof was presented that Doubleday had nothing to do with baseball's origins, it didn't matter to organized baseball. In 1939, to mark the so-called centennial of baseball, the Baseball Hall of Fame opened in Cooperstown. To commemorate the occasion, the U.S. government issued a statement commemorating the birth of the national game.[27]

As comical as the Doubleday story seems in hindsight, its emergence represented the culmination of defining the ethos of baseball as the American national pastime, and also helped codify baseball's role as a distinct manifestation of civil religion.

Baseball as Civil Religion

Francis Richter, editor of *Sporting Life* magazine, remarked around the turn of the twentieth century that baseball was more than just a game. It was "a great sport, representative and typical of the people who practice it . . . one that stimulates all the faculties of the mind; keenness, invention, perception, agility, celerity of thought and action, adaptability to circumstances—in short all the qualities that go to make the American man the most highly organized, civilized being on the earth."[28] Richter's assertion, like Bart Giamatti's almost a century later, speaks to the same theme. Baseball was the national pastime because it represented, in some fashion, the "soul" of America.

Understanding the connection between baseball and civil religion rests in how arguments for the game's origins and popularity led proponents to speak of baseball as a uniquely transcendent phenomenon—yet a phenomenon that was grounded in the ethos of America itself. The emerging late-nineteenth-century ideology of baseball as the national pastime follows the pattern of what Martin Marty calls a "priestly civil religion." As he reveals, "when the language of civil religion shifts from talk about the promise *to* America (from a transcendent deity) to the promise *of* America, and national self-transcendence, the signal of priestly civil religion is raised."[29] Yet at the same time, the civil religion of baseball made its own selective use of deity language, turning baseball, like other institutions in the nation, into an instrument to carry out God's will on earth.

How can these attributes of civil religion be fleshed out in baseball, and what do they suggest to us about contemporary efforts of those like Bart Giamatti to canonize baseball as an intrinsically American game? The rhetoric of baseball as civil religion suggests that Giamatti was accurate when he noted that baseball was part of "America's plot." But baseball's plot developed in ways in the nineteenth century that had little to do with how he later envisioned the American ethos of the game.

First, the civil religion of baseball was rooted in the consistent paradox that the game was to be played by boys but mastered by men. Many of the attributes Spalding attached to baseball had to do with the way that the sport contributed to the development of individual virtues—virtues that Spalding believed were inherently American. "I claim that Base Ball owes its prestige as our National Game to the fact that as no other form of sport it is the exponent of American Courage, Confidence, Combativeness; American Dash, Discipline, Determination; American Energy, Eagerness, Enthusiasm; American Pluck, Persistency, Performance; American Spirit; Sagacity, Success; American Vim, Vigor, Virility."[30] More succinctly, the playing of baseball "demands Brain and Brawn, and American manhood supplies these ingredients in quantity sufficient to spread over the entire continent."[31] In an age synonymous with the virtues of "rugged individualism," baseball crafted its own symbols surrounding the uniqueness and virility of American manhood, symbols that have acted in particular to keep two groups outside the parameters of organized baseball: women and African Americans. For

Spalding and for many of his contemporaries, baseball was only meant for "the sterner sex" to play. "Base Ball is too strenuous for womankind, except as she may take part in grandstand, with applause for brilliant play, . . ."[32] Spalding's perspective was hardly unique, as he articulated a dominant middle-class Victorian perspective that put women in the stands and not on the playing field. Such athletic exertion on the part of the fairer sex was simply anathema for the male middle class of that time.

Even as contemporary commentators wax poetically about the unique skill and acumen required to play baseball, it is necessary to remember how the language of masculinity has been used over the years to shut other Americans out of the game. In the case of African Americans, who suffered over sixty years of exile from the playing fields of organized baseball, the issue of exclusion centered not on brawn, but on brains. In 1945, just prior to the announcement that Brooklyn Dodgers owner Branch Rickey had signed an African American, Jackie Robinson, to play for the Dodgers organization, Larry MacPhail, owner of the New York Yankees, gave expression to the prejudices of many white Americans by noting in a *Sporting News* editorial that, in his view, few blacks were qualified to play in the major leagues, because they lacked "the technique, the co-ordination, the competitive aptitude and the discipline usually acquired only after years of training in the smaller leagues."[33] In the mythology of baseball civil religion, baseball trained young American boys in the virtues of hard work and perseverance; yet it was apparent from the perspective of many late-nineteenth-century baseball moguls that that ideal would and should not apply equally to all Americans.

Second, while baseball requires unique athletic skills, the civil religion of baseball connected the origins of baseball to a sense of pastoral purity. Although it took God seven days to create the world, it took Abner Doubleday only one day to create baseball. In Spalding's history, baseball out of necessity evolved out of the "pastoral" garden of Cooperstown; its fall from grace was represented by the efforts of both players and gamblers to compromise the integrity of "clean" competition. Yet the game's redemption occurred because of the wise and benevolent leadership of baseball men (led by Spalding) who proved that ballplayers could not "at the same time direct both the business and the playing ends of the game."[34] From Spalding's perspective and others within major-league baseball, the future of the game in the early twentieth century looked promising because the game had once again achieved an Eden-like state, reflective of its pure American origins. In an article written to commemorate the twenty-fifth anniversary issue of *Sporting Life,* the magazine's editor, Francis Richter, compared baseball's purity to that of his news weekly. "No unclean or doubtful advertisement is ever to be found in 'Sporting Life' columns to bring offense to men, blushes to women or evil suggestions to youth—thus making the paper safe for boys, acceptable to their elders, and fit for admission to any family circle whatsoever. We say, advisedly, that 'Sporting Life' is not only one of the cleanest papers issued, but that it is absolutely the cleanest paper on earth. . . . But what more fitting than that the one absolutely honest professional sport on earth should have the cleanest organ?"[35] Baseball rose to prominence in a historical era when white middle-class Americans literally believed that cleanliness was next to godliness. Instead of viral germs or bacteria, baseball's cleanliness meant that it was free of the vilest toxins of class and culture that would pollute and corrupt middle-class sensitivities.

Ironically, this theme of purity was also used by Spalding and his allies to advocate for abolishing Sunday bans on organized baseball games. "I know it is the one day in the week when a great many of those who care for the game can have leisure, without too great loss, to witness the sport. . . . I know that boys and men, by hundreds and thousands, who regularly patronize Sunday ball would be engaged in practices much more inimical to their wellbeing if no games were played on Sunday."[36] The idea that baseball was and is somehow intrinsically and morally pure has reflected a powerful mythology throughout the course of the twentieth century. At the height of the infamous Black Sox scandal, when eight Chicago White Sox players went on trial for allegedly conspiring with gamblers to throw the 1919 World Series, the sentiment of baseball organs like *The Sporting News* was zealous in its call for a renewed "cleansing" of the national game. Bemoaning the "moral degradation" brought upon baseball by the accused ballplayers, the magazine called for a renewed effort to rid the game of those who would corrupt it. As *The Sporting News* noted, not without a tinge of moralism, "we are not forgetting that 'while the light holds out to burn, the vilest sinner may return . . .'"[37] Even as organized baseball was a sport connected directly to urban America, the image of idyllic purity and primitive simplicity was always used to accentuate the sport's exclusive American identity.

Finally, the civil religion of baseball permeated with a zealous patriotism that connected the exclusive claims of American uniqueness to world redemption. For Spalding, the values of manliness, teamwork, competition, brains, and brawn inherent in baseball reflected the larger genius of American society. When Mark Twain spoke at the banquet honoring the homecoming of Spalding's touring teams in 1889, he noted that there was an irony about trying to bring baseball "the very symbol, the outward and visible expression of the drive and push and rush and struggle of the raging, tearing, booming nineteenth century . . . to places of profound repose and soft indolence."[38] For Twain, baseball's values reflected the uniqueness of American society, a uniqueness that would be impossible for other nations to fully understand and embrace. Yet baseball's virtues were also synonymous with American virtues, in particular that the game, like the country, was governed by a just God. When a leader in the Chicago National Guard gave an address honoring Spalding's traveling teams, he invoked "baseball's role in making 'men that we are proud of.'" The same speaker called America "'a country mighty in people of courage'" and urged his audience to "'help . . . God in building up a country of men all powerful in protecting a country such as this. Long life to baseball and athletics. Long life to the National Guard. Long life to America, the freest land on earth.'"[39] This sentiment strikes at the heart of another one of the roles for a priestly civil religion: Americans are a nation under God whose greatness is ordained by an almighty creator.[40]

For Spalding and for many of his contemporaries, baseball embodied what was sacred about American society. "The genius of our institutions is democratic; Base Ball is a democratic game," he wrote. And even though the rest of the world couldn't measure up to American standards of manliness and virility, baseball was a means to show the world what it was like to be American. For Spalding the ascendency of American international prominence in the second half of the nineteenth century was inseparable from the march of baseball to its status as the national game. "Ever since its establishment in the hearts of the people as the foremost of field sports, Base Ball has 'followed the flag.' It followed the flag to the front in the sixties [the Civil War], and received then an impetus which has carried it to half a century of wondrous growth and prosperity . . . and wherever a ship floating the Stars and Stripes finds anchorage today, somewhere on a nearby shore the American National Game is in progress."[41] As turn-of-the-century politicians believed in America's manifest destiny and as American Protestant leaders believed in "Christianizing" the masses, so baseball symbolized an American faith

The Faith of Fifty Million

that the world could be subjugated by the superior values of the United States. Baseball symbolized not only American uniqueness, but in its own way reinforced a message that God was on our side.

A Lost Faith?

Like those who criticized Philip Schaff for suggesting that the Protestant Reformation had any historical connection to Catholicism, baseball's nineteenth-century prognosticators were set to re-create the game's past in a way that the sport embodied its own distinctive proclamation of Americanism. For just as New England Puritans believed that they served as a light to all nations, so did the civil religion of baseball preach its own gospel of redemption, whereby those who "believed" would experience through the game all that was unique and righteous about America. Organized baseball became its own priestly cult, using the game not only to promote the American virtues of the sport but to use those virtues as a way of limiting access to membership in the cult.[42]

Fortunately, there are also examples of movements within baseball that have turned baseball's sacred language against itself, seeing the game's call of American uniqueness as a summons to open the game up to greater participation among the nation's (and the world's) citizens. Nevertheless, many who have advocated for change in baseball's power structure throughout the years have linked their struggle to the larger theme that baseball is intrinsically American, standing for fairness, community, and equality. To paraphrase from Martin Marty, America is a nation under God, but God expected more of a chosen people than of others.[43] As represented especially by the struggle of men like Jackie Robinson to integrate organized baseball, the theme of baseball being intrinsically "American" has, at times, been a redemptive theme that has set the tone for the rest of society.

But even in those occasions when baseball has served as a social compass for the rest of America, baseball's appeal to pastoral purity has often come at the expense of seeking to understand the larger sources of "tradition" from which the game arose. Enshrined on a plaque in the Baseball Hall of Fame Library at Cooperstown is an inscription by Bart Giamatti reading, "Baseball is one of the few enduring institutions in America that has been continuous and adaptable and in touch with its origins. As a result baseball is not simply an essential part of this country; it is a living memory of what American culture at its best wishes to be." From one angle of American history, Giamatti's statement is totally false. Baseball certainly was a grand game in capturing the public's imagination in the nineteenth century, with its conception of team competition, its rivalries, and (much like professional wrestling today) its propagation of heroes and villains. But it also reflected the ethos of a nation that saw itself on the move, a nation that would supplant others by virtue of the superiority of its government, its culture, and even its forms of recreation. When we at the dawn of the twenty-first century speak of baseball as the national game, we are paying homage more to the residue of a sacred mythology concocted by a relatively small number of persons, as opposed to anything that borders on realities that can be quantified (after all, one could easily argue that a sport like basketball requires greater athletic and intellectual acumen to play than baseball).[44] There is nothing wrong in claiming that baseball has an intrinsic appeal related to larger metaphysical, philosophical, or theological realities, so long as we are cognizant of the fact that these intrinsic appeals emerge from historical realities.

Like contemporary Americans who cannot conceive of Christianity without the virgin birth or the factual reality of the creation narrative in the book of Genesis, baseball still evokes upon America the exclusive claim that it is the only definitive national pastime. In part, these claims of exclusivity are reinforced by the fact that the game can appeal to a "sacred mythology" of the past—something that other sports in America simply cannot evoke.

Similar to the arguments used by many Christian communities in American religious history, who extolled the unique virtues of their beliefs as representing the one, true faith, baseball was remarkably successful for a long time because it propagated a claim that it offered to Americans a unique gift of imputed righteousness that no other sport could offer. In a time when few other professional team sports existed, or had the ability to appeal to middle-class virtues in the same fashion as baseball, it was easy for baseball to make exclusive claims about its greatness. In our era of increased pluralism in professional sport, it is not so easy for the game to claim an exclusive hold on the nation's soul.

Yet all is not hopeless for those who come to baseball seeking redemption. For some, baseball will always just be a consumer product, something to manipulate in order to make money. Others will take the language of A. G. Spalding and his contemporaries and recast baseball's sacred mythologies in ways that suit their own personal ends. Others, however, will see in the game's imperfect and soiled history the opportunity to become more than what we are today. Just as baseball has served its priestly role in American culture, so too out of the game has come the cry of a few voices in the wilderness of a prophetic hope. For these visionaries, baseball was not just a means of celebrating the virtues of American greatness. Baseball was a means of holding out hope that Americans, regardless of class, race, or gender, could discern the fuller meaning of the words "liberty and justice for all."

The cynic might call this perspective myopic; the baseball fan and the person of faith might call this perspective saving grace.

1	2	3	4	5	6	7	8	9	R	H	E

Chapter 2

The Kingdom of Baseball in America:
The Chronicle of an American Theology

Christopher H. Evans

"Then I saw a new heaven and a new earth; for the first heaven and the first earth had passed away, . . ."

Revelation 21:1

Recently, I made a pilgrimage to Cooperstown, New York, home of the Baseball Hall of Fame. Walking through the Hall of Fame players' gallery, I stood next to a father who reverently pointed out to his son the plaques of the great players he cheered for as a kid. Listening to this man talk about the likes of Bob Gibson, Sandy Koufax, Mickey Mantle, and Willie Mays made me search my own memories of the players I revered as a kid. In its own way, Cooperstown invokes for the baseball fan a feeling of transcendence, a sense that one has entered into a timeless realm of heroic deeds and eternal bonds between parents and children. For a few precious hours, my visit to Cooperstown transported me into a realm where the stresses of my own life seemed insignificant. For an all-too-brief period, I had entered the kingdom of baseball.

Since the 1988 motion picture *Bull Durham,* it has become fashionable to speak of baseball's significance in American popular culture as analogous to an institutional religion—what the Annie Savoy character in the film calls "the church of baseball." To speak of the "church of baseball," as David Chidester observes, is to reveal how the game embodies the qualities of an organized religion. "Like a church, with its orthodoxy and heresies, its canonical myths and professions of faith, its rites of communion and excommunication, baseball appears in these terms as the functional religion of America."[1]

The church of baseball metaphor helps one understand the mythological appeal of baseball in American popular culture. There exists, however, another metaphor to understanding baseball's place as America's "national pastime." It is a metaphor equally rich in symbolic meaning, but one with much deeper and visible roots in America's theological past. It is a metaphor sculpted by one of the most important doctrines in the history of American Christianity: the kingdom of God.

Within American religious history, especially within American Protestantism, the kingdom of God doctrine affirmed that America was a divinely anointed nation—a nation judged by a righteous God. Historically, the kingdom of God expressed hope that God would transform human and institutional relationships. In H. Richard Niebuhr's words, "The kingdom of God in America is neither an ideal nor an organization. It is a movement which . . . appears in only partial and mixed manner in the ideas and institutions in which men seek to fix it."[2]

Niebuhr's characterization relates to how baseball at the turn of the century embodied a distinctive liberal-Protestant theological vision: *the kingdom of baseball.* For many, caught up in the liberal-Protestant currents of the turn-of-the-century Progressive Era, baseball epitomized both a faith in America's unique standing as a nation and the hope that the game could open a door leading to a better future. The kingdom of baseball contributed to the game's mythic stature by depicting the sport as a transcendent phenomenon that enabled Americans to clarify their nation's past, embrace a shared vision of the present, and affirm a common hope in the future.

The roots of the kingdom of baseball reveal how baseball embodied the residue of a distinctive liberal-Protestant theological worldview—a residue that contributed to the popular mythology of baseball as a uniquely American phenomenon. A critique of the kingdom-of-baseball metaphor reinforces two themes. The kingdom paints a portrait of a distinctive American theology, a theology that reflects the historical worldview of the era that spawned it. The kingdom of baseball also transcends its historical context, reflecting the possibilities and limitations of a peculiar theological vision of American culture. At the beginning of the twenty-first century, the kingdom of baseball in America accentuated the sins of the past, but also points to the hope of a better future.

The Kingdom of Baseball in Historical Context

Baseball's coronation as the American national pastime represented the convergence of a number of historical factors in the mid- to late-nineteenth century.[3] The game reached the height of its public identity as the national pastime during the turn-of-the-century Progressive Era.[4] In an era defined by a variety of social-reform initiatives, baseball became a symbol of postmillennial liberal-Protestant zeal that contributed to the personal and social uplifting of all Americans. Turn-of-the-century Protestant church leaders preached a gospel of a new millennial civilization, where faith in the kingdom of God meant faith that the virtues of an Anglo-Saxon civilization would spread the Gospel and lead to unprecedented social advancement in the western world. In short, baseball encapsulated Protestant hopes to usher in the kingdom of God in America.

These hopes were especially evident among many church leaders associated with the social gospel movement in the United States. Church leaders, like Josiah Strong, Shailer Mathews, Washington Gladden, and Walter Rauschenbusch, shared a vision that the task of Protestant Christianity was to build "the kingdom on earth." Washington Gladden reflected this vision fervently when he commented that the kingdom of God was the controlling factor for all personal and social transformation. "Every department of human life,—the families, the schools, amusements, art, business, politics, industry, national politics, international relations,—will be governed by the Christian law and controlled by Christian influences. . . . The complete Christianization of all life is what we pray for and work for, when we work and pray for the coming of the kingdom of heaven."[5] The emergence of baseball as the American national pastime reflected Gladden's faith that popular amusements, like baseball, served as clear signs of God's kingdom on earth. These liberal-Protestant hopes laid the foundations for the kingdom of baseball.

There were three predominant themes within the rhetoric of liberal-Protestant, Progressive-Era reformers that point to the origin of the kingdom of baseball in America. These themes mirrored baseball's enshrinement as the national pastime during the late-nineteenth and early-twentieth centuries. First, Progressive Era liberals were united behind a strong vision of social progress, where social reform initiatives were viewed as movements closer to the kingdom of God. This progressive ideology reveals itself in terms of how Protestant liberals equated the advancement of the kingdom with the pastoral virtues of rural life.

The theological liberalism of the social gospel epitomized the tendency of Progressive Era reformers to speak of how rural-pastoral virtues could "Christianize" the excesses of urban America. In Gladden's words, the kingdom could be brought to the hearts of an ailing humanity, "just as the spring is here when the crocuses open and the violets and the spring beauties are first in evidence."[6] Social gospelers shared a strong faith that rural-pastoral virtues would "Christianize" cities by "cleansing" and "sweetening" the excesses of urban-industrial life. For social gospelers, like Gladden, God's kingdom was synonymous with the idyllic virtues of small-town America.[7]

The construction of major-league baseball's first generation of "permanent" steel and concrete ballparks between 1909 and 1915 reveals an important dimension of this pastoral ruralism. G. Edward White observes that the steel parks, besides being safer than their wooden predecessors, were viewed as providing stability and aesthetic beauty to growing urban centers.[8] The construction of these new ballparks echoed the sentiment behind turn-of-the-century Progressive Era zeal that spawned the development of urban public parks throughout the United States. Social gospelers like Walter Rauschenbusch saw these parks as a sign of how rural virtues could redeem the excesses of the city. Through the support of "enlightened moral sentiment," Rauschenbusch observed that recreational urban parks were "beginning to offer sand-hills for the little children, swimming baths in summer, skating in winter, music on holidays, gymnastic apparatus, and open-air games. Instead of warning people to 'keep off the grass,' they are bidding the inflow of people."[9] The social gospel fed the Progressive Era drive to redeem urban areas. The first wave of permanent ballparks emphasized this urban "redemption" on a grand scale.

The permanent ballparks accentuated another aspect of this pastoral ruralism in that bringing the kingdom of God upon the earth was the task of middle-class elites. Although professional baseball for much of its history was a sport played by the working class, the new ballparks enhanced the image that the game was a uniquely middle-class institution. The new ballparks were designed to attract the middle class *and* to make working-class fans mindful of higher cultural values. Ben Shibe, the owner of the Philadelphia Athletics and whose name graced the first permanent ballpark in 1909, commented that Shibe Park was " 'a lasting

The Faith of Fifty Million

monument; built to endure, with a grandiose beauty that should express continuing prosperity and assured advance."[10] Baseball offered Americans something beautiful and artistic that contributed to an enlightened social order. As one historian observed, "The creed of the old ball game stood for fair play, gentlemanly virtue, self-reliance, middle-class decorum, community pride, and rural traditions."[11]

Second, turn-of-the-century liberal Protestantism believed baseball embodied the virtues of Christian recreation. The obsession of many social gospelers with positive models of recreation mirrored a general trend of the Progressive Era.[12] By the late nineteenth century, liberal clerics saw popular amusements like baseball as a means of developing moral character. The Rev. Charles Sheldon, author of the famous social-gospel novel *In His Steps,* affirmed baseball as an American symbol of hard work and youthful zeal—all virtues of the Christian life.[13] For many secular and religious Progressives, baseball was a spiritual tonic that offered solace and relief to a tired and "overworked" nation.[14]

The emphasis on baseball as a recreational tool went beyond promoting healthy lifestyles, however. For many liberal Protestants, to play baseball (especially for young boys) was to learn important lessons essential to Christian moral development—lessons necessary to survive the growing complexities of twentieth-century life. "Amusement is not only a great fact and a great business interest, it is also a great factor in the development of the nation character," observed Washington Gladden. Gladden's comments reflected a shared assumption among liberal-Protestant leaders who believed that popular amusements like baseball developed models of masculinity for young boys and adolescents. Through baseball, "the robust virtues are nurtured under the discipline of work; if the diversions can be kept healthful, a sound national life will be developed."[15]

Baseball's language of masculinity reflected a spirit of Protestant triumphalism that being a Christian was about winning. Shailer Mathews, dean of the University of Chicago Divinity School, affirmed that vision by observing that baseball modeled for the Protestant middle class the importance of playing on a winning team.[16] In this regard, the New York Giants star pitcher Christy Mathewson, "the Christian Gentleman," was the ideal representative for the kingdom of baseball in the early twentieth century. Mathewson showed Americans that being a Christian did not preclude being a fierce competitor, and most of all, a winner.[17] No better affirmation of this Protestant worldview can be found than through the words of baseball's greatest turn-of-the-century promoter, Albert G. Spalding. In comparing baseball to the "genteel," feminine qualities of Great Britain's national pastime, cricket, Spalding asserted that baseball demanded intelligence, physical ruggedness, and mental toughness. "Base Ball, I repeat, is War! And the playing of the game is a battle in which every contestant is a commanding General, . . . who having gained an advantage, must hold it by the employment of every faculty of his brain and body, by every resource of his mind and muscle."[18] Spalding's outlook reflects the tenets of the "muscular Christianity" movement, popular in many Protestant reform circles in both Great Britain and the United States at the turn of the century. For "muscular Christians," healthy athletic competition signified the virtues of male ruggedness and Protestant piety.[19] Baseball's connection to the development of healthy American males was noted in a 1919 Protestant Sunday school publication. "[Baseball's] problems, its ethical and social questions are the big questions to him. . . . In the game his conscience will be tried, his will tested, his ideals strained. If the [Sunday] school cannot help him in the experience that is so real, so vital and so potent for his life, how can it help him to live as a religious person?"[20]

Finally, baseball embodied what many liberals saw as the chief cornerstone of the kingdom of God in America—a faith in Christian democracy. In spite of the fact that social-gospel liberals like Gladden, Mathews, and Rauschenbusch differed significantly on matters of a just political-economic order, they were united in a common faith that American democracy represented the embodiment of the kingdom of God on earth. To see the Christian church as a democratic institution was to reclaim, they thought, the church's true identity as an apostolic faith community. In this regard, baseball was not just a game that depicted an abstract belief in American creativity. The game served as an illustration of how Americans from different class and ethnic backgrounds could work cooperatively to build a better society—striving for a shared vision of the kingdom of God. Citing baseball as the perfect embodiment of teamwork, Gladden observed that the essence of Christianity could be taught to those who grasped the cooperative aspects of the game. "So you need not expect to convert any man to Christianity unless you can show him Christianity at work in human society. . . . The team work is all there is of it."[21]

The Faith of Fifty Million

Segments of liberal Protestantism, reflected notably in the tradition of the social gospel, saw part of its mission to train future generations of Christian men for leadership in the church and society. Susan Curtis illustrates that social-gospel leaders repeatedly affirmed baseball as the perfect model for an emerging twentieth-century society. With its emphasis on cooperation and the need to master the intricacies of the game, baseball modeled a democratic Christian commonwealth that many social gospelers yearned to create. "Life on the diamond raised ethical and social questions, tried young consciences, tested adolescent wills, and strained youthful ideals."[22]

The uplifting of social progress, healthy masculine recreation, and democratic virtues served as cornerstones of a Protestant vision for the kingdom of God. Baseball embodied the ends of the kingdom of God to bring Americans together under the rubric of a male-Protestant worldview. In many respects, baseball served as an ideal alembic in which social and cultural differences would disappear. The baseball writer Hugh Fullerton summarizes this liberal-Protestant hope by affirming that baseball "is the greatest single force working for Americanization."[23] For Fullerton, like many Protestant church leaders, Americanization meant conformity to the cultural norms of white-Anglo-Saxon Protestant America. This assimilationist perspective, however, did not include women and African Americans. As one historian reflected, "The national pastime encouraged people to think that the United States was a democratic country where *all white men* were entitled to equal social justice, equal political rights, and equal opportunities for advancement" (*italics mine*).[24]

Kenesaw Mountain Landis, baseball's first acting major-league commissioner, affirmed the essence of the turn-of-the-century kingdom of baseball in America by noting that "baseball is something more than a game to an American boy. It is his training field for life work. Destroy his faith in its squareness and honesty, and you have destroyed something more—you have planted suspicion of all things in his heart."[25] The culture of turn-of-the-century Protestantism saw the kingdom of baseball in a way that the game embodied hope in a divinely inspired future. That future vision, however, was very conservative, as social and cultural differences were minimized and ignored, absorbed within a white-Protestant cultural worldview. What is most revealing today is the resiliency of this uniquely turn-of-the-century Protestant vision of the kingdom of baseball.

Christopher H. Evans

The Kingdom of Baseball Today

Many contemporary commentators proclaim baseball's death as the American national pastime. However, signs of the kingdom of baseball in America are everywhere. We see signs in the fact that so many major- and minor-league ballparks built over the past decade are styled after the classic parks built in the Progressive Era. We see signs in the way that baseball has been depicted as a vehicle of supernatural transformation in contemporary popular culture, including films and novels. We see signs of the kingdom of baseball in the way that scores of contemporary writers and scholars depict baseball as a symbol of personal and social transformation.[26] John Thorn, noted author on baseball and American culture, captured a predominant sentiment by affirming baseball's status as an enduring symbol of hope for Americans. "[Baseball] is the game of our past, our nation's and our own; it is the game of our future, in which our sons and daughters take their places alongside us, and replace us. It reflects who we have been, who we are, and who we might, *with the grace of God,* become" (italics mine).[27]

Thorn's imagery strikes deep into the American imagination. His characterization resonates powerfully with the historical mythology that the kingdom of baseball offers Americans a unified vision of the future. In effect, Thorn affirms a central ideal of the kingdom of baseball—that the game is an agent of some type of redemption for Americans.

At the same time, the twentieth century had not been kind to the kingdom of baseball. History has shown that baseball is not impervious to the social problems that have plagued twentieth-century America. Baseball has been beset by fierce battles between players and owners. It has embodied excesses of greed, reflected by recalcitrant owners who steadfastly resist any innovation that they fear will take money out of their pockets and by ballplayers whose escalating salary demands not only put them at odds with owners, but with fans. Most especially, the game has been torn apart by the sins of racism, epitomized by the galvanic struggle of Jackie Robinson and other African Americans to integrate the game in the late 1940s.

No greater indictment of the kingdom of baseball's failure can be found than professional baseball's mass exodus from the very centers in America that it was enshrined to redeem: the cities. Professional team franchise movements to predominantly white, middle-class suburbs in the 1950s and 1960s saw the death of most of the great early-twentieth-century "permanent" major-league ballparks. By the end of the 1960s, the rural-pastoral game that Americans once believed could redeem their cities was in full retreat from the very centers it was enshrined to save. Given these historical realities, is the kingdom of baseball simply a metaphorical relic of America's past?

In a review in *Christian Century* of Ken Burns's 1994 PBS documentary *Baseball*, David Heim warned readers about the sin of inflating the "mythic, quasi-religious themes" in sports. "We want [sports] to provide lessons for life, metaphors of some larger reality, stimulants for the emotions. Sports encompass all those things, but the danger in concentrating on them is that we trespass on the true mystery and the source of fascination: sports are fundamentally useless. . . . Work is not accomplished, mouths are not fed, the world is not improved, but we want to do these things anyway."[28]

Heim strikes a cord of truth. By embellishing baseball in myth, we risk losing a grounding in any kind of historical discourse, enslaving ourselves to a myopic portrait of the past. However, part of the significance of the kingdom-of-baseball metaphor at the beginning of the twenty-first century is how it focuses attention on the often ambiguous relationship between "history" and "memory." Historian Bruce Kuklick affirms that even romantic memories of the past have the power to recreate better incantations of the present. "We know from experience that at some time a dismal past has turned into a better present. And we know that a terrible here-and-now may not truly indicate a final condition for us or for our community."[29] John Thorn adds that baseball has manifested hope in a better future through a delusional sense about contemporary realities. "There is nothing terribly evil in this, for the lie is sometimes all that sustains the dream. Undelivered promise is, when viewed one way, the tragedy of both the nation and its pastime; viewed another, it is the measure of their souls—an uncaring nation or game would feel no compulsion to rationalize its failures."[30] America's great social prophets in the twentieth century have understood the truth behind Kuklick's and Thorn's assertion. Without a unified vision of a better future, a vision clear enough to hold together a disparate following, social movements collapse and die. Baseball allows diverse groups of Americans to feel as if we share a common past, destiny, and purpose. A place like the Baseball Hall of Fame is meaningful because it provides Americans from a variety of backgrounds with a sense that we embrace a unified destiny, within a largely fragmented society.

Christopher H. Evans

At the same time, however, the kingdom of baseball, like early-twentieth-century liberal-Protestant theology of the kingdom of God, fails to take into account the social, ethnic, and cultural differences that fragment our society. Like the kingdom of baseball, the liberal-Protestant legacy has insisted on the imperative for evolutionary social progress in America. It has ignored the differences that fragment Americans along the lines of gender, race, ethnicity, class, and culture—insisting that these differences can be absorbed within the great American mythology of "the melting pot."

What is most missing from the kingdom of baseball is an embrace of Martin Luther King Jr.'s vision of the "beloved community." King's beloved community relied on earlier Protestant notions of the kingdom of God by insisting that all Americans were tied together within an interconnected fabric of a common destiny, the imperative that we are all linked to a common American "dream." Yet he pushed beyond the parameters of the kingdom of God by insisting that a truly just society required redemptive suffering from both victims and oppressors. The most radical aspect of King's beloved community was a belief that living together as one people didn't just mean meritorious sacrifices of those victimized by oppression. It required those with power to sacrifice that power in hope that both oppressed and oppressor would experience redemption. Challenging the optimism of white-liberal Protestantism, King argued that historical time was neutral to the plight of humanity. Time became redemptive only when individuals pushed constantly for the moral imperative of change. Baseball's tragedy mirrors America's in that the game's history reflects a persistent faith in evolutionary change, at the expense of embracing the transformative vision of redemptive suffering that King's beloved community demands. It has replicated the sin of liberal Protestantism, summed up by H. Richard Niebuhr's famous admonition, "A God without wrath brought men without sin into a kingdom without judgment through the ministrations of a Christ without a cross."[31]

These tensions within the kingdom of baseball are depicted in the contemporary fiction of Canadian author W. P. Kinsella. His book, *The Iowa Baseball Confederacy*,[32] tells of a titanic ball game in 1908 between a team of minor-league all-stars and the world champion Chicago Cubs. Set in the fictitious rural town of Big Inning, Iowa, the game is played against the backdrop of Progressive Era America that would make social gospelites like Shailer Mathews and Washington Gladden proud. But as the game stretches into a two-thousand-plus inning affair, and as days turn into weeks, the players engage in their battle—oblivious to the fact that their idyllic surroundings are being washed away by a torrential flood.

The game is orchestrated by Drifting Away, the spirit of a Native American chief who uses baseball as a weapon of revenge against the white descendants responsible for his wife's murder. "Baseball is the one single thing the white man has done right,"[33] he explains to the book's main character, Gideon Clarke. Drifting Away admires the order, ritual, and harmony produced by the game. At the same time, he exploits these rituals to expose the absence of true community in white America.

As the town is literally erased from historical memory by the flood, a group of people called *The Twelve-Hour Church of Time Immemorial* repeatedly sing the great missionary hymn, "I Shall Not Be Moved."

> The Church of God is marching,
> I shall not be moved
> I shall not be moved
> I shall not be moved.[34]

But the irony is that everyone is moved, even as an entire community stubbornly refuses to move in the face of the massive flood. Drifting Away explains to Gideon Clarke about the obsession that drives both teams to keep playing.

> "Then what causes all this?" I wave a mud-encrusted hand to show I mean the flood and the endless game.
> "Pride," says Drifting Away. "What else?"
> "Is it so bad not to be moved? To stand by what you believe, no matter what? To have an obsession?"
> "It is when obsession overrides love, takes precedence over brotherhood."[35]

The Iowa Baseball Confederacy reveals the paradox of the kingdom of baseball today. Baseball can still conjure for us images of a shared American past—the same images held up by segments of turn-of-the-century Protestant America. However, baseball accentuates the social sins that historically fragmented Americans along lines of race, class, ethnicity, and gender. Kinsella reminds us that a game that can produce pastoral feelings of togetherness, social harmony, and love can also bring out resentment, anger, and destruction. The bucolic Protestant ideal of the game—that we are one people in a unified nation under God—is literally washed away by the book's end.

Kinsella's best-known novel is *Shoeless Joe*,[36] which inspired the popular film *Field of Dreams*. This book also displays a unique manipulation of Progressive Era kingdom-of-baseball imagery. However, unlike the antediluvian outcome of *The Iowa Baseball Confederacy*, *Shoeless Joe* offers the reader a vision of hope stemming from tragedy.

The book and the movie follow a similar trajectory. Farmer Ray Kinsella hears a voice that beckons him to build a baseball field in the middle of his Iowa cornfield, where long-dead members of the banished 1919 Chicago White Sox play again. Both the book and the film follow the path of telling a story of a reconciliation between a father and son, where baseball is the central force responsible for bringing two estranged persons together. *Shoeless Joe* and *Field of Dreams* are deeply eschatological works, that is, they crystalize for their audiences a clear portrait of a divine order "enthroned" on the earth—literally a heaven on earth. But entering into this state of earthly perfection does not bring easy peace to the central characters in *Shoeless Joe*. Seeing the legendary Joe Jackson and his dead teammates play again seems like a good payoff for Ray and Annie Kinsella, who sacrifice their livelihood to build the field. However, Ray soon enters a "dark night of the soul" that leads him into a valley of suffering (his own and that of others) before his dream of healing and reconciliation is realized at story's end—symbolized by Ray's reunion with his dead father.

In *Shoeless Joe*, the kingdom of baseball is not just a place where "dreams come true." It is a place where dreams die and subsequent redemption occurs. This theme is powerfully displayed by the character of Eddie Scissons. Eddie is the original owner of the farm that Ray and Annie buy. Eddie's claim to fame is that he is the oldest living member of the Chicago Cubs, claiming to be part of the Cubs' great championship teams of the early twentieth century. Eddie fills Ray's days with stories adorned with Progressive Era images of the game, making Ray believe that Eddie is indeed a divine messenger from a sacred past.

But as time goes by, Ray learns that Eddie's stories are nothing but tall tales told by a man of unfulfilled dreams. It turns out that Eddie was only a mediocre minor leaguer who never came close to playing in the major leagues. In effect, Eddie is nothing but a false prophet. After Eddie's secret has been exposed, Ray and Eddie watch a game featuring an array of ghostly ballplayers. Suddenly Eddie is shocked when he recognizes that the relief pitcher coming to the mound from the cornfield is himself as a young man!

From the standpoint of an elderly adult looking back on his life, Eddie has a chance to see what would have happened if his elusive dream of playing for the Cubs had actually come true. What he sees breaks his heart. In less than an inning, "Kid" Scissons is hammered by batter after batter and is unceremoniously taken out of the game. The elder Scissons experiences the devastation of learning that often dreams, like memories, are more appealing when they remain dreams. As Eddie later tells Ray, "Success is getting what you want, but happiness is wanting what you get. . . . You saw what happened to me. I got what I wanted, but it wasn't what I needed to make me happy."[37]

The experience deeply wounds Eddie, but it doesn't destroy him. Just prior to his death, Eddie delivers what amounts to his eulogy to an assemblage of characters in the middle of the ballfield. As Eddie speaks, it is clear that while he failed to live out his own personal dream, a larger dream lives on in him and in others. Like a frontier revivalist, Eddie speaks of baseball as an incarnate spirit at work in America. He presents a vision that offers humanity the hope of new life, amidst pain and suffering.

> Praise the name of baseball. The word will set captives free. The word will open the eyes of the blind. The word will raise the dead. Have you the word of baseball living inside you? Has the word of baseball become part of you? Do you live it, play it, digest it, forever? Let an old man tell you to make the word of baseball your life. Walk into the world and speak of baseball. Let the word flow through you like water, so that it may quicken the thirst of your fellow man.[38]

Eddie's speech is not just to glorify baseball for nostalgia's sake. It is to remind his audience that baseball, like faith, makes possible for others a shared vision of hope—even in the face of broken dreams.

Shoeless Joe and *The Iowa Baseball Confederacy* bring into focus the paradox of the kingdom of baseball's turbulent existence in the twentieth century. On one hand, the kingdom can promote a false myth of history, attempting to justify a bygone Protestant mythology that we are one people of one blood. Kinsella helps us see through this myth, by showing how baseball highlights a world of pain and estrangement, where the game is nothing but a reminder of our sin—that which keeps us from realizing Martin Luther King's dream of the beloved community.

However, baseball also attests to the power to be transformed by forces greater than our limited dreams. Eddie Scissons serves well as an illustration of divinely inspired hope. Even as Eddie's dream dies, he enables a community to find its dream. His vision of America's national pastime helps the book's characters to experience a new birth in their lives. In effect, they receive from baseball the gift of redemption.

Conclusion

As David Heim observes, it can be dangerous to take sports, like baseball, too seriously. By the same token, we need to take stock of how American history has framed baseball metaphorically as something transcendent, something permanent, and something sacred. One of the characters in *Shoeless Joe* observes that "America has been erased like a blackboard, only to be rebuilt and then erased again. But baseball has marked time [as] America has rolled by like a procession of steamrollers."[39] This passage breaks through the illusion of the liberal-Protestant perspective that viewed baseball as a symbol of evolutionary social progress. Yet the quote also reflects the yearning of many Americans to believe that certain institutions—yeah, even a sport—can embody qualities of the eternal.

The kingdom of baseball can easily enslave Americans to a sanitized past, where racial, cultural, and social differences are whimsically dismissed through a false white-male Protestant vision of national and cultural unity. The kingdom of baseball can also lift up a vision of America's past that reveals the game as a communal symbol of hope. In John Thorn's words, baseball "opens a portal to our past, both real and imagined, comforting us with intimations of immortality and primordial bliss. But it also holds up a mirror, showing us as we are. And sometimes baseball serves as a beacon, revealing a path through the wilderness."[40] This ongoing faith in baseball reminds us that the age-old American Protestant quest for a new heaven and new earth just might be in our grasp.

Part II

Saints and Sinners

1	2	3	4	5	6	7	8	9	R	H	E

Chapter 3

"Matty" and "Ol' Pete":
Divergent American Heroes

Donald K. McKim

The names of Christy Mathewson (1880–1925) and Grover Cleveland Alexander (1887–1950) are emblazoned in baseball's record books. They were two of the premier pitchers of the early twentieth century. They both won 373 games, tying them for third on the lifetime wins list, behind Walter Johnson (416) and Cy Young (511). Both were inducted early into the Baseball Hall of Fame. Matty was among the first five chosen, in 1936, and Alexander was elected in 1938. So both earned a place among baseball's elite. Both captured America's attention for their baseball skills during the course of their careers. Both are bona fide baseball heroes.

Yet despite much that binds "Matty" and "Ol' Pete" together, they are divergent American heroes. Both served in World War I and had experiences that affected their health for the rest of their lives. Mathewson died tragically at age forty-five of tuberculosis. He had a continuing association with baseball after his retirement as a player. The eyes of the nation were fixed on his battle for life. Alexander, however, lived until he was sixty-three, fighting battles against epilepsy and alcoholism, and barely eking out a living, largely depending on the beneficence of others. He died of an apparent heart attack in his room, alone.

These divergent American heroes represent two different strains in American culture. Mathewson is an "ideal hero"—handsome, college-educated, a "Christian gentleman" whose legend portrays pure baseball as its fans idealized it to be. Alexander is the "flawed hero," beset by the limits of life and character. His legacy reflected a reality of "life beyond baseball," a tragic figure whose death a quarter of a century later—at mid-twentieth century—reflected a changed ethos in the country and a changed status of the game of baseball itself. In these two figures, common images of "saint" and "sinner" emerge; the "ideal" and the "real," the "ideal" hero and the "flawed" hero.

The biographies of these two baseball greats are also a rich source for reflection on significant theological themes in the Christian tradition. Both represent streams in understanding of the human condition and Christian anthropology. Elements of character, virtue, tragedy, defeat, loss, suffering, and the struggle for redemption are part of these two lives. In considering "Matty" and "Ol' Pete," we are also drawn into reflection on our own existence and experience as we are confronted by themes that raise theological questions for our understanding and for our own lives. Baseball is the galvanizing metaphor that holds Mathewson's and Alexander's lives together—both for their enduring love of the game and as a central influence as each pursued diverging paths. Thus baseball opens the door to understanding their struggles and as a prism for exploring issues of faith and meaning for our own lives and times.

Matty

When Christy Mathewson was born on August 12, 1880, in Factoryville, Pennsylvania, the northeastern Pennsylvania town had approximately 650 inhabitants. Nestled near the coal-mining centers of Scranton and Carbondale, it was seventy-five miles from Lewisburg, the site of Bucknell University. Gilbert and Minerva Mathewson, Christy's parents, were committed to the Baptist faith and hoped that Christy would grow up to be a preacher. They considered smoking and drinking to be evil; Minerva was a member of the Woman's Christian Temperance Union (WCTU). Christy's grandmother had founded Keystone Academy, a junior preparatory academy that both Christy and his brothers attended.

During his teenage years, Christy participated in football, basketball, and baseball. At six feet, one and one-half inches and 196 pounds, the young man became known for his skills at kicking a football and for pitching a baseball. During the summers, Christy earned cash playing on the diamond and spent the summers of 1898 and 1899 playing for the Honesdale team near the New York border. In July 1899, he joined a small industrial team in Tauton (part of the New England League). It was here that he may have learned his famous "fadeaway" pitch, a kind of reverse curveball that would break away from a left-handed batter and break in on a right-handed batter when thrown by a right-handed pitcher. It was to become a pitch forever associated with the Factoryville hurler.

When he was eighteen, Mathewson enrolled in Bucknell University along with seventy-one other freshmen. This university, on the banks of the Susquehanna River, had been founded by Baptists, and when Mathewson matriculated in 1898 featured competitive teams in the three sports that Matty liked. He became an excellent student, busy with campus activities, including the literary society, Glee Club, the Phi Gamma Delta fraternity, and Theta Delta Tau, an honorary leadership society. He established a sterling record at the university and was nicknamed "the infant phenomenon," "Rubber Leg," and "YMCA"—this moniker probably given in reference to his religious nature. He was an outstanding football player but also attracted the eye of a baseball scout, who signed him to pitch for Norfolk in the Virginia League from May to September, 1900.

By the end of his junior year, Matty decided to leave Bucknell. His 20–2 record as a pitcher for Norfolk attracted the eye of the New York Giants, who paid $1,500 for his contract. After some further dealings with the Cincinnati Reds and Philadelphia Athletics in the upstart American League, Mathewson became a Giant again and launched his magnificent career. From 1903 to 1914, he never won fewer than twenty-two games a season.

Mathewson flourished with the Giants under manager John J. McGraw, the fiery "Little Napoleon" who, as a brilliant strategist and one of the top managers of the early twentieth century, was also roundly disdained and hated for his profanity and brutality. Mathewson became like a son to McGraw. Blanche McGraw said that for her husband, "life without baseball had little meaning for him . . . it was his meat, drink, dream, his blood and breath, his very reason for existence." Mathewson, however, had wide-ranging interests that included reading, chess, checkers, and bridge played at championship levels. He had an exact memory, was a skillful writer, and could hardly have been more an antitype to the rough McGraw, who managed the tough "old Orioles" of Baltimore in baseball's earlier days. Yet, they both shared a love of baseball and a passionate desire to win. Perhaps this is the only explanation for the bond that enabled them to maintain their special relationship through the years—their common "faith" as baseball. One writer noted,

> It is difficult to account for the firm ties that developed between this early twentieth-century odd couple—the well-educated man of equable disposition, the near-saintly pitcher with supposedly spiritual dimensions, on the brink of canonization in the minds of fans, press, and players alike, teaming up with his mentor McGraw, the vitriolic angry, pot-bellied (in his later years), short-armed figure always on the verge of an auto-da-fé by a hostile outside world.[1]

While the two unlikes admired each other, their bonds were also strengthened by the warm relationships of their wives, Blanche McGraw and Jane Mathewson. The two couples lived together for a summer in McGraw's New York apartments. The Mathewsons had been married in Lewisburg on March 4, 1903, and spent their honeymoon at the Giants' spring training camp in Savannah, Georgia. Matty had left his Baptist faith to become Presbyterian in order to marry Jane. She had promised that if he became Presbyterian, she would become a Republican.

Matty's personality and baseball career were unparalleled. During his seventeen seasons, he led the league in wins and shutouts four times, won the strikeout title five times, and pitched four shutouts and ten complete games in World Series competition. He led the league in Earned Run Average (ERA) five times. He won twenty games thirteen times and thirty games four times. He won at least twenty games for twelve consecutive years (1903–1914). His best regular season was 1908 when he led the league in wins (37), ERA (1.43), games pitched (56), games started (44), complete games (34), innings pitched (390 2/3), strikeouts (259), and shutouts (12) while amassing a 37–11 record. His 373 wins tie him with Grover Cleveland Alexander for third best of all time.[2]

Mathewson's popularity with the fans gave him the nickname "Big Six." While the origins of this name have been debated (it had nothing to do with the number on his jersey since in his day players wore no numbers), it most probably originated with sportswriter Samuel Newhall Crane. According to Ray Robinson, in New York "there was an antique horse-drawn engine called Big Six, used by the volunteer fire department, that was effective in dousing out fires. Some said it could pump more water than Niagara Falls. Since Crane often had dubbed Matty as a 'great flame-thrower,' he carried the metaphor a step further by naming him the 'Big Six of all pitchers.'"[3] In burgeoning industrial America, Matty was a "pitching machine."[4]

The year 1914 was Matty's last great year as a pitcher for the Giants. Under McGraw the Giants had been fantastically successful, winning pennants in 1911, 1912, and 1913. Matty's fame was legendary and in Marlin Springs, where the Giants trained for a number of years, "old black people would get off the sidewalks and take off their battered hats whenever 'Marse Matty' walked down the streets."[5] By 1915, Matty, who had by then pitched over 4,700 innings and 623 games, was tired. His 8–14 mark that year indicated he was in decline, and in 1916, after getting off to a 3–4 start, he was traded to Cincinnati with Edd Roush and Bill McKechnie for Buck Herzog and Red Killefer. Matty was to become manager of the Reds. Giants fans were sad, their grief captured by Ring Lardner, who wrote:

> My eyes are very misty
> As I pen these lines to Christy
> Oh, my heart is full of heaviness today.
> May the flowers ne'er wither, Matty
> On your grave at Cincinnati
> Which you've chosen for your final fadeaway.[6]

Mathewson managed the Reds for three years, establishing a 164–176 (.482) record. In 1918, with America deeply involved in World War I and many ballplayers enlisting in the armed forces, Mathewson accepted a commission as captain in the chemical warfare division of the Army.[7] He, with others, was given accelerated training against the use of poisonous gas and became an instructor in the Gas and Flame Division.

Matty was averse to ocean travel and on the way to France became dreadfully seasick. He also contracted flu and reached France barely alive. Two divergent accounts of Matty's experience with poison gas following a training exercise at Hanlon Field in Chaumont, France, have emerged. One is from Ty Cobb, the other from Branch Rickey. Cobb recalled that after a test exercise, Matty missed the signal to snap on his gas mask for self-protection. When the gas was released, men began screaming and in a "hopeless tangle" sought to get out of the room. Cobb inhaled gas and had a hacking cough and drainage from his chest for weeks. Mathewson said, according to Cobb, "'Ty, when we were in there,

I got a good dose of that stuff. I feel terrible.' He was wheezing and blowing out congested matter." Yet according to Rickey, who said he had the same training as Matty and was with him immediately afterward, "to my knowledge Matty had no mishap. In fact, Matty took part in an impromptu broad-jump contest, after the field training exposure, and outleaped everyone in our group who cared to try, by a comfortable margin."[8]

Despite these divergencies, there is more agreement that later, Matty was examining ammunition dumps and other sites left behind by the Germans in Flanders Field when he was exposed to lingering amounts of mustard gas. Thus,

> his lungs already weakened by flu, Matty may have been more vulnerable to the gas fumes lurking in the trenches. However, though poison gas is terrible, as well as deadly to the lungs, it did not cause the tuberculosis which later struck Matty, as it had other members of his family.[9]

Matty was in the hospital when the Armistice was signed on November 11, 1918. He never responded to the Cincinnati club's inquiry as to whether he would return as manager, and the job was given to Pat Moran, who had managed the Phillies to the 1915 National League Pennant. When Matty returned home, he was hired by McGraw as a coach for the Giants. But his health was suffering and his demeanor changed. His coloring was pasty and he coughed frequently, bringing beads of sweat to his forehead. His wife Jane insisted he see a specialist, who told Matty that he had chronic bronchitis.

For the 1919 World Series that featured the Cincinnati Reds against the Chicago White Sox, Matty was hired by the New York *Evening World* to write columns about the games. He worked with veteran writer Hugh Fullerton of the *Chicago Tribune*, with whom he roomed. When rumors swirled that the Series might be fixed, Fullerton enlisted Matty to sit beside him in the press box and draw a red circle on his scorecard for every play he suspected might represent a deliberate attempt to help lose a contest. While Matty never wrote about his suspicions in his column, he did play an important role as Fullerton revealed the infamous Black Sox scandal.[10]

By 1920, Matty's body was shrunken, his coughing heavy and constant. He was told he had tuberculosis, the dreaded scourge of the Great War era. Robinson indicates that "there was no likelihood that Matty had gotten TB from his exposure to mustard gas. However, such exposure could have weakened his resistance to the disease, decreasing his immunity to it."[11] Matty and Jane moved to Saranac Lake, sixty miles from the Canadian border and nine miles from Lake Placid in upstate New York. There a famous sanitarium for tuberculosis victims was started in 1885 by Dr. Edward Livingston Trudeau.

Matty's progress at Saranac Lake was slow. By the time of the World Series in 1921, he was allowed to take brief walks and rides in the countryside by automobile. His friend McGraw had frequently telephoned him throughout the season. In September, the Giants had played a doubleheader benefit in Matty's honor with a crowd of 20,000 on hand at the Polo Grounds.[12] Matty sent a message of appreciation to the crowd. His presence in the town always generated a crowd, and while at Saranac, Matty received hundreds of letters often addressed to "Big Six" or "Matty." When well enough, he played checkers at the St. Regis hotel, taking on challengers from across the country.[13] In June 1922, Matty threw out the first ball in a season opener between Saranac Lake and Plattsburg. In the fall he visited his parents in Factoryville, and by December he returned to New York City to launch the annual Christmas Seal sale—and was hailed as an example of the "Saranac Miracle" for his apparent recovery.

Through McGraw, Matty—against the advice of his wife—was persuaded to become president of the Boston Braves, recently acquired by Judge Emil E. Fuchs, a former attorney for the Giants. Yet Matty became a figurehead, due to his lack of energy and need to return to Saranac Lake for rest and further treatment. Polo Grounds fans were shocked when he occasionally appeared, looking pale and walking with a cane, to watch the Braves play the Giants.

In 1924, Matty and Jane moved into a five-bedroom, three-bath colonial house at Saranac Lake. In the summer, he was involved in a two-car collision and injured his arm, setting back his health still further. He covered the 1924 World Series between the Giants and the Senators—McGraw's last Series. Walter Johnson pitched the Senators to victory, leaving Matty saddened for his mentor. Matty wore glasses and sat slumped in the press box throughout the Series.

In 1925, Matty severed connections with the Braves as his strength lessened considerably and he was mostly confined to bed. When rumors of his impending death circulated in July, his doctor quoted Matty as saying, "Just say for me that I'll fan Death again. He can't touch me, I'm sure of that. I want my friends to know that I am fighting and will continue until I come out on top."[14]

But he didn't. On October 7, 1925, Matty told Jane, "It is nearly over. I know it and we must face it. Go out and have a good cry. Don't make it a long one. This is something we can't help."[15] That evening, after pitching great Walter Johnson defeated the Pittsburgh Pirates in the first game of the World Series, Matty died. His cause of death was listed as tuberculous pneumonia.

Matty's death was a national event. Before the second game of the Series started, the flag was lowered to half-mast and many of the 44,000 fans began to sing, "Nearer My God to Thee." Each ballplayer wore a black armband.[16] McGraw, attending the Series, left immediately and, joined by his wife Blanche, traveled to Saranac Lake. On October 10, Matty was buried near the Bucknell campus in Lewisburg, Pennsylvania. McGraw served as a pallbearer while other baseball luminaries attended the service.

The Matty Legend

Matty's legend, begun in life, lived on. It was fitting that "America's first unalloyed baseball hero was going to his death on an ipso facto American holiday—the opening day of the World Series."[17] The day after his death, *New York Herald Tribune* writer W. O. McGeehan wrote that Matty was "the best loved and most popular of all American athletes . . . if baseball will hold to the ideals of this gentleman, sportsman and soldier, our national game will keep the younger generation clean and courageous and the future of the nation secure."[18] Other tributes were similar: Matty's life was "a vindication of our love for sport" (*New York World*); he was "the symbol of the highest type of American sportsmanship" (*Philadelphia Inquirer*). Grantland Rice, premier sportswriter, said that Matty was "the only man I ever met who in spirit and inspiration was greater than his game."[19]

A few weeks after Matty's death, the mayor of Boston, James M. Curley, a longtime friend of Matty's and a director of the Boston Braves, offered a memorial resolution to Matty at the ball club's annual meeting. Curley said that Matty's life was an ideal and inspiration for youth and "a stainless record of loving service for God and country." He exemplified the qualities of resourcefulness, science, and ingenuity. He raised the game to new and higher standards. Curley said, "His game of life was called by the darkness of death, but the Great Manager of all, releasing him from mortal pain and travail, has taken him home, and signed him to an eternity of light and happiness."[20]

Matty was called "the Christian gentleman."[21] Fullerton described him as a "clean, right-living man."[22] Yet, to avoid an image of the pitcher as a saint that was totally "out of this world," his wife Jane remarked that while her husband was a good man, "he was not a goody-goody."[23] Along the same lines, Fullerton indicated that Matty was "100 percent male he-man. He smoked a bit, drank a bit, at times gambled and swore."[24] He had promised his mother not to play Sunday baseball. But when he was manager of Cincinnati, in 1917, he and McGraw had their teams play a Sunday game in defiance of the local law, as a benefit for Army men.[25]

Baseball writers of the time, especially Ring Lardner, waxed rhapsodic about Matty's character as well as his abilities. Some of his teammates thought Matty to be shy and standoffish, a bit of a prig. He was known to pull the shades in the Pullman car in which his team was riding when it stopped to prevent those on the platform from gazing at him. But nearly all would agree with Matty's battery mate for seven seasons, Chief Meyers, who said, "How we loved to play for him! We'd break our necks for that guy."[26] Fred Snodgrass exclaimed, "And Mathewson! The great pitcher that he was! . . . Matty was the greatest pitcher who ever lived, in my opinion. He was a wonderful, wonderful man, too, a reserved sort of fellow, a little hard to get close to. But once you got to know him, he was a truly good friend."[27]

At Matty's alma mater, Bucknell University, the Christy Mathewson Memorial Gateway was erected at the campus's main entrance in 1928. The year 1989 saw the rededication of the Christy Mathewson Memorial Stadium, not far from Matty's grave in the Lewisburg cemetery.[28]

Matty's legend gained further currency through Eric Rolfe Greenberg's 1983 novel, *The Celebrant*. By mixing the facts of Matty's life with the fictionalized account of a Jewish immigrant family of jewelers, Greenberg creates a character, Jack Kapp, who designed team championship rings—initially in celebration of Mathewson's no-hitter on July 15, 1901, against the St. Louis Browns—and who becomes a "celebrant" of Matty's achievement and character.[29]

Interestingly, the Matty legend continues today through professional actor Eddie Frierson, who performs "Matty: An Evening with Christy Mathewson" throughout the nation. Frierson presents a one-person, two-hour stage play, in character as Matty, with virtually all the dialogue coming from Matty's own words. Frierson says that "using baseball as a backdrop, Mathewson draws his experiences in the Big League as a metaphor for life. He raises many questions. Some are answered, some are not. But, according to him, 'That's the way life is. You can sum it up with the title of the Cohan song, *Life's a Very Funny Proposition, After All.'*[30] Characteristically, Mathewson is quoted as saying, "You can learn little from victory. You can learn everything from defeat."[31]

In the life and character of Christopher Mathewson, the idyllic myths of baseball, American values, Christian virtues—purity, integrity, dedication, and saintliness—converged. In the years prior to World War I, in the optimistic opening decades of the twentieth century and all the progress it portended, America's national pastime found its perfect hero, its first truly national media star who in himself embodied the ideal elements of all that baseball, (Christian) religion, and America represented. As baseball gave meaning to Mathewson's life, so his own personal example gave faith to his fans that "America's game" signified the best in the American character and culture. "Matty" was an American hero.

Ol' Pete

If Christy Mathewson was the ideal American hero of baseball, his counterpart, Grover Cleveland Alexander, was the flawed hero. Spoken of in the same breath, along with Walter Johnson, as the premier trio of pitchers, Alexander matched Matty in pitching prowess and stature, yet did not capture a nation's attention for his virtues. As Donald Honig wrote of Alexander:

> Equal in glory with Mathewson and Johnson, he outdid them in drama and tragedy. His is the most poignant superstar story in all of baseball, a story that began with matchless talent and beguiling innocence and kept going through an ever-deepening and darkening abyss of horror, illness, and self-degradation. We, who prefer our heroes to be luminous with purity, cannot condemn the fall from grace of the one known, inevitably, as Alexander the Great, because he became suddenly a prototypical victim of a world and a time he never made and was utterly unprepared for.[32]

Grover Cleveland Alexander was born on a small Nebraska farm near Elba, outside of St. Paul, Nebraska, on February 26, 1887. He, like Matty, was six-foot, one-inch tall, but was thin, shy, and possessed an early love of throwing rocks. According to his mother, young "Dode" could hit a chicken in the head with a stone while it was running outside the henhouse. Alex explained his superior pitching control as having come from knocking clothespins from the neighbor's wash lines with pebbles.[33]

As a teenager, Alex naturally became a baseball pitcher. He played on weekends for local teams. In 1907, he moved to St. Paul to work as a hole-digger for the telephone company. The Galesburg, Illinois, team in the Class D Illinois-Missouri league offered Alex a contract for $100 a month for the 1909 season. His record was 18–5 when his season ended; he was hit in the head by a thrown ball when he failed to slide into second on a double-play ball. Alex was in a coma for thirty-six hours and remained in the hospital for three weeks. When he returned home, he had double vision and had to close one eye to see properly.

The Galesburg team sold Alex's contract to Indianapolis for $700. Alex reported to that ball club, but his wild pitching one day broke the ribs of the club's manager, Charlie Carr. An Indianapolis eye specialist said Alexander had damaged optic nerves behind his left eye and that only rest would lead to a return of normal vision. Manager Carr sent Alexander to the Syracuse club when Alex's right vision returned, and he won twenty-nine games.

While waiting for the return of his vision, Alex threw a baseball every chance he got. It seems that Alexander

> kept pitching and pitching, in his pain and his anguish like some fanatical supplicant calling on the one agency he believed in, performing day in and day out his ritualistic act of faith. And who are we to say that the grimly repetitive ritual, the faith, did not enact restoration, for suddenly and for no logical reason, in the midst of pitching to a friend in the St. Paul schoolyard, his plural world abruptly flashed singular again, and the tall, lanky Nebraska farm boy was heading east once more, to become part of the mighty litany: Mathewson, Johnson, and Alexander.[34]

Despite his sterling record at Syracuse, major-league teams passed on Alexander until the Philadelphia Phillies bought his contract for $500. Veteran catcher Pat Moran (who was later to replace Matty as manager of the Cincinnati Reds) was the first to realize Alexander's potential and insisted he be allowed to pitch regularly. Alexander's 1911 rookie season was the best ever for a pitcher. He led the National League in victories (twenty-eight), in innings pitched and complete games, as well as shutouts (seven, four of them in a row). He was second in strikeouts.

From there, Alex's pitching feats made him Mathewson's successor as the best pitcher in the National League. Through his career he had three thirty-game seasons, leading the National League in wins six times (including four straight years, 1914 to 1917) and in ERA five times, with six years of an ERA under 2.00 (1.22 in 1915). He led the league in complete games six times, strikeouts six times, and shutouts six times, ending with a National League record of ninety shutouts, bested only by Walter Johnson. Alexander was called "Old Low-and-Away" because of his ability to nip the corner of the plate with knee-high fastballs and a sharp-breaking curve that acted much like today's sliders. His pinpoint control and lively fastball kept batters guessing.[35] Alexander's fantastic success was achieved in the Phillies' Baker Bowl, which featured a right-field wall just 280.5 feet from home plate.

On December 11, 1917, after three straight thirty-game-win seasons, Alexander was traded to the Chicago Cubs along with his battery mate, Bill Killefer, for $55,000 and two players. In May of that year, a national conscription law was passed, and in June, the first United States troops set foot in Europe. America had entered World War I.

Alexander pitched three games for the Cubs in the 1918 season before being drafted. He entered the service with the 342nd Field Artillery of the 89th Division and reported to Camp Funston in Kansas. He was named a sergeant and assigned to an outfit that was bound for overseas. Before leaving, however, Alexander married Amy Arrants in a civil ceremony. Alex and Amy had met on a blind date in St. Paul and from then on their lives were intertwined. On June 28, Alex's liner sailed from New York and reached Liverpool, England, on July 9. They reached Le Havre, France, and were sent to a camp outside Bordeaux.

Alex was a sergeant, but more, a premier major-league pitcher who had already established himself as a superstar. Like Mathewson, Alexander was to suffer long-lasting effects of war. His unit consisted mainly of Kansas and Nebraska farm boys, of which Alex was one. In a photograph of Alex on the liner, the thirty-one-year-old pitcher is in

> . . . overseas cap, knee-length overcoat with sergeant's chevrons on the right sleeve, canvas leggings, and ankle-high boots. He is squinting in the sunlight, in his face still some of the guilelessness

of the Nebraska farmboy. He knows he is going to cross an ocean and fight a war, he has heard of the new weapons and the awesome slaughter; still, he is a portrait of the unsuspecting. There are other doughboys in the picture, and they are staring not at the camera but at Grover Cleveland Alexander, at that moment a treasured and unsullied demigod in khaki, fresh off of three thirty-game seasons, in the prime of his life and at the peak of his fame, who might have been squinting at a red sun setting behind the Nebraska sandhills.[36]

The 342nd Field Artillery moved onto the front during the last week in July. Alex was there for seven weeks. The firing never stopped. The weather was horrible. Alexander insisted a young lieutenant, shivering alongside him, take his gloves to keep his hands warm. Alexander used his hands to cover his ears, but the sound of guns was incessant. When he returned from France, Alex was deaf in one ear, "his soul shaken into epileptic seizures that plagued him for the rest of his life, and with a desperate helplessness that only whiskey could exorcise."[37] The story is told that a dozen years later while Alex was sitting on a bench during spring training, some kids were igniting fireworks in the grandstand. Some of the players gave a little start with each explosion, but, according to a teammate, "Alex never budged. He just sat there stiff as a board, teeth clenched, fists doubled over so tight his knuckles were white, staring off into space like he was hypnotized. When finally somebody came and chased the kids off and the noise stopped, he turned and looked at me with a sad little smile."[38]

After the Armistice, Alex spent five weeks in Germany with the Occupation Army. He returned to the Cubs for the 1919 season. Was he as good as he had been? Alexander believed he wasn't. In an interview, he said:

> When I went to France I fully believed I had not yet reached my prime. I had had three great years in succession and confidently expected the fourth would be as good as any of them, if not better. I have never regained the pitching form I had in 1917. My endurance has never been what it once was. In short, service abroad not only deprived me of one of my best seasons in baseball but it prevented me from ever regaining my former pitching strength and skill. The Great War put an end to my day dreaming of various records.[39]

Alexander was still a formidable pitcher and in 1919 led the league in ERA. The next year he led with twenty-seven wins, ERA, games started and completed, innings pitched, and strikeouts. In 1923 he won twenty-two games. But despite his outstanding control as a pitcher on the field, Alexander increasingly became less able to control himself off the field. He drank Prohibition whiskey and fell down in epileptic seizures. His wife, Amy, sought to minimize his drinking, and when Alex would disappear for several days at a time, Amy would explain, "Almost always they were epileptic seizures. He carried a bottle of ammonia and took sips when he felt a fit coming on."[40] Under Cubs manager Bill Killefer (Alex's friend), Alexander's behavior was tolerated. He was hugely valuable to a perennially second-division team. But when Joe McCarthy became the Cubs manager following the 1925 season, trouble was ahead for Alex.

McCarthy thought Alex was a bad influence on the team, especially on the young players. Alex would keep liquor hidden in the locker room and sneak in to have a drink during a ball game. So, after some absences from the team, McCarthy and the Cubs asked for waivers on the aging superstar.[41]

The St. Louis Cardinals picked up Alexander for $4,000, and he journeyed to St. Louis to join "two of the game's most notable teetotalers—general manager Branch Rickey and manager Rogers Hornsby."[42] Hornsby, baseball's greatest right-handed batsman, ignored Alex's problems with alcohol, arguing that Alex was free to do as he wished as long as he put in a good day's work on the mound.[43]

1926 was a year the Cardinals won the pennant, and Alexander's nine victories gave a big boost to the cause. In the World Series, the Cards faced the New York Yankees, led by Babe Ruth. The Series turned out to be dramatic and suspenseful, each of the seven games won by a Hall of Fame pitcher.

Alex was to win two games in the Series and save a third as the Cardinals triumphed over the New York team. But it is the seventh game of the Series that lives in lore and is a major piece of Alexander's legend.

The story of the dramatic confrontation of Grover Cleveland Alexander and Yankee Tony Lazzeri in the seventh inning of that seventh game is surrounded in myth. In the bottom of the seventh inning at Yankee Stadium, the Cardinals were leading 3–2. Two were out but the bases were loaded, and slugger Tony Lazzeri came to bat. Hornsby put out the call to the bull pen: Bring in Alexander. It took Alex a bit of time to make the long walk, prolonging the anticipatory agony of the Yankee batter who knew that out of the shadows was emerging the awesome and monumental Grover Cleveland Alexander.

Les Bell, who as a thirteen-year-old had first seen Alexander pitch in 1915, was playing third base for the Cardinals. He recalled what happened as Ol' Pete came into view:

> I can see him yet, to this day, walking in from the left-field bull pen through the gray mist. The Yankee fans recognized him right off, of course, but you didn't hear a sound from anywhere in that stadium. They just sat there and watched him walk in . . .
>
> Yeah, I can still see him walking that long distance. He just came straggling along, a lean old Nebraskan, wearing a Cardinal sweater, his face wrinkled, that cap sitting on top of his head and tilted to one side—that's the way he liked to wear it.
>
> We were all standing on the mound waiting for him—me and Rogers Hornsby (who was our manager and second baseman) and Tommy Thevenow and Jim Bottomley and Bob O'Farrell. When Alec reached the mound, Rog handed him the ball and said, "There's two out and they're drunk"—meaning the bases were loaded—"and Lazzeri's the hitter."
>
> "Okay," Alec said, "I'll tell you what I'm gonna do. I'm gonna throw the first one inside to him. Fast."
>
> "No, no," Rog said. "You can't do that."
>
> Alec nodded his head very patiently and said, "Yes I can. Because if I do and he swings at it he'll most likely hit it on the handle, or if he does hit it good it'll go foul. Then I'm going to come outside with my breaking pitch."
>
> Rog looked him over for a moment, then gave Alec a slow smile and said, "Who am I to tell *you* how to pitch?"[44]

Donald Honig adds, "The master of masters was telling exactly how it was going to be, speaking from layers of experience so whorled by time that not even the greatest of right-handed hitters could make contradiction."[45] And Les Bell thought, "Doggone, there wasn't another man in the world I would have rather seen out there at that moment than Grover Cleveland Alexander."[46]

After conferring with Hornsby, Alexander threw only three warm-up pitches. His first toss to Lazzeri was a curve for a strike. His second was off the plate and Lazzeri checked his swing. Alexander's third pitch was a fastball tight on the inside, and Lazzeri knocked it long and foul by ten feet down into the left-field bleachers. A few feet to the right and Alex would have given up a grand-slam home run. Then with another curve, snapped off to perfection, Lazzeri awkwardly tried to connect as the ball zipped into the catcher's mitt for strike three.[47] The aging master Ol' Pete had beaten the young Yankee slugger.[48] What Alex is quoted of as saying about Tony Lazzeri in that situation can also be applied to him in many aspects of his own life: "Less than a foot made the difference between a hero and a bum."[49]

Alexander worked the next two innings, putting away all the Yankees until he at last faced Babe Ruth (who had already hit four home runs).[50] Ruth walked. But mysteriously he tried to steal second—and was thrown out. The Cardinals had won the Series; Alex the Great was the hero! This was the apex of his career.

Some believe that Alexander was recuperating from a night of drinking and was under the influence of booze when he struck out Lazzeri.[51] Yet this is vigorously disputed from a number of sources including third baseman Les Bell, who called such stories "a lot of bunk." Bell explained: "I saw him around the hotel the night before, for goodness sakes. I don't say he didn't have a drink, but he was around most of the night. . . . No man could have done what Alec did if he was drunk or a little soggy. Not the way his mind was working and not the way he pitched. It's true that he was a drinker and that he had a problem with it. Everybody knows that. But he was not drunk when he walked into the ball game that day. No way. No way at all, for heaven's sake."[52]

Next season's spring training in Avon Park, Florida, featured celebrations for the Cardinals and for Alexander. Gifts, speeches, and a dinner were held. In a comment that proved sadly untrue, Alexander said on the occasion of his fortieth birthday: "The first forty years are the hardest." Going on, he told the audience: "You know, I love baseball. Always have. It's still a game to me—not a business. I'd like to play from morning 'til night. Maybe I'm foolish but I always did like baseball. Too many fellows think of how much they are going to get for pitching. When a man doesn't love to play baseball for the game's sake, then he's handicapped."[53] In June, the World Series rings were passed out and what became Alex's most-prized possession was given to him by another hero, Colonel Charles A. Lindbergh. With twenty-one wins to his credit in 1927, this was to be his last twenty-game season.

The Cardinals won the pennant again in 1928 with Alexander going 16–9. But the Yankees swept them in the Series, with Alex losing the second game.[54] In 1929, Alexander was beginning his nineteenth season and needed eight victories to tie Mathewson's record of 372 wins and one more to break it. Alex's drinking had gotten worse and had become an embarrassment to the Cardinal team and to Alex's wife, Amy. By midseason, Alex had checked into the Keely Institute, the "Betty Ford Clinic of its time."[55] Two weeks later, he was back with the team under new manager Bill "Deacon" McKechnie. On August 2, Alex won, and it was announced that he had tied Mathewson's National League record of 372 lifetime wins. On August 10, Alexander beat the Phillies to push him past Matty with 373 wins.

By August 19, McKechnie announced Alex had broken training once too often and was suspended.[56] Owner Sam Breadon sent Alex home on full pay, in gratitude for what he had done for the Cardinals. But on October 3, Amy Alexander obtained a divorce; Alex did not appear in court either in person or by attorney. Amy told of long drinking parties prior to their separation the preceding January when she ceased to believe Alex's promises that he would stop drinking. She later said she hoped the divorce would shock Alexander into a reformation.

Alex got one more try when he was sold along with several other players to the Philadelphia Phillies for the 1930 season. In January 1930, Alex was twice arrested by the Grand Island, Nebraska, police for drunkenness and disorderly conduct and was named in a suit for stealing the affections of the wife of Roy H. Masonnof.

By May 28, Grover Cleveland Alexander had made his last appearance in a major-league uniform. He lost three games for the Phillies and was given his unconditional release. After pitching for a couple of minor-league teams, Alexander joined the House of David baseball team, representatives of a religious sect who spread their Old Testament beliefs as they toured the country playing baseball at a minor-league level during the days of the Great Depression.

Alex also sought Amy's forgiveness, and promised to reform his drinking yet again, and they were remarried on June 2, 1931. She and Alex traveled apart from the rest of the team, and he was the only player granted permission not to wear a beard—a trademark of the House of David's religious beliefs. Frequently Alex would pitch against teams from the Negro Leagues, including Satchel Paige.

But Alex's drinking continued, and by 1934, Amy had had enough—again. Alex had become a public nuisance, and baseball figures at the highest levels deplored his circumstances.[57] Stories about him appeared in newspapers, leading some to criticize baseball for not taking care of

Alex. Reporters invariably asked him about whether he was sober when he entered the seventh game of the 1926 World Series and what the experience was like. Alex eventually started to reply, "I'm getting mighty tired of striking out Lazzeri."[58]

Newspaper accounts also began to appear about Alexander being found in alleys, passed out from either alcohol or epilepsy. It was arranged for Alex to stay with a farmer in St. Paul, Nebraska, but he soon left. He appeared in Louisville, Kentucky, in a strange partnership with a local woman who sold cosmetics and who wanted him to appear on a radio program to advise young boys about baseball. The program would be sponsored by the cosmetics enterprise. After six weeks of unpaid bills, the radio station cancelled the program.[59]

Through the 1930s Alex drifted from town to town, from job to job. Cardinal President Sam Breadon and General Manager Branch Rickey both took an interest in Alex, offering him positions with the club—but according to Rickey, Alexander never responded.[60] One bright spot was Alex's election to the Baseball Hall of Fame in Cooperstown, New York. He gathered 212 of the 262 votes cast and was on hand in 1939 when the Hall was opened. He joined the other legends in the Hall as the sixth player chosen.[61] When Alex was given a replica of the tablet that was hung in his honor in the Hall, he told writer Fred Lieb, "You know I can't eat tablets or nicely framed awards. Neither can my wife. But they don't think of things like that."[62]

A year later, Alexander was employed for a time at a "flea circus" in New York City, giving talks and answering questions every hour from noon to midnight, along with all the other "attractions" at Hubert's Museum. He was also receiving a small veteran's pension and $100 from the Cardinals' Sam Breadon.[63]

In the summer of 1940, Alex advertised for a job in *The Sporting News*. He took a short stint as clubhouse manager at various racetracks but by spring 1941 was back in New York in the Veterans' Hospital. In July, he was found near midnight by a cab driver, unconscious on a sidewalk, and was taken to Bellevue Hospital for lacerations and a possible skull fracture. A $2,500 fund was raised for him by *The New York Daily Mirror*. During that same year, Amy divorced him for the second time. Alexander continued to squeeze out a living through odd jobs. He worked in a billiard academy, as a security guard, and as a floor manager at a cafe. His right ear eventually was removed due to cancer.

In 1943, baseball historians agreed that in 1902, Christy Mathewson

The Faith of Fifty Million

actually deserved one more win than what was credited to him. When Alexander had won his 373rd game on August 10, 1929, he was hailed as having surpassed Mathewson. But by 1945, the official records were changed so that Alexander and Mathewson were now tied with 373 wins.

In 1946, a United Press story indicated that Alex had suffered a heart attack as he left Sportsman's Park in St. Louis after seeing the Cardinals win their sixth World Series. On his sixtieth birthday, February 27, 1947, he had a quiet dinner with old friends and held a short radio broadcast from his home in which he said that the day was "one of the happiest in many years."[64]

The next year Alex appeared in Long Beach, California, where he was scheduled to collaborate with a writer on the story of his life. But that collaboration never took place. He moved to Los Angeles—near to where Amy was living—but was hospitalized in October and again in December, after he was found unconscious behind the building where he lived. The Associated Press said he was broke, seriously ill with cancer, and wanted to teach kids how to play baseball.[65]

Alex recovered enough to return home and attend a luncheon held in his honor when he was inducted into the Helms Hall of Fame in Los Angeles, soon after his sixty-third birthday. In 1950, with his health failing and his finances meager, Alex moved to St. Paul, Nebraska, where he rented a room in the home of Mrs. Josie Nevrivys. Amy also left California and moved to Omaha, and she kept in touch with Alex through letters.

The 1950 Phillies "Whiz Kids" won the National League pennant and faced the Yankees in the World Series. Friends in Chicago convinced a local radio show to provide Alex with an all-expense-paid trip to the World Series to see his old team play. Alex saw the two games in Yankee Stadium but had to stand for three innings in the first game until someone recognized who he was.

When Alex returned home to St. Paul, he had three letters from Amy awaiting him. On October 25 he wrote to her: "Yes the day is gone and I am in my room. . . . I have this to say, if there is another Hell in this world I don't want to ever get there. St. Paul is enough."[66] Alex's bar tab was reportedly cut off, and he was shunned by his fellow-townspeople, a "gaunt old shadow fading wordlessly in and out of the local saloons."[67] On November 2, he wrote to say he would see Amy in Omaha on Friday. He had received an invitation from the governor of Nebraska to come to Lincoln for a visit. He was waiting for his government check and a promised topcoat from a benefactor back East. But Grover Cleveland

Alexander never left St. Paul. On Saturday, November 4, 1950, he suffered a heart attack and died. Alone. His death certificate said: "Found dead on the floor of his room face downward. No signs of a struggle." His last letter to Amy, which he had just mailed, said, "Am still sorry that I did not get to Omaha, but more later. Love, Alex."[68]

Three hundred people attended Alex's funeral, and he was buried in the Elmwood Cemetery, one mile from St. Paul, next to his parents.[69] A large floral wreath in the shape of a baseball diamond was sent by the St. Louis Cardinals, who also paid for the funeral.

Alex the Great

The Cardinals recognized Alexander's greatness with the building of a memorial in his honor at Sportsman's Park. Baseball historian Lee Allen, who contributed to the project, said, "The failing that Alex had was medical and therefore understandable. The failing of his detractors, meanness, is non-medical and inexcusable."[70]

Alexander's image of a tragic hero, who like Christy Mathewson was so deeply affected by World War I, is forever connected with epilepsy and alcoholism. While attending the 1950 World Series, Alex told Fred Lieb:

> I lasted long in the big leagues—twenty seasons—and won more games than any other National League pitcher except Christy Mathewson. We are tied at three hundred seventy-three victories. But I should have had more. I don't feel sorry for myself, or excuse my drinking. I guess I just had two strikes on me when I came into the world. My father back in Nebraska was a hard drinker before me, and so was my grandfather before him. Sure, I tried to stop—I just couldn't.[71]

Branch Rickey said:

> I doubt that I ever felt sorrier for any man who ever worked for me than I did for Alexander. He was a perfectly wonderful fellow and his only enemy was himself. I had many a long talk with him. "I don't want to drink," he told me and I believed him. "I've tried and I've tried. But once I take that first sip I'm lost."[72]

When asked if he had spent much time with his uncle, Alexander's nephew told Dave D'Antonio: "Oh, sure. We hunted and fished . . . (H)e had his regular crew here and his bootleg whiskey down by the river." The nephew said that he "often led his staggering uncle home after dusk. He was frequently drunk but that 'was his business.' "[73]

Ol' Pete's legend and tragedy drew national attention again when the motion picture *The Winning Team* was released in 1952.[74] Future President Ronald Reagan played Alex and Doris Day played Amy. Amy Alexander herself was a paid consultant for the film. She was in large part responsible for how the story was shaped. She emphasized the role of epilepsy in Alex's life and believed that it was a final epileptic seizure on November 4, 1950, that had caused Alex to fall and strike his head in his room, unaided because no one knew he needed help.[75] According to one film critic,

> The script rearranges the chronology of Alexander's life, suggests incorrectly that the Lazzeri strikeout was the last play in the deciding Series game, and—most amusingly—depicts the unlovable Rogers Hornsby as a 100% sweetheart. Otherwise, *The Winning Team* provides an excellent showcase for Ronald Reagan—though in later years he expressed some reservations about the script, noting that, by adhering to Warner Bros.' insistence that the word "epilepsy" never be spoken, the picture confused audiences as to the true nature of Alexander's affliction.[76]

Alex was a hero, all right. But his life beyond baseball was filled with disappointments, suffering, and the criticism of those who believed he should be able to overcome his alcoholism and epilepsy to triumph in his later years the way he had on the baseball diamond.

"Saint and Sinner"

While Christy Mathewson and Grover Cleveland Alexander were united in baseball greatness, each being bona fide baseball "immortals," their lives diverged radically beyond the baseball fields. This contrast is seen in regard to their personal paths and legends, but also in regard to the ways in which their lives helped shape the relationship of baseball to "religion" and to American culture.

Personal Paths

The personal contrasts between Matty and Alex are many. Matty was the son of a gentleman farmer and had the advantage of attending college, where he was an outstanding student and star athlete. Alexander was the son of a poor Nebraska farmer, one of thirteen children, who worked as a farmer and a lineman with the local telephone company before signing his first professional contract.

When he broke in with the Giants, Christy Mathewson was one of the few "college boys" to be in the major leagues. In 1900,

> . . . ballplayers, in the order of their social acceptance, were lower even than circus clowns, itinerant actors, and train robbers. On the whole, they were crude, roistering, disreputable folks full of foul oaths and beery smells. Few would have recommended them for entrance into a decent caravansary.[77]

Matty's rise to stardom and heroic status helped change that image and make it possible for a sports figure to be a role model in American culture. As Robinson notes:

> The word "hero" comes from the Greek word *heros,* which means the embodiment of composite ideals. Yet the Greeks always knew their gods were not perfect; they knew they were fallible and possessed character flaws. Many Americans, however, preferred to view Mathewson as a hero without warts. In this public thirst for a saint among ballplayers Mathewson became someone entirely apart from his own rowdy fraternity. He was an idealized, cardboard figure—the first to come from the baseball ranks.[78]

Alexander, on the other hand, was known for his "warts"—most notably his drinking. The saga of his later life, with his arrests, drinking binges, and other difficulties, made the newspapers so that both the baseball establishment and the baseball public looked upon him with pity or judgment or as a hero with a "character flaw." No one ever said of Ol' Pete that he was a "Christian gentleman" or "role model" for young boys.

Further contrasts in the paths of life followed by Matty and Alex involve three significant dimensions of the human experience: love, suffering, and death.

Love

Christy Mathewson married Jane Stoughton, a "lively intelligent young woman, who dressed circumspectly, as a Sunday school teacher should," whose family was "society" in Lewisburg, Pennsylvania, and who was regarded as an extremely "good catch."[79] Theirs was apparently a devoted, loving marriage, with Jane caring for Matty in his battle with tuberculosis at Saranac Lake. In one of his last utterances, Matty told his wife, "It is nearly over. I know it and we must face it. Go out and have a good cry. Don't make it a long one. This is something we can't help."[80]

Alexander, on the other hand, was married just before he went off to war and twice divorced afterwards. Though devoted to each other through the years, Alex and Amy Alexander faced the consequences of Alex's alcoholism and inability to find steady, secure employment. Theirs was a difficult relationship, but Amy had always been Alex's biggest fan and supporter. She once said that "Alex always looked to me for advice, help, and encouragement. I don't think he ever considered we were divorced."[81] A paid consultant for *The Winning Team,* the story of Alexander's life, she used her fees to commission a monument for Alex's grave to be erected by May 31, 1952—the thirty-fourth anniversary of their first marriage.[82] But the personal paths in love and marriage of the two baseball greats, Matty and Alex, significantly diverged.

Suffering

So too in tragedy. Both men had experiences in World War I that greatly affected their future health. Both suffered the consequences of their participation in the Great War. Matty's life was tragic in the sense that his tuberculosis, which claimed his life at the young age of forty-five, was a disease that came upon him. And "the suffering that is of particular concern for tragedy is that which has the effect of destroying its victims and which cannot be understood as being deserved."[83]

Alex also suffered—from epilepsy, alcoholism, and cancer. In the end he died of an apparent heart attack. His sufferings over the course of his sixty-three years, especially after he left baseball, also included the breakup of his marriages, his drifting from job to job, and his dependence on the benevolence of others for his livelihood. Alex exercised his freedom and responsibility as a human in terms of his life choices. He admitted his own mistakes, but in regard to his epilepsy and alcoholism he also saw himself as imprisoned within his own finitude as when he tellingly told Lieb, "I don't feel sorry for myself, or excuse my drinking. I guess I just had two strikes on me when I came into the world. My father back in Nebraska was a hard drinker before me, and so was my grandfather before him. Sure, I tried to stop—I just couldn't."[84] In this regard, Alexander was recognizing what theologian Wendy Farley has pointed out that "the conditions of finite existence are tragically structured. Multiplicity, embodiment, mortality, historicity make human existence possible—but each of these structures makes certain kinds of suffering inevitable."[85] Alexander was a tragic figure because "whatever else is entailed in tragedy, suffering lies at its very heart."[86]

But in the eyes of the baseball public, Matty's suffering and tragedy only enhanced his stature as an icon of American culture because what he faced was seen as purely undeserved. The "ideal hero" had no "warts"—he was felled by the ravages of a disease over which he had no control. Matty, in a sense, became an innocent "martyr." As a heroic ideal, Matty was an example—of how to live and how to face adversity, even how to die.[87] The "Matty Legend" lives on—from *The Celebrant* to Eddie Frierson's "Matty: An Evening with Christy Mathewson." Frierson quotes Matty as once saying, "I feel very strongly that it is my duty to show those youth the good, clean, honest values that I was taught by my Mother when I was a youngster. That, really, is all I can do."[88] The "salvation" of American youth and American culture—mediated by a baseball hero—lies in following his example and adopting his values, even when faced with innocent suffering and ultimately, death.[89] Matty is the "saint."

Yet in the eyes of the baseball public—writers and fans—Alex's tragedy and suffering also included those factors over which people expected him to have control—his life decisions, as well as his epilepsy and alcoholism. Alex was a "sinner" in that his troubles were seen largely to be of his own making. Branch Rickey, widely regarded as a truly religious man and devout Christian, told Arthur Daley that Alex's "only enemy was himself." Alex said he didn't want to drink and repeatedly tried not to do so, but claimed that "once I take that first sip I'm lost."[90] For Rickey—and for sportswriters and probably the general baseball public in America prior to 1950—Alexander was responsible for his own life and he simply did not have the "strength of character" or "self-control" to resist drinking to excess. This is the poignancy surrounding the myth of Alex being drunk or hung over when he struck out Lazzeri in the 1926 World Series. Honig writes that by 1926, Ol' Pete had "become a multiple legend: Alexander the pitcher and Alexander the drinker."[91] In 1926,

> . . . alcoholism was not understood to be a disease and Alcoholics Anonymous was still a gleam in the bloodshot eyes of the afflicted. It was expected that you made fun of a staggering drunk. Jokes about morning afters were a trademark of the Prohibition era.

The Faith of Fifty Million

Alexander's reputation made him a convenient target for claims that he had fallen into the gutter the night after bringing the World Series to a final game.[92]

So, Alexander's alcoholism was widely regarded as fully his own fault. He was a "sinner." Therefore, while both Matty and Ol' Pete shared tragic dimensions in life, the perceptions of their "tragedies" were much different. Another divergence.

Death

A third element in the differences between these two heroes is in terms of their deaths. Matty's struggles were very much in the public eye. He received hundreds of letters at Saranac Lake, many addressed simply to "Big Six" or "Matty." The declining health of the beloved "Christian gentleman" was widely reported in the press and, even in his suffering, Matty insisted, "I always think how much better off I am than most other people."[93] When the end came, it was on October 7, 1925—a hallowed day—the opening day of the World Series. Matty's passing was nationally acknowledged, and in an American culture that now seems much more than merely three-quarters of a century from our own, a crowd could sing the hymn "Nearer My God to Thee" when the flag at the World Series game the next day was lowered to half-mast.[94]

But Grover Cleveland Alexander died alone. He died in a rented room, face down on the floor, on Saturday, November 4, 1950. His old team, the Cardinals, paid for his funeral, and it was his baseball friends who raised money to honor Ol' Pete with a memorial at Sportsman's Park. Alexander's passing marked the end of his struggles. He lies buried in the Alexander plot, but again, alone, because Amy is not buried with him. His was not the "ideal family life," and so his grave near his parents is still set apart.[95]

Alexander must have died with a sense of futility. He was remembered by pitcher Robin Roberts—who succeeded him in the affections of Philadelphia Phillies fans—as being brought to Roberts' little red schoolhouse in Springfield, Illinois, by a saloon keeper after Alexander's playing days were ended. Alex's message to the children was: "Boys, I had my day and made big money for the times, but I wasted the years and the money. Don't let it happen to you."[96] Alex felt he had let it happen to himself. If his great "redeeming moment" came in the 1926 World Series when he struck out Lazzeri—and showed the world that even as an aging alcoholic he still possessed the mythic power of baseball greatness—then the rest of his life, even his death, must have felt like a continuing downhill slide. When battling the forces of epilepsy, alcoholism, and cancer, Alex must have many times felt that his statement about Lazzeri's foul ball was also true for the bigger picture of his life: "Less than a foot made the difference between a hero and a bum." Alex's own choices in life, limits, and failures, coupled with those forces beyond his control, all contributed to his perception as a baseball "hero" who was also "flawed" by the decisions he made in life—so "close," but yet "so far."[97]

Baseball, Religion, and American Culture

The lives of American heroes Matty and Ol' Pete are filled with important theological and religious themes that relate to the human condition and its struggles with issues of character and virtue, suffering, loss and tragedy, and the quest for redemption.

Matty

Christy Mathewson as the "ideal hero" embodied religious and cultural ideals that most Americans embraced in the early twentieth century. He fit the popular image of a "hero" and a "saint" by his superlative exploits on the diamond and the reputation he developed off the field. He was the first truly national baseball figure who captured the country's admiration and hero worship by combining all the ideal elements of baseball, religion, and American culture. He was the premier pitcher in the major leagues and the saintly "Christian gentleman" who defined baseball in a new way for millions of people. He placed baseball "firmly in a new and unrivaled position in the nation's imagination."[98]

The strength of Matty's character was exemplified even further in his later life as the baseball hero and American war veteran struggled valiantly against the ravages of tuberculosis. He died a tragic "martyr's" death under the watchful, tearful eyes of the American nation during the high holy days of the 1925 World Series. His family values, virtues, and larger-than-life persona epitomized the myth of what "baseball" was supposed to be and contributed to its unchallenged status as the "national pastime" and America's "civil religion" at a time when the "kingdom of baseball" reigned supreme.[99] The Mathewson myth symbiotically fueled and was fueled by the secular/sacred elements of the larger "baseball myth" as Matty himself epitomized all its values and strengths. Baseball's pure, idyllic status was taken to a new level by the

"Christian moralist" who so gracefully combined skill, intelligence, virtue, and patriotism within himself.

The only "evil" in the Matty world was that of undeserved suffering. His exposure to deadly gas in World War I—while serving his country—spiraled into the tuberculosis that ultimately took his life. This was his tragedy; the great man was dead at age forty-five. Matty was "the first of the twentieth century's great baseball idols, and the first to die."[100] Commissioner Landis opined, "Why should God wish to take a thoroughbred like Matty so soon and leave some others down here that could well be spared?"[101] Matty's death would have raised the vexing theological question of suffering and evil in the national consciousness. Why *should* the good die young? When such an "intrusion" entered the kingdom of baseball, it was all the more important to keep the myth alive and to rise up to embrace new heroes.

Matty was a "baseball redeemer" by bringing respectability to the game and embodying its virtues and values as a model of what a real ballplayer should and could be. In a broadly "religious sense," he epitomized humanity as it was created to be in the Garden of Eden (Genesis 2). He lived and played in a "garden paradise," a pure specimen of the ideal ballplayer and created being. He was in no need of "redemption" (in this sense) for himself. The "evil" that intruded into Matty's life was not of his own making or fault. He was an "innocent" who was felled by forces outside himself. Yet even in the face of his tragic suffering, this role model of the American nation and the American sport heroically fought and maintained his dignity, continuing to wed cultural and religious values as he showed the country how to play baseball, how to live, and even how to die. One tribute at Matty's death said it simply: "He had proved you could play professional baseball and remain a gentleman."[102]

Ol' Pete

Grover Cleveland Alexander presents a different American hero. Although he was equal to Mathewson in baseball skill and legendary accomplishment, Ol' Pete's life took a divergent path, one that extended longer in terms of lifespan and which led to its own sad end. He too struggled with issues of character and virtue, suffering, loss, and tragedy in a quest for redemption. His was not the life of the "ideal hero," but the "flawed hero." He succeeded Matty as the best right-handed pitcher in the National League. But his reputation for drinking pointed to his human frailties even as he struggled against disease and spent years wandering from place to place in search of personal stability and security. He could never find a job in baseball after he retired, as Mathewson did. Alexander's drinking reinforced a bleaker image of baseball players, and as a reason for his being traded and derided, it functioned as a counter and an influence that in many ways diminished his achievements. After he left baseball, his notoriety was chiefly associated with his quest to find satisfactory employment—whether with the House of David traveling ball team or at the flea circus in New York City. Alexander became a pitied and pathetic figure to the baseball establishment which sought to protect Ol' Pete from himself.[103]

To look at Alexander in and out of baseball is to see baseball not as a sport of mythic idealism but as a human enterprise of brutal realism. The frailties and perversities—"evils" of the human condition—are to be found both on and off the baseball diamond. Alexander and his alcoholism was a prelude to drug abuse and other scandals among professional ballplayers during the last century. Baseball is played by humans who display character traits that are not always laudatory and that do not embrace all the ideals of "the Christian gentleman" of earlier years in a more homogeneous American culture.

Religiously or theologically, this realism is associated with "sin," which traditionally has been seen to establish its reign among humans in the mythic biblical story of the Garden of Eden as it is conveyed after Genesis 2—in Genesis 2–3. Here the humans created by God "fall" into a perversion of the true humanity the Creator intended humans to enjoy. Here "sin" enters the picture and causes a disruption of the divine/human relationship with its legacy extending through the further progeny of the human race. Here the effects of sin begin to show up in the ways that humans treat one another and in the attendant disorders of human relationships. The "ideal" gives way to the "real," and the "real" is marked by human perversity, frailty, egoism, selfishness, and a host of other symptoms. Self-destructive behavior, meaninglessness, and the loss of self-esteem manifest themselves also. In this "sin," a savior is needed for redemption.[104] Community needs to be restored; humans need to be healed.

To see Grover Cleveland Alexander against this backdrop is to recognize profound relationships among baseball, religion, and American culture. Alexander's life and system of meaning were thoroughly connected to baseball. He played for the love of the game and would like to play, as he said, "from morning 'til night." He believed that "when a man doesn't love to play baseball for the game's sake, then he's handicapped."[105] While his feats on the field and the records he amassed were superior and "heroic" in status—tying him with the great Mathewson at 373 wins—Alexander's life and legend was "more" than baseball. And the "more" of his life turned out to be a tale of hardship, loneliness, illness, and disappointments that are the lot of humans in general and which poignantly coalesced in the series of difficulties Ol' Pete experienced through the years. Alex's "heroism" did not carry over into his life beyond baseball. Public perceptions of him, his difficulties in marriage and divorce, his checkered existence, and his tortured struggles present the image of a "flawed" hero who experienced failures, losses, and tragedies for which he himself bore a level of responsibility. The "evil" in his life was not only that over which he had no real control—such as his epilepsy. It also included those elements over which he exercised some manner of choice, and thus accountability. Alex was in need of healing and wholeness—as all humans are. But his needs were played out on a wider American stage than most people's. His legendary status as a supreme pitcher made his failures more public and visible—and more poignant than those of lesser mortals.

By the time of Alexander's death in 1950, baseball had embraced other heroes—the greatest being Babe Ruth, Alexander's contemporary—who with his monumental appetites and off-the-field exploits created his own legend. In the heroic Ruth we see the very definition of "*humanity coming to bat*"! Baseball legends after Ruth could be "human"—recognized with "warts and all." America and its national pastime had lost an innocence and idealism that Mathewson embodied. Alexander's appetites and exploits were not exemplary. He stands as a "flawed hero"—remembered for his stellar baseball achievements, but known too for the other aspects of his struggles that brought him grief and sorrows. Even his great moment for "redemption" on the ballfield in striking out Lazzeri is forever linked with the legend of his drinking—thus casting its reflection, rightly or wrongly, on Alexander's character. This is the "realism" of Ol' Pete's heroic feat. Now he needs "redemption" from his legend as well as for the rest of his life.

The Faith of Fifty Million

The story of Matty and Ol' Pete, while portraying poignant religious themes, points to one further recognition about baseball, religion, and American culture.

Theologian Brian Gerrish has pointed out that the term "faith" has both a theological or religious as well as a secular sense. "Saving faith" refers, in a Christian context, to belief and trust in God, known in Jesus Christ, and "perceiving one's experience under the image of divine benevolence (*fides*) and . . . a consequent living of one's life out of an attitude of confidence or trust (*fiducia*)."[106] But Gerrish argues that by living this "faith," Christians are "doing in their own way what everyone does all of the time." There is a "secular faith" in which faith may be seen as a "generic concept" in which "faith is a personal relation to transcendence that enables one to find meaning in one's life."[107] Faith is thus "not a peculiarly Christian concept but a generically religious, indeed universally human, phenomenon, and that it has to do with the discovery of personal meaning in one's existence."[108] Put directly: "Generic faith is the perception of meaning and purpose in one's life through commitment to an object of ultimate loyalty in which one finds security."[109]

If this is so, the allusion in F. Scott Fitzgerald's *The Great Gatsby* to baseball as "the faith of fifty million people" takes on a profound meaning. The context there was the 1919 Chicago Black Sox scandal, when public confidence in baseball was severely tested.[110] But what if "baseball" really is "faith"—secular, generic "faith" in the sense defined earlier as "the perception of meaning and purpose in one's life through commitment to an object of ultimate loyalty in which one finds security"? Baseball—with all its myths and legends, its victories and defeats, its "ideal hero" and its "flawed hero," Matty and Ol' Pete—what if this "game" really does function in American consciousness and experience as "faith"? Baseball, the national pastime, is perceived to bring meaning and purpose to life. Baseball is a game, a "reality" that is an "object of ultimate loyalty." Baseball is an experience "in which one finds security." Baseball is "meaning construction" that gives structure and purpose to one's existence.[111] Without it—with "no faith"—loss of order, meaning, and purpose, "chaos" results! The Chicago Black Sox in 1919 could rock "the faith of fifty million people." If baseball tottered, a whole culture could be plunged into the abyss of confusion!

Thus baseball is literally "the faith of fifty million" who find meaning and purpose in what baseball provides in a tremendously significant way.[112] Commitment to baseball as "faith" is not the only "faith commitment" we may hold. But baseball functions as such—as generic "faith." Through all ethos and pathos, this "faith" remains—the "faith of fifty million" and more.

Without doubt, baseball functioned as "faith" in this respect for Christopher Mathewson and Grover Cleveland Alexander. Both loved the game. For both it provided meaning, purpose, and security. Baseball was, for Mathewson, the perfect form that united his strength of character, values, and virtues—all elements that provided meaning and stability for his "faith." Conversely, Alexander is a dramatic example of how outside of baseball, meaning and purpose seemed to evaporate and existence was plainly chaos. The lives and identities of the two pitchers congealed in the baseball experience. Their lives and legends are forever intertwined with baseball records, statistics, and lore. Their status as great American heroes is secure because they are important parts of the tradition that is the kingdom of baseball, which endures through all the vicissitudes of American culture.

Matty and Ol' Pete are divergent American heroes. Their lives were quite different and followed dissimilar paths. Yet their stories reflect important religious and theological themes that can nudge one into personal self-reflection even a century after Matty threw his first big-league pitch for John McGraw's Giants. But despite the dissimilarities, Matty and Ol' Pete are united in the "field of dreams" that is baseball. Baseball holds these two heroes together, and baseball holds them in our hearts.

1	2	3	4	5	6	7	8	9	R	H	E

Chapter 4

The World of Spirit or the World of Sport?

Figuring the Numbers in Hemingway's
The Old Man and the Sea

C. Harold Hurley

Several commentators are aware that the opening sentence of Hemingway's *The Old Man and the Sea*[1] depends for its effectiveness on the number eighty-four.

> He was an old man who had fished alone in a skiff in the Gulf Stream and he had gone eighty-four days now without taking a fish.[2]

In addition, the exchange several pages later between Santiago and Manolin emphasizes the significance of the number eighty-five.

> "Do you think we should buy a terminal of the lottery with an eighty-five? Tomorrow is the eighty-fifth day."
> "We can do that," the boy said. "But what about the eighty-seven of your great record?"
> "It could not happen twice. Do you think you could find an eighty-five?"[3]

The presence of these numbers has posed the following questions related to Hemingway's use of the specific figures eighty-four and eighty-five throughout the novel:

1. Does the number eighty-four carry some tone of despair or loneliness not expressed so well by, say, eighty-six or by some vaguer indication of time, such as "for almost three months now"?

2. Were the numbers selected on the basis of mere euphony?
3. Is there some vague mathematical or symbolic significance to the arrangement of the digits: eight followed by four and eight followed by five?

Scholarly responses to these questions have covered a range of options. One simple proposal suggests that "Hemingway . . . could not resist the sly little joke of having the Old Man 'better' by one day the wonderful [eighty-three-day] fishlessness record set by Zane Grey."[4] One complex reading holds that Hemingway is "counting the number of days since Christmas" so that "the events of the novel take place in a period corresponding to Holy Week"[5] for the year 1951. A more esoteric interpretation holds that Hemingway's "mythical and mystical associations [of numbers] . . . are symbols mirroring the collective unconscious of Santiago or the conscience of Hemingway, which provided an Ariadne thread out of the dark labyrinth of death to light, life and freedom."[6] But the recent discovery that the novel's chronology corresponds exactly to the second full week of the September 1950 American League pennant race reveals that the numbers eighty-four and eighty-five derive—not from some sly fishing joke or some obscure religious anagoge—but from Hemingway's allusions to actual baseball games played several months prior to his writing of the novel.

Afforded brief treatment in several of his short stories and novels, Hemingway's lifelong interest in baseball finds its ultimate expression, albeit allusively, in *The Old Man and the Sea*. The moving account of an old fisherman who has gone eighty-four days without a catch and Santiago's ordeal on the Gulf Stream derives its significance, in part, from his near obsession with "the baseball."[7] Inspired by the record-breaking achievement of Joe DiMaggio in the Yankees' eighty-fourth victory of the season, recognizing that the number corresponds with his own eighty-fourth day of disappointment, and aware that the Yankees with their eighty-fifth win would secure a first-place tie with the Detroit Tigers, the old fisherman places himself in fictive competition with the great DiMaggio. Confident that "eighty-five is a lucky number,"[8] Santiago vows to fish well on his eighty-fifth day on the Gulf Stream, not only to assure his success but also to make DiMaggio proud of him. Purposefully set, then, against the background of specific games played during the American League pennant race of September 1950 in which the Yankees achieved their eighty-fourth and eighty-fifth victories,

Santiago's heroic feats at sea, especially when measured against DiMaggio's exploits on the playing field, come to epitomize Hemingway's theme "of what a man can do and what a man endures."[9]

Seeking to explain the significance of eighty-four in the opening sentence of the novel, Robert N. Broadus has discovered what he believes is the definitive reason for the number's selection, a reason "revealing something of the Hemingway personality."[10] It is to be found in one of Zane Grey's books on fishing. "Among Grey's fishing adventures—described so colourfully in several books on the subject," Broadus recounts, "was an extended trip to Tahitian waters in 1928."[11] Complaining vehemently of his misfortunes, Grey writes:

> My long and unparalleled streak of blankety-blank days was broken on November 14. I had caught my last fish around August 22. Here was a stretch of eighty-three days without catching a fish. I know quite well it cannot be beaten. There is a record that will stand.[12]

However attractive on the surface this explanation appears to be, Broadus's argument is weakened by his lack of proof that Hemingway knew of Grey's account,[13] by the joke's incompatibility with the seriousness of the novel's opening sentence, and by his failure to note that Santiago, having previously endured eighty-seven days without a fish, has already surpassed by four days Grey's record to establish a "great record" of his own.[14]

The majority of commentators attach greater significance to Hemingway's use of figures than Broadus does, seeing in them matters of numerological and anagogical import. After observing that "Hemingway's numerology is often so subtle that it is easy to miss" and equally "easy to over-interpret," William Adair, for example, indicates that

> "Eighty-five is a lucky number," Santiago tells the boy, and asks him to get a lottery number ending in eighty-five (though their constant fiction-making game implies that the boy never gets the number). And it is obvious that Santiago considers this lottery number lucky for the next day will be his eighty-fifth day of trying to get a fish. But eighty-five is lucky for another less obvious reason. And we need not be accused of over-reading when we point out that eight and five, subtracted, added, and multiplied,

result in three, thirteen and forty, all "significant" numbers. Whether eighty-five turns out to be lucky or unlucky for Santiago is another question.[15]

Adair, unfortunately, explains neither the underlying reasons for Santiago's trust in the number eighty-five nor the significance to the text of the numbers three, thirteen, and forty.

Working with several of the same numbers as Adair, Joseph Waldmeir sees in *The Old Man and the Sea* a rather intricate numerology carefully set forth that both depends on and reinforces Christian symbols in the novel's text. After noting the extent to which Hemingway makes "judicious use" of the numbers three, seven, and forty, all "key numbers in the Old and New Testaments, and in religion," Waldmeir concludes that what appears to be a Christian allegory is really a decisive step on Hemingway's part to elevate "what might be called his philosophy of Manhood to the level of a religion."[16]

As with Waldmeir, John Halverson finds "major allusions to Christ and the Christian tradition in *The Old Man and the Sea*" that "are inexact but certainly inescapable."[17] But unlike Waldmeir, Halverson seeks to link the religious implications of the numbers, specifically eighty-four and eighty-five, not to Hemingway's "philosophy of Manhood" but to his association of the novel's chronology with the Christian calendar for the year 1951:

> We may begin with Hemingway's insistence on the precise number of days preceding the events of the novel. Why eighty-four days of bad luck and not some other number, or some vaguer indication of time, say, "For almost three months now . . ."? It is the kind of tightly sequential narrative that, once underway, demands a strict chronology, so it is not surprising that the time of the action itself is carefully accounted for. But is there any reason for beginning the novel exactly on the eighty-fourth day? It is possible that Hemingway picked his calendar out of the air, but it is also possible that he was counting the number of days since Christmas, for the calendar of the novel corresponds almost exactly to the religious calendar commemorating the life of Christ from the Nativity to Easter. The date of Easter of course varies from year to year, so that the number of days from Christmas varies accordingly. But one year fits the time scheme of the novel: the year 1951 when Hemingway was writing it.[18] Santiago's homecoming–his carrying

of the mast up the hill, his stumbling under its own weight, his collapsing in a cruciform position—seems to allude clearly to the events of Good Friday. This homecoming takes place on the eighty-eighth day of the novel's calendar; Good Friday was the eighty-ninth day from Christmas in 1951. The closely approximate correspondence may be fortuitous. If not, the discrepancy of a day may be a deliberate inexactness (close enough to be very suggestive, not exact enough for completely confident identification); or Hemingway may have made the common mistake of subtracting 25 from 31 to get the number of days from Christmas to the end of December and arriving at the number 6, forgetting that you have to add one more day to get the right inclusive number.[19]

As we shall soon see, Halverson is correct about the novel's tightly sequential narrative demanding a strict chronology, but he is misguided in linking the novel's chronology to Holy Week of 1951. If we put aside for a moment the fact that Hemingway's calendar corresponds precisely not to the Christian year but to the American League baseball schedule for the second full week of September 1950, Halverson's argument rests on a weak foundation, depending as it does on the "deliberate inexactness" of the parallels, "approximate correspondence[s] [that] may be fortuitous"[20] and on the notion that Hemingway may have erred in subtraction. Hemingway, of course, is not beyond erring, but one might think he would exercise greater care for accuracy if, as Halverson argues, he were purposefully paralleling the novel's chronology with the Christian calendar. And to believe that "Hemingway was actually thinking of Eastertime while writing 'September,'"[21] as Halverson later suggests, strains credibility.

Edward H. Strauch, one of the most recent commentators linking numerological implications of *The Old Man and the Sea* with religion, begins on firm footing with the observation that "Undoubtedly, Hemingway's use of numbers in his novel had the immediate artistic intention of arousing reader response to the old man's bad luck and of awakening admiration for Santiago's tenacity."[22] Indeed, "ordinary men," as Leo Gurko reminds us, "are seldom afflicted with disaster so outsized."[23] But the soundness of Strauch's responses to his own question— "yet why precisely eighty-four days and the story itself taking place on the eighty-fifth day?"[24]—begins to weaken as soon as the question is asked. Although the number eighty-five is of importance, as Strauch suggests, he is amiss in believing that the novel, which traces the eighty-fourth through the eighty-eighth days of Santiago's ordeal, takes place only on the eighty-fifth day. To support his contention that *The Old Man and the Sea* "is a modern Christian exemplum,"[25] Strauch argues that

> if for the moment we accept at face value the need to decipher the meaning of numbers in any given text with mythical or religious connotations, as numerologists would contend, then we can further explore the hints such numbers augur.[26]

Through a series of correspondences, neither easily summarized nor commented upon, between Moses' forty years of trial and tribulation in the desert and Jesus' forty days in the wilderness with Santiago's quest for a "new beginning"[27] after forty days alone at sea, Strauch's attempts to prove the primacy of numerology in understanding the old fisherman's ordeal in the Gulf Stream are to my mind neither convincing nor adequately explicatory of Hemingway's text.

But rather than comment on the entirety of Strauch's lengthy numerological argument, let us concentrate instead on those ideas directly related to the numbers eighty-four and eighty-five. Having shown that the numbers three, four, seven, and twelve hold special meaning in Christian numerology, Strauch contends that Hemingway arrived at the number eighty-four by multiplying seven and twelve and that "astrologically speaking, the successive positions of the seven planets of the solar system timing the rotation of the twelve signs of the zodiac could account for Santiago's bad luck."[28] Continuing his argument, Strauch writes,

> The number twelve has another association. On [a] clock, in a calendar year, or as the final number of the astrological cycle, twelve designates the end of the old but indicates also the beginning of the new. Furthermore the number twelve, associated with Artemis, guardian of the unborn, is a promise of a new beginning or of a new life. If we divide that twelve into the eighty-fifth day of the actual story, we get seven with the number one left over. This fact leaves us to ask what "one" represents. In the ancient zodiac "one" meant unity. In Christian doctrine, the trinity is the union in one Godhead of three persons: Father, Son and Holy Ghost. When we recall that the Virgin gave birth to the one and only Son of God in the twelfth month of the year (at the winter solstice, December 22,

The Faith of Fifty Million

which is the beginning of the earth's new solar cycle) and that she first learned of her destiny through the seven words of the angel, we come to understand the meaning of the eighty-fifth day.[29]

Although allusions to Christianity interwoven throughout the text, especially allusions to the crucifixion, so abound as to suggest an allegorical intention on Hemingway's part,[30] Strauch's insistence that "numerology . . . provide[s] a key to deciphering the hermeneutics of Santiago's story,"[31] typified by the notion that Christ's birthdate can be ascribed to a specific day and month, is more ingenious than convincing.

Each of the preceding arguments attempting to account for Hemingway's selection of the numbers eighty-four and eighty-five is beset with difficulty. But the genesis and significance of the numbers make far greater sense when tied, not to some sly joke or religious anagoge, but to Hemingway's references to major-league baseball and its heroes, which occupy such a prominent place in the inner stitching of the novel. Seen in the context of events transpiring during the second full week of September 1950 in the American League pennant race, the numbers eighty-four and eighty-five derive meaning from the world of sport rather than from the world of spirit, for Santiago's sympathies and allegiances throughout his three-day encounter with the great fish lie less with Christ, savior of humankind, than with Joe DiMaggio, star outfielder for the New York Yankees. As I have indicated at length in "The Facts Behind the Fiction: The 1950 American League Pennant Race and *The Old Man and the Sea*," Manolin's comment to Santiago in their exchange about "the baseball"[32] that "they [the Yankees] lost today"[33] coupled with the old fisherman's lament on his second day at sea that

> He felt very tired now and he knew that night would come soon and he tried to think of other things. He thought of the Big Leagues, to him they were the *Gran Ligas,* and he knew the Yankees of New York were playing the *Tigres* of Detroit.
> This is the second day now that I do not know the results of the *juegos,* he thought . . .[34]

place the opening day of the novel on Tuesday, September 12, 1950. Corresponding historically to the day of the Yankees' loss to Cleveland, the loss to which Manolin refers, Tuesday, September 12, also precedes by two days the beginning of the Yankees' three-game series with the Tigers, to which Santiago alludes at sea. In short, the novel's action begins on Tuesday, September 12, Santiago's eighty-fourth day without a fish; extends through Wednesday, September 13, Thursday, September 14, and Friday, September 15 (Santiago's three days at sea); and ends on Saturday, September 16, with Santiago's return to port after doing battle with the great fish.

On the novel's first day and Santiago's eighty-fourth without a catch, the old man prepares to sit in the sun in the doorway of his shack and read about "the baseball" in "yesterday's paper"[35] while Manolin makes preparations for his aged friend's departure early the next morning. As a result of Hemingway's allusions to baseball, we discover that "yesterday's paper," dated Monday, September 11, recounts the events of the preceding day, Sunday, September 10, a day that not only proved momentous for Santiago's hero, Joe DiMaggio, and his beloved Yankees but also provided Hemingway a basis for the much-debated numbers.

On that day in history, the sports headlines, box scores, and team standings reveal that the New York Yankees, led by Joe DiMaggio's record-breaking three home runs in spacious Griffith Stadium, have triumphed over the lowly Washington Senators by an 8–1 score. After a sluggish start for the team and their thirty-five year-old star, the Yankees, with eight wins in their last eleven games and on a torrid winning pace since mid-August, recorded their *eighty-fourth* victory against forty-nine defeats to move into second place, one-half game behind their first-place rivals, the Detroit Tigers.[36]

The New York Times, below sports headlines proclaiming "DiMaggio Sets a Record" and "First Player to Hit 3 Homers in One Game at Griffith Stadium—Also Doubles," provides the following account of Sunday's events:

> The opener [the second scheduled game was rained out], during which DiMaggio drove his three circuit clouts into the distant left field bleachers, went to Casey Stengel's Bombers, 8–1. It marked the third time in his career that the Clipper had clubbed three in one game and the first time any batter, left or right handed, had been able to gain this distinction in the 30-year history of the present arena. All three clouts traveled well over 400 feet.[37]

Inspired by the account of the Yankee Clipper's assault on the record books and armed with the twofold awareness that the Yankees' eighty-fourth victory coincides numerically with his own eighty-fourth day of defeat and realizing that the Yankees, should they record at least one win against Washington in their scheduled doubleheader on Monday, September 11, would with their *eighty-fifth* victory secure at least a tie for the American League lead with the idle Detroit Tigers, Santiago determines that today of all days he will not drift and sleep with a bight around his toe.

Superstitious—"he knew that if you said a good thing it might not happen"[38]—a great believer in luck—"when luck comes you are ready"[39]—and willing to gamble—"if you were my boy [he says to Manolin] I'd take you out and gamble"[40]—Santiago, having read of the great DiMaggio's record-breaking exploits and of the Yankees' eighty-fourth win, realizes, nonetheless, that if he is to secure his own good fortune and garner the respect of his hero, then, today, his eighty-fifth without a catch, he must fish well.

Whether the result of coincidence, of his reliance on "tricks,"[41] of his skill and experience, or of his illogical faith in the efficacy of the number eighty-five,[42] Santiago succeeds, nonetheless, in hooking his long-awaited big fish, which is two feet longer than the skiff itself and with a sword longer than a baseball bat. For the next two days, the great fish tows him and his boat north and then east into the Gulf Stream. Despite his claim that he is not a religious man, Santiago, confused, exhausted, and faint as a result of his strenuous ordeal, promises nonetheless to "say ten Our Fathers and ten Hail Marys" and "to make a pilgrimage to the Virgin of Cobre"[43] in return for success in catching the great fish. But without success and "suffering exactly as much as before"[44] his prayers, Santiago eventually turns from thoughts of religion to thoughts of baseball and its heroes for strength and courage, as he often did when the "bad time[s]"[45] came.

In his never-ending quest to prove to himself just "what a man can do and what a man endures,"[46] Santiago, Hemingway implies, can find no better role model than the Yankees' Joe DiMaggio, "who does all things perfectly even with the pain of the bone spur in his heel,"[47] as attested to by his recent home run spree that led the Yankees to their eighty-fourth win. In a world that not only breaks but crucifies everyone, leaving many scarred in the hands, the most important thing, as Philip Young reminds us, is to be pretty good in there like DiMaggio and Santiago.[48]

Given the book's not-so-subtle allusions to Christianity, it is understandable, then, that commentators would seek to explain the numbers eighty-four and eighty-five in religious terms. But Santiago, though in many ways a spiritual man, seems to derive greater strength and sustenance from baseball than from the Bible. Rather than turn to personages of the Old and New Testaments to teach his young disciple lessons of courage and faith and to sustain himself during the "bad time[s]"[49] at sea, Santiago turns instead to the larger-than-life figures of the sports pages, well aware that his own victories depend less on divine intervention and petitionary prayer than on the kind of human strength and endurance displayed by men like the great DiMaggio. So profound, in fact, is Santiago's love and respect for the Yankees and their star player that the coincidental numerical correspondence of the Yankees' eighty-fourth and eighty-fifth victories to his own eighty-four-day span without catching a fish provides the superstitious old fisherman with the impetus needed to endure and prevail over his lonely encounter with the marlin and the sharks in the Gulf Stream.

Running parallel to the internal action of the novel, the games of baseball's "September Stretch," and especially the Yankees' eighty-fourth and eighty-fifth victories, serve not only to heighten and intensify Santiago's heroic encounter with the great marlin and the sharks, but also to place that encounter against the heroes of a sport that in the mythic sense is emblematic of humanity's struggle to endure and prevail. For Santiago, as we have seen, it is the constant measuring of self against the yardstick of the incomparable DiMaggio that sustains him in the agony of his ordeal, and it is his thoughts of the game itself that console and divert him when that agony becomes too great.

From the outset, Santiago and Manolin, by sharing their countrymen's passion for baseball, discover in their bantering about the exploits of Sisler and Durocher, Luque and Gonzalez, but especially of DiMaggio,[50] topics of mutual interest that not only solidify the bond between the old master and the aspiring apprentice but also strengthen the resolve of the aged fisherman when, after eight-four days without a catch, he struggles with the biggest fish "he had ever seen and bigger than he had ever heard of."[51]

Frequently comparing himself with the great DiMaggio, whose father was also a fisherman, Santiago repeatedly conjures up the image of the Yankee Clipper to win, despite the limitations imposed by infirmity, age, and pain, a hard-fought victory, first over the great fish itself and then over the sharks that would strip him of his record-breaking prize. It is small wonder that the beleaguered old man, buoyed by the newspaper accounts of the ballplayer's own record-breaking feats, longs "to take the great DiMaggio fishing"[52] with him. DiMaggio, the old fisherman implies, is the kind of man who in the batter's box or in an open boat "makes the difference."[53]

To increase his strength and confidence in his efforts to land the fish and to defend it from its attackers, Santiago, though he clearly knows the facts from following the newspaper accounts, purposely perpetuates the fiction that DiMaggio is still hampered by a painful bone spur on his right heel that cut short his play in the preceding season. Although he does not know if the pain in his "hands were as great a handicap as bone spurs,"[54] Santiago's suffering is such that he wonders whether "the great DiMaggio would stay with a fish as long as I will stay with this one."[55]

But if it is Santiago's fictional competition with the skilled but injured DiMaggio that sustains him when "the bad time" comes, it is his thoughts of the game itself that comfort and distract the old fisherman when those hard times test the limits of his endurance. Joined with the fish since noon of the first day and with no one to help him, Santiago turns repeatedly to thoughts of the big leagues and to the results of the games, thoughts that along with those of the boy and the lions serve him well until such time that his pain and confusion make it increasingly difficult to "think about something cheerful."[56]

On his final day at sea and his third with the fish, Santiago, weak and exhausted, succeeds nonetheless in harpooning his worthy opponent and lashing him beside the skiff for the long journey home, content that the great DiMaggio would have been proud of him that day. But then the sharks strike. Again seeking consolation from thoughts of baseball and its heroes and defending his catch until nothing remains but the head and tail and skeleton, Santiago, destroyed but not defeated, catches at last the reflected glare of the lights of the city at ten o'clock that night and sails into the harbor in the early hours of morning.

Secure in his shack, the old fisherman, asleep on the newspapers on his bed and with his arms out straight and the palms of his hands up, is discovered some hours later by Manolin. Overwhelmed by what Santiago has obviously endured, the boy, amidst plans to rejoin Santiago at sea, prepares for his sleeping friend a pot of hot coffee. As Manolin leaves to bring the old man something to eat and a clean shirt, Santiago's lone request is for "any of the papers of the time that I was gone,"[57] not to read the front-page headlines of the day, but to learn of the great

DiMaggio and the fate of his beloved Yankees. When the young boy returns, the old fisherman is asleep and dreaming about the lions.

We do not know, of course, the dates of the papers that Manolin will provide. Unless an early-morning edition of Saturday's paper is available, Friday's paper (September 15) will report that the Yankees won both the final game against Cleveland (played on Wednesday, September 13) and the first game against Detroit (played on Thursday, September 14) to move into first place by half a game. With Friday's sports headlines proclaiming that "Yanks Regain League Lead by Downing Tigers" as "DiMaggio Blasts no. 29" (*Times,* September 15), Santiago is doubtless pleased to learn that in the three days he was doing battle with the greatest foe of his long career, alone on the Gulf Stream, the great DiMaggio and his Yankees, in one of the most exciting weeks of the 1950 season, were before thousands of jubilant fans in Yankee Stadium proving themselves victors in contests of another sort.

Readers familiar with Hemingway's larger vision know, of course, that every story if followed long enough ends not in victory but in defeat, that ultimately even winners take nothing. Whether for Santiago, whose determination and courage in the face of danger and despair on the Gulf Stream enabled him to overcome the worthiest opponent of his career, or for Joe DiMaggio, whose skill and grace against opponents of another sort and in another arena led his team to glory and earned him the adoration and respect of the nation, the time will come when determination and courage, skill and grace prove to be insufficient. Despite his contention that man was not made for defeat and despite his resolve to repair the broken rudder of his skiff to return with Manolin to the sea, Santiago, with increased age and failing strength, will not live to fish many more seasons. Similarly, Santiago's worthy counterpart, Joe DiMaggio, who in September 1950 at age thirty-five contributed mightily to the Yankees winning the American League pennant and ultimately the World Series, will, for reasons comparable to Santiago's, retire at the end of the 1951 season, after posting numbers that did not approach the standards of excellence he established for himself over the course of a brilliant career.

As his biographer, Michael Reynolds, so eloquently reminds us, Hemingway's constant message throughout his canon was simple and true: "We are doomed to lose, so we must lose on our own terms. It is all that is left us, we exiles from the garden of Eden";[58] but, for a brief moment at least, we are heartened by Hemingway's stirring portrayals of an aged fisherman and an aged ballplayer who through strength of will and passion for excellence have left us with the nobler, more hopeful message of "what a man can do and what a man endures," even in the face of ultimate defeat.

Far more, then, than some sly fishing joke or some obscure religious anagoge, Hemingway's allusions to baseball through the numbers eighty-four and eighty-five set Santiago's efforts at sea against the larger world of the game's "September stretch drive" to achieve for the novel a single, thematic whole. Santiago and Manolin's musings about baseball, its heroes, and their achievements, when examined within the framework of an old fisherman's solitary struggle, serve not only to date the internal events of the book, but, more important, to allow that struggle to achieve both temporal and thematic resonance with a world of sport whose contests for many seem a paradigm of the human condition. Whether for an aged fisherman alone in an open boat testing his skill and endurance against marlin and sharks on the Gulf Stream, or for an aging baseball player measuring his strength and courage against the Indians of Cleveland or the Tigers of Detroit in Yankee Stadium, the contest is the same; and in the application of skill and strength, endurance and courage lies humankind's only hope for victory, short-lived though it may be.

C. Harold Hurley

1	2	3	4	5	6	7	8	9	R	H	E

Chapter 5

From Scapegoat to Icon:
The Strange Journey of Shoeless Joe Jackson

William R. Herzog II

The story of Joe Jackson and the Black Sox scandal of 1919 are intricately interwoven, and it is difficult, if not impossible, to discuss Shoeless Joe without engaging the larger issue of the fix. While this essay concentrates on Jackson and argues that he was wrongfully accused of participating in the fix, it also deals with the scandal as the framework needed to understand the strange journey of Shoeless Joe Jackson. It needs to be said that this is but a sketch of a longer and more detailed project that, owing to space constraints, cannot be presented here.[1]

The Story of Joe Jackson[2]

Joe Jackson was born in the spring of 1887 or 1889. Inaccurate records do not allow a more precise dating, although the *The Baseball Encyclopedia* (1974) lists his birthday as July 16, 1887, while *Total Baseball,* 7th edition (2001) lists his birthday as July 16, 1889.[3] He was born to Martha and George Jackson, who lived in Pickens County, South Carolina. George worked at a sawmill with his three brothers, and he may have been a tenant farmer as well. When work became scarce, he moved his family to the new mill towns that were then being built, eventually settling down in Brandon Mills. When his family arrived in Brandon Mills, Joe was six or seven years old, so he went to work in the mill along with his father. George Jackson worked in the engine room of the mill, and

Joe probably swept floors. Mill owners used child laborers as a matter of course, although they felt defensive enough about their practice to justify it by noting that children under twelve worked only sixty-six hours a week (as opposed to the seventy-hour weeks put in by adult workers) and worked in jobs that required less heavy work.

Mill owners encouraged the formation of mill baseball teams because they believed that these teams would help to keep mill workers and would build loyalty to the mill town. It didn't take the local team long to discover Joe's talents, but they waited until he was twelve to recruit him for the team. Joe was probably earning $35 a week, so the $2.50 he would earn for each game he played was a welcome addition to his income. In addition, the folks who attended the games would "pass the hat" for any player who hit a home run. Joe specialized in hitting these "Saturday specials" and earned a hatful of change when he did. Because he was so well liked by the folks of Brandon Mills, Joe usually received a generous offering.

His play in the mill league attracted the attention of local baseball scouts, and eventually Joe was recruited to play professional baseball in a variety of minor-league teams, such as the local team, the Greenville Spinners, and others farther away, including the New Orleans Pelicans of the Southern League and the Savannah Indians of the South Atlantic League. It was during his sojourn in the minor leagues that Joe Jackson acquired his nickname. He was breaking in a new pair of spikes and found them too tight and uncomfortable, so he played a game without shoes. A spectator is said to have noticed and remarked, "Look at that shoeless sonovabitch." The nickname stuck, although Joe never liked it very much. In time, his contract was purchased by Connie Mack of the Philadelphia Athletics. Joe made his debut in the major leagues at the end of the 1908 season, when he played five games for the team, but his relationship with the veterans on the team was cold and hostile. When he reported, they baited him mercilessly, no doubt because he was illiterate. Recognizing his enormous talent, Connie Mack tried to make him feel at home, but his efforts were undercut by his own players. Mack tried for two years to integrate Jackson into the team but failed miserably. Jackson kept returning to the South where he felt at home.

Finally, in 1910, Connie Mack traded Jackson to the Cleveland Naps, where Joe and his wife Katie were well received and felt at home. In his first full season for Cleveland, Jackson hit .408, the only player in major-league history to hit .400 in his rookie season. The Naps' fans appreciated Jackson's defensive play as well as his hitting. Joe hit .408, .395, .373, and .338 for Cleveland. During the 1915 season, when he was hitting .331, he was sold to the Chicago White Sox, a team then on the rise. The move from Cleveland to Chicago was not traumatic, but Jackson never liked Chicago as much as Cleveland. The years there, from 1910 to 1914, were the happiest years of his professional life.

Jackson's sale to Chicago made headline news. In March of 1916, *Baseball Magazine* devoted virtually an entire issue to Joe Jackson, telling his rags-to-riches tale. It was a Horatio Alger story with a strange and fatal twist—the hero was an illiterate Southerner! Jackson continued his productive years for Chicago, hitting .341, .301, .354, and .351. He was hitting .382 when he was suspended just before the end of the 1920 season. In 1915, when Charles Comiskey purchased Jackson's contract for the unheard-of price of $65,000, he declared to the baseball world just how much Joe Jackson was worth. The scandal, however, would change everything. In 1920, Joe Jackson could look forward to several more seasons of continued success. After the scandal broke and he was scapegoated for it, his career was over. The success story had become a strange journey indeed.

The Cover Story

For eighty years, organized baseball has perpetuated a cover story to explain the so-called Black Sox scandal. The cover story blames the "eight men out"[4] who colluded with gamblers to fix the 1919 World Series but reserves special censure for Shoeless Joe Jackson who becomes, in this version of events, the scapegoat for the entire affair. Nowhere in recent times has the official cover story been told more effectively or more erroneously than in Ken Burns's *Baseball*.[5] From the beginning sequences of his documentary to his portrayal of the scandal, Burns subjects Joe Jackson to unremitting calumny and obloquy. The character assassination begins in the prologue of the documentary, where Jackson is first introduced to the viewer in one of a series of still photographs. As Jackson's picture fills the screen, a voice-over intones, "a mill hand, who could neither read nor write, and who might have been one of the game's greatest heroes if temptation had not proved too great."[6] The film begins by declaring Jackson guilty and hinting that his poverty and illiteracy were contributing factors.

The actual portrayal of the scandal follows from the acceptance of the cover story. Burns introduces the six conspirators whom Chick Gandil, the instigator of the fix, has purportedly recruited through a series of quick snapshots and a brief identifying phrase until he comes to the final "conspirator," Joe Jackson. While the camera holds on a picture of Jackson batting, the voice-over continues,

> and the idol of schoolboys all over the Midwest, Joseph Jefferson Jackson. In two years, he had risen from a poor millhand to the rank of a player in the major leagues. The ignorant mill boy had become the hero of millions. . . . There came a day when a crook spread money before this ignorant idol and he fell. For a few dollars, which perhaps seemed like a fortune to him, he sold his honor . . .[7]

The narrator is quoting from Hugh Fullerton's article in *The New York Evening World*, (September 30, 1920), which Fullerton wrote shortly after the news of Eddie Cicotte's and Jackson's Grand Jury "confessions" had made front-page news and at the moment when the case against them appeared to be airtight. All Fullerton had to go on were excerpts of Jackson's supposedly privileged testimony leaked to the press, excerpts that either distorted what Jackson had said or fabrications that were placed in his mouth. More to the point, the article reflects Fullerton's longstanding animosity toward Jackson. In 1911, when Jackson was developing his reputation as a fledgling major leaguer, Fullerton wrote, "a man who can't read or write . . . simply can't expect to meet the requirements of big league baseball as it is played today."[8] Like so many others who wrote about Joe Jackson, Fullerton confused illiteracy with ignorance and a working-class background with incompetence. It was as though Fullerton could not forgive Jackson for being poor and illiterate. Yet, Burns introduces this biased material as though it were sober and reasoned historical reflection on Jackson's character and role in the scandal.

Having prejudged Jackson, the film turns to the games of the 1919 World Series. In the description of Game One, the narrator notes that Joe Jackson "seemed to throw wide from the outfield and deliberately to slow down to miss balls hit near him."[9] The source of this misinformation is found in the newspaper versions of the testimony that Jackson reputedly gave to the Grand Jury. As Harold Seymour notes,

The newspapers printed different versions of their confessions, none of them complete. . . . Jackson told of moving slowly after balls hit to him, making throws that fell short and deliberately striking out with runners in scoring position.[10]

The New York Times reported Jackson as saying that "throughout the series, he either struck out or hit easy balls when hits would mean runs."[11] Nowhere does the actual transcript of Jackson's Grand Jury testimony make any of these assertions.[12] Can the narrator's assertions about Jackson's performance in Game One and the alleged, self-incriminating confessions of Jackson survive the scrutiny of what actually happened in the World Series? A closer examination of Jackson's role in the 1919 Series will help to answer this question.

One thing is clear. In Game One, Jackson did nothing of the kind. A contemporary pitch-by-pitch description of the game indicates that Jackson handled every chance in the field flawlessly.[13] Evidently, the creators of the documentary *Baseball* decided that they could not convict Jackson on the basis of his performance at bat, so they attempted to convict him on his fielding. After the description of Game Four, the narrator observes, "Only at bat did Jackson evidently forget the script. He would bat .375 in the Series." Yet, a more detailed look at Jackson's fielding opportunities in the Series reveals an incontrovertibly fine performance.[14]

A brief look at Game Four will illustrate the pattern for the entire series. Game Four kept Jackson busy. In the first inning, he barely missed Morrie Rath's foul ball that dropped near the temporary boxes in left field. In the third inning, Rath lofted another foul ball to the same place. A contemporary description of the play says that "Jackson was after the ball like a deer but missed the catch after a hard run."[15] Hardly the description of a slacker throwing a game! Jackson made neither catch in foul territory, but his effort was unquestioned. He retired Edd Roush on a fly out in the second inning and Rath on a short fly in the fourth, because he was playing shallow as outfielders often did in the dead ball era, and he caught Jake Daubert's line drive in the ninth. But the play that most reveals Jackson's relationship to the conspirators came in the fifth inning. Pat Duncan bounced a grounder off Cicotte's glove and reached first. When Cicotte, who was committed to the fix, threw wildly to Chick Gandil, Duncan took second. Larry Kopf followed with a sharp single to left field. Jackson charged the ball and, assuming that Duncan would try to score, threw to the plate. "The throw was sailing straight and true" toward the catcher Ray Schalk when Cicotte attempted to cut off the throw and deflected the ball with his glove. "The move was disastrous. The ball, traveling with the speed of a bullet . . . rolled to the stand back of the plate."[16] Duncan then scored. Why would Cicotte make such an obvious effort to interfere with Jackson's throw and bungle the cutoff attempt unless he assumed that Jackson was playing to win? This is why he had to cut off Jackson's throw.[17] In an article published in *Sports Illustrated,* Gandil said that he told Cicotte to cut off Jackson's throw to the plate because he thought it could not get Duncan heading toward the plate while they might get Kopf, who was taking second on the throw.[18] Gandil's memory of the play, like many other reminiscences in the article, is self-serving and suspicious, but if he did call for the cutoff, then he too believed Jackson was playing to win. The majority of those who witnessed the play agree that, had he gone home, Duncan would have been thrown out at the plate. No play shows more clearly than this play how hard Jackson was playing to win. It took a conspirator (Cicotte) to compromise his throw to the plate and allow a run to score. However, on the next play, Jackson did make a mistake by playing Greasy Neale too shallow in left. Neale hit one over Jackson's head, and in spite of his best efforts, it landed just out of the reach of his glove in deep left field. In the October 1949 issue of *Sport Magazine,* Jackson told his version of the 1919 Series. When asked if he saw any suspicious plays, he singled out this play.

> [N]ow that I think back over it, Cicotte seemed to let up on a pitch to Pat Duncan, and Pat put it over my head. Duncan didn't have enough power to hit the ball that far, particularly if Cicotte had been bearing down.[19]

Jackson confuses Duncan, the runner he nearly gunned down at the plate, with Neale, the next batter who hit the ball over his head, but he does reveal why he made the mistake. He assumed Cicotte was pitching to win, and he positioned himself in left field working on this assumption. Neale, a .242 hitter for the 1919 season, was a left-handed batter not known for his power. He did, however, have a banner series, hitting .357, though eight of his ten hits were singles. Clearly, Jackson thought a finely tuned Cicotte could handle Neale, and on this occasion, he was wrong. The same pattern of defensive excellence continues throughout the rest of the Series.

One conclusion clearly emerges from descriptions of Jackson's defensive play. Joe Jackson played to win. He was consistently praised for his effort even on plays that he failed to make, and he played errorless ball throughout the Series. In Game Four, he made one mental error by playing Neale too shallow in left and allowed a double to be hit over his head. But Jackson played Neale where he did on the assumption that Cicotte was pitching to win. It was an erroneous assumption. All of this means that Burns's theory that Jackson hit to win but fielded to lose is false. The facts speak for themselves, and with one voice, they exonerate Joe Jackson.

Some have tried to make the case that Jackson's hitting was less convincing than his fielding. He did hit .375 (12 for 32) in the Series, and he would have hit .406 (13 for 32) had the official scorer not changed his mind and scored Jackson's sharp grounder to Rath, which he knocked down, as an error. He had originally scored it as a hit. On its Internet site, ESPN made the case that Jackson "sure didn't do much to help his team win."[20] This conclusion was based on his reputed failure to hit with runners on base. Yet, using the very statistics that ESPN took from David Neft and Richard Cohen's *The World Series*, Jackson hit .353 (6 for 17) with runners on base, and this figure omits the single-turned-error that advanced Eddie Collins to second base (Game Four). In addition, Jackson advanced runners by hitting the ball to the right side of the infield, including the ground out to first that advanced runners to second and third (Game One), from second to third (Game Four), and from first to second (Game Seven). In the dead ball era, players sacrificed and hit to the right side to advance runners, so a batter's effectiveness needs to include more than his number of hits. In the sixth inning of Game Two, Jackson did strike out once with a runner in scoring position, and he failed to sacrifice in the third inning of Game Three.

Jackson was a model of consistency throughout the series. He batted .500 (4 for 8) when leading off an inning and .250 (2 for 8) when hitting with the bases empty but not leading off. He hit .375 (6 for 16) with runners on base.[21] This means that Jackson hit .375 (6 for 16) with the bases empty and the same with runners on base. The ESPN Web site criticizes Jackson for hitting to the opposite field and, in fact, many of his hits were to left field. In Jackson's era, good hitters used the entire field. No player could hit for a lifetime batting average of .356 and not use the whole field. However, this doesn't tell the full story. When hitting to the right side would advance runners, Jackson did so. As already noted, he hit to the right side to advance runners in Games One, Four, and Seven. Jackson had six runs batted in (RBIs) and scored five runs, and he scored these runs even though the hitters behind him (Happy Felsch, Gandil, and Swede Risberg) were not playing to win. Four times Jackson reached third and was stranded there by one of these three players. The ESPN Web site notes that Jackson failed to score from third on a ground ball hit to the shortstop, but the contemporary account observes that Kopf, the Cincinnati shortstop, was "playing in on the grass," perhaps to cut off the run at the plate.[22] Jackson held at third because he was an alert base runner, not because he was playing to lose.

With runners on base, Jackson was two for nine in the five games the White Sox lost, and he was four for seven in the three games they won. However, he scored three runs and drove in three runs in the five games the Sox lost, while he scored two runs and drove in three runs in the three games that the Sox won. All in all, his five runs scored and six RBIs accounted for ten of the twenty runs that the Sox scored in the series.[23] Some critics have noted that Jackson's home run and double came in the final game, a decisive 10–5 loss. But his home run came in the third inning, making the score 5–1, and his two RBIs came in the eighth inning as part of a four-run rally that narrowed the score from a 10–1 rout into a 10–5 game and kept alive the possibility of victory, however slight. What better time to hit than when your team needs runs or faces elimination?

The only condition under which anyone could conclude that Joe Jackson played to lose would be to assume that he had the ability to get hits at will and to make outs at will, a proposal that is patently absurd. In an interesting study, Victor Luhrs has argued that the White Sox lost the Series because the regular players who were *not* in on the fix played so poorly, especially their lack of hitting, and because the team was thin on pitching.[24] Urban "Red" Faber, one of the White Sox's best pitchers, developed a sore arm late in the season and could not pitch in the Series, and the Sox relief pitching was suspect, as their collective performance in the Series would demonstrate. No less a luminary than Christy Mathewson made the same point in his series of special reports to *The New York Times*. In his column for September 30, 1919, the day before the Series opened, he noted that both teams had strong starting pitching but added,

. . . if it comes to using relief pitchers, I think the Reds have the advantage. Their staff is generally stronger on the whole. . . . [B]ut when it comes to the balance of the staff, the Reds have the better men on the average.[25]

In his column for Sunday, September 28, 1919, Mathewson had noted how often teams that depended on one pitcher as heavily as the White Sox were depending on Cicotte were disappointed. It seemed obvious to Mathewson that Hod Eller, Dutch Ruether, Jimmy Ring, or Slim Sallee could "prove [to be] the master of Cicotte or Williams." In addition, he gave the definite offensive edge to the Reds, based on their hitting prowess. Since so much has been made about Mathewson sitting in judgment on the series, it is interesting to note that he did not view a White Sox victory as a foregone conclusion. He even predicted a Reds victory before the Series began!

If the historical situation of the 1919 World Series was as ambiguous and unclear as it seemed to Mathewson, and if Jackson's performance was as good as it was, why did Burns's documentary make such a concerted effort to slander Jackson's memory? The excerpts from Jackson's Grand Jury testimony are edited to make it seem as though Katie Jackson is condemning her husband for participating in the scheme. Inevitably, Burns uses the "say it ain't so" story, even though Jackson denied it ever happened.[26] Whether Jackson was right in attributing the origin of the story to Charley Owens of the *Chicago Daily News* is an open question. The writer who popularized the story and spread it across the country was Hugh Fullerton, a figure whose animosity toward Jackson is well established. The documentary continually emphasized the larger implications of the scandal as a way of underlining its heinousness. This approach reinforces Judge Kenesaw Mountain Landis's observation:

> Baseball is something more than a game to an American boy. It is his training field for life work. Destroy his faith in its squareness and honesty and you have destroyed something more; you have planted suspicion of all things in his heart.[27]

It requires little imagination to guess how the section on the Black Sox scandal will cover Judge Landis's verdict on the eight men out. With the camera slowly moving in for a tight closeup of Jackson's face, the voice-over recites the familiar words of Landis's last judgment:

Regardless of the verdict of juries, no player that throws a ball game; no player that undertakes or promises to throw a ball game; no player that sits in a conference with a bunch of crooked players and gamblers where the ways and means of throwing games are planned and discussed and does not promptly tell his club about it, will ever play professional baseball.[28]

By the coordination of the script and the visual, the full weight of Landis's verdict falls on Jackson; the other seven men out have faded into oblivion. Although he should have known better, Daniel Okrent opines that "a man as simple as Jackson" could have no sense of the consequences of his actions. "His livelihood was taken away and, with it, his life. He lived another thirty years but not very happily." The fact that none of this is true seems not to have disturbed either the speaker or the creator of this section of the documentary.

Why was this the case? What did Burns think he was doing? Fortunately, he gives an insight into his conception of his work in a story carried in *The Greenville News* on August 7, 1994. In the article, Burns made it clear that he was "not interested in just facts and dates but how facts and dates and human lives in collision cause emotion." He and his crew were doing the work of "emotional archaeologists." This apparently means, then, that Burns found the conflict created by the cover story of the 1919 World Series, leading to the collision of Landis and Jackson, and he developed it because it was emotionally satisfying. The fact that he and his crew conspired to destroy Jackson's memory and defame his character one more time must have seemed a secondary consideration. At one level, Burns's approach has a certain logic and reflects a truth. Our emotions do enliven historical inquiry, and our passion to understand the past persuades us to revisit the past and reinterpret its meaning. This very essay is an example of that pursuit. But when its emotionally satisfying character becomes the criterion on which historical inquiry is based, it can pervert the quest for a fuller accounting of the past and its complexities as well as frustrate the search for justice. In the end, Burns could not resist the portrayal of Landis as, in George Will's words, "Jupiter in a very bad mood," confronting the frail and finite illiterate millhand from the South, passing final judgment on him, and thereby vindicating baseball and redeeming its future.

The permanence of the final triumph of the baseball establishment is portrayed in the encounter between Ty Cobb and Joe Jackson that occurred when Cobb stopped to buy a fifth of bourbon at Jackson's liquor store. After selling him the bourbon without an acknowledgement, Cobb asked Jackson, "Don't you know me, Joe?" Jackson answered, "Sure, I know you, Ty. I just didn't think anyone I used to know up there wanted to recognize me again."[29] Thus was the banishment and exile of Joe Jackson complete and the prophecy of Hugh Fullerton fulfilled. It would appear that the emotional dig of the archaeological tell was complete, but the truth is that Burns's documentary did not even begin to scratch the surface, to say nothing of exposing the layers hidden beneath the surface of the cover story.

The Fix

It was important to begin with the World Series as it was reported. The description of Joe Jackson's performance in the Series makes a prima facie case that Jackson played to win and establishes a framework for reconstructing Jackson's role in the events that preceded and followed the Series. If Jackson played to win, then he was not one of the players who conspired to throw the Series, a status he shares with Buck Weaver. Indeed, if the players who were not in on the fix had supported the efforts of Jackson and Weaver, both of whom led the team in hitting and fielded well, and if the Sox relief pitching had had any success at all, then the White Sox might have won the Series even with the fix on. But some important questions about Jackson remain to be answered. What did Jackson know about the fix? When did he know it? What did he do about it? Why was he condemned? To answer these questions requires some knowledge of how the scheme to fix the Series evolved.

The more immediate origins of the fix trace at least to mid-July of the 1919 season, when the White Sox players threatened to strike unless their salaries were readjusted to reflect baseball's postwar prosperity. During the 1918 season, the baseball owners had shortened the season from 154 to 140 games because the nation was at war. Believing that baseball might not be as popular in the aftermath of the war as it had been before, the owners shortened the 1919 season as well. Because baseball players were paid by the month, the shortening of the season meant that all contracts would be reduced by a proportionate amount. This had happened in 1918, and the practice was repeated for the 1919 season. But, as usual, the baseball owners were wrong. Baseball was more popular than ever in 1919, and attendance hit new highs. Realizing that the owners were making record profits, the White Sox players threatened to strike unless their salaries were adjusted to reflect this unexpected popularity and profit. The manager of the Sox, Kid Gleason, promised to take the players' concerns to the owner, Charles Comiskey, who was, by any measure, one of the stingiest owners in baseball. He habitually underpaid his players because he compared their salaries not with the salaries of their professional peers but with what they could make if they worked in a factory or a mill. He was, in the words of Okrent, "a man of small mind, a tight fist and a nasty temperament" who abused his players horribly.[30] The stories of his cheap and abusive behavior are well known. He charged his players for cleaning their uniforms, provided $3 a day for meals rather than the standard $4, and negotiated contracts by invoking the reserve clause, thus depriving his players of any negotiating power whatsoever. After promising Cicotte a $10,000 bonus if he won thirty games in 1919, he benched him after he won twenty-nine on the pretense that he was resting him for the World Series. It is probably no accident that Cicotte demanded $10,000 before the series began as his condition for participating in the fix. He would get his bonus one way or another.[31] Chick Gandil remembered Comiskey as "a sarcastic, belittling man who was the tightest owner in baseball."[32] Asinof summarized his character succinctly when he observed that "he was a cheap, stingy tyrant."[33] In light of these character references, it will come as no surprise to learn that Comiskey crushed the near strike. Cicotte was so furious that Gleason decided not to pitch him that afternoon, a reaction noted by Gandil. It is quite possible that Gandil saw this aborted strike as the goad he needed to recruit players to throw the World Series, but it was too early to know whether the Sox would win the pennant, so he bided his time.

Although the White Sox did not clinch the pennant until September 25, just three days before the end of the season, it was clear, as early as mid-September, that they were very likely to do so. On September 14, *The New York Times* carried an analysis of the White Sox team, which had "all but clinched the honors for which they have been battling since last April," in order to assess its chances against the Cincinnati Reds of the National League. It was on the Sox's last Eastern trip of the year that the fix began to take shape.[34] It is no longer possible to say with certainty whether the players pitched the gamblers or the gamblers approached the players. Gandil claims that Sport Sullivan approached him about a week before the series and proposed that, if he could form a "syndicate" of seven or eight players to throw the series, he would pay each player

$10,000. In his testimony before the Grand Jury, however, Sleepy Bill Burns said that the players had actually initiated the contact on September 16 and 18. Burns, a former major-league pitcher who played for both the Reds and White Sox among other teams[35] and a small-time gambler, ran into Cicotte in the lobby of the Ansonia Hotel in New York and, sensing that something big was in the making, asked the players to let him bid for their services. On September 18, Gandil along with Cicotte pitched the fix to Burns. The Sox would throw the series for $100,000. The discrepancy between the two accounts may be more apparent than real, since there were, in fact, two groups of gamblers working with the players. Sport Sullivan represented the interests of Arnold Rothstein, who put up $80,000 to buy the fix, and Abe Attell, an associate of Rothstein's, headed another group of gamblers that used Rothstein's name but operated without his permission or his money. The Attell group was the group with whom Sleepy Bill Burns and Billy Maharg worked. They acted as mediators between the players and the gamblers. It is possible that Sullivan approached the players while the players approached Burns and Maharg. Whatever the case, both groups of gamblers double-crossed the players, who received very little of the money promised.

It is probable that Gandil had initiated serious efforts to recruit a cadre of players to participate in the fix sometime in early to mid-September. His first two targets took some convincing. Cicotte was especially bitter about Comiskey's treatment of him but he was not certain that he wanted to throw the Series, so Gandil cultivated him slowly. Gandil knew that, if he could get Cicotte, then he could enlist Claude "Lefty" Williams. He didn't need more than two pitchers since Red Faber would be unable to pitch in the Series. Gandil then recruited Swede Risberg, Oscar "Happy" Felsch, and Fred McMullin. Whether Buck Weaver was part of the group this early is an open question. It is no longer possible to know the detailed tactics of Gandil's recruiting efforts, but his strategy is clear. The 1919 White Sox were divided into two hostile camps, one centered around Eddie Collins and Ray Schalk, the other around Chick Gandil and Swede Risberg. The Gandil-Risberg camp included Eddie Cicotte, Lefty Williams, Happy Felsch, Fred McMullin, Buck Weaver, and Joe Jackson. Gandil recruited exclusively within the confines of his faction on the team. It was not a tightly knit group of close friends; the bonds of the faction were weak enough. As Gandil remembers, "there was a common bond among most of us—our dislike for Comiskey."[36]

During the recruiting period, Gandil approached Jackson twice. The first contact was in Boston. Jackson was walking in Kenmore Square when Gandil approached him and invited him to join the fix. He promised Jackson $10,000 if he would participate. Jackson refused, and Gandil left. This first contact occurred on September 19, 20, or 21, on the Sox's last road trip to Boston.[37] On the basis of this brief encounter, Jackson had no idea whether or not there really was a fix. Gandil felt him out, and Jackson slammed the door in his face. Gandil evidently believed that Jackson would be a willing participant but was forced to reconsider his situation after their brief encounter. But Gandil was nothing if not persistent, so he made a second approach after the White Sox returned home, most likely on September 24 or 25 but possibly as late as September 26. He intercepted Jackson on the "small wooden bridge leading to the White Sox clubhouse."[38] This time he offered Jackson $20,000 and pressured him to participate. He told Jackson that the fix was going to happen whether he joined the conspiracy or not. Why be a fool, he asked Jackson, and be left out of the money? Jackson refused, and Gandil left.

This meeting occurred at least a week after the meeting in Gandil's room at the Ansonia Hotel in New York on September 16 or 17, the first time the seven conspirators gathered together to plot their moves. Jackson was not present at the meeting; indeed he could not have been, since Gandil had not even approached Jackson about participating in the fix and would not do so for another day or two. In fact, Jackson was never present at any of the meetings where the conspirators gathered. Bill Burns, whose testimony proved to be so damning, admitted that Jackson was not present at the meetings on September 16 and 18.[39] Nor was he present at any of the subsequent meetings. How then did his name get associated with the seven conspirators? Why did they use his name? The answer to the second question is evident. They needed to use Jackson's name to convince the gamblers to put up the big money they were demanding. It would do no good to attempt a fix without the team's leading hitter. So Lefty Williams presented himself as representing Jackson. He did this without Jackson's knowledge or permission. In Jackson's 1924 suit against Comiskey for unpaid back wages, Ray Cannon, Jackson's attorney, placed Lefty Williams on the stand, and under oath, Williams confessed to using Jackson's name without his permission.[40]

When could Jackson have known that a fix was on? The answer is readily available. On the morning of October 1, the day that the Series was to open in Cincinnati, Jackson was in the lobby of the Sinton Hotel when Bill Burns saw him and began to talk excitedly about the fix. Jackson was confused because he had no certain knowledge that a fix was on or who was in on it. Burns sensed his confusion and, realizing his mistake, disappeared into the crowd. This was, as Donald Gropman notes, "the first corroboration he got that the fix was actually in."[41] Gandil's approaches had been just feelers, but Burns spoke of a fully developed plot, so, on the morning of October 1, 1919, Jackson knew the series was rigged. What did he do? The very thing he was condemned for not doing. He went to Kid Gleason and/or Charles Comiskey and notified the ball club.[42]

At this point, the historical record lacks critical details. On the basis of Bill Burns's easy assumption that he was in on the fix, Jackson must have suspected that his name was being used in connection with the scheme. Jackson had only two real choices: he could speak to Kid Gleason or to Charles Comiskey. Gropman believes that Jackson went straight to Comiskey and asked to be benched. When Jackson told him why,

> Comiskey refused. . . . He laughed off the rumors and reminded Joe that similar stories circulated almost every year and told him not to worry. But we don't know if Comiskey questioned Joe to learn if he knew more, or promised to protect Joe if anything came of his fears.[43]

After Comiskey refused, Jackson remembers saying, "Tell the newspapers you just suspended me for being drunk, or anything, but leave me out of the Series and then there can be no question."[44] Asinof constructs a different picture, but it is based on his assumption that Jackson, an easily manipulated ignoramus, had reluctantly gone along with "the boys" to throw the Series. Now, on opening day, he was beginning to feel the effects of his decision. He was conflicted and, driven by his feelings of inferiority and ignorance, he tried to stay on the bench. However, Kid Gleason told him to play.[45] The difficulty with Asinof's scenario is that it makes unwarranted assumptions about Jackson's participation in the fix so that it is misleading and, in light of what has been said above, simply wrong.

In spite of the confusion, it is possible to suggest what probably happened. Jackson went to Comiskey, as he would attempt to do again after the Series was over. Since his own knowledge of the fix was garbled and uncertain, based as it was on the hurried comments of Bill Burns in the crowded lobby of the Sinton Hotel, Jackson could communicate little more to Comiskey than his fears and apprehensions. He did not want to be painted with the brush of conspiracy. Believing that Jackson was passing along rumors and not much else, Comiskey dismissed the conversation. He did not have a high regard for Jackson in any case. It is unlikely that Jackson would have gone to Kid Gleason because he was more difficult to find alone, and Jackson would not want to talk about his fears in a public place, especially where any of his teammates might overhear him. However, once he had gone to Comiskey, Jackson knew that he would be under scrutiny. He had to play to win so that "there can be no question" that he participated in the fix. I have suggested that a detailed analysis of his play in the Series exonerates him from such suspicions. In later years, Jackson always pointed with pride to his hitting and fielding.[46]

To summarize: In the weeks preceding the World Series, Chick Gandil approached Jackson twice about participating in the fix. Jackson refused both times, even though Gandil had doubled the amount offered. The six players who were committed to the fix (Cicotte, Gandil, Williams, Risberg, Felsch, and McMullin) and Buck Weaver, who met with them but eventually decided not to join the conspiracy, met on September 16 or 17 to discuss the details of their scheme for throwing the Series. The seven players met at the team hotel in Chicago, the Warner, on September 29, and probably earlier (between September 24 and 28) with each set of gamblers. Jackson knew about neither meeting. Not until October 1, as the result of a chance encounter with Sleepy Bill Burns in the lobby of the Sinton Hotel in Cincinnati, did Jackson learn that a fully developed scheme was in place. When he did learn this, he reported the information, however incomplete, directly to his team, probably through a meeting with Charles Comiskey. Comiskey dismissed Jackson's fears and ordered him to play.

It is interesting to note that, after the first game of the Series, Comiskey had a change of heart and decided that something was so wrong with his team that the matter had to be brought before the National Commission, the committee of three that oversaw major-league baseball. But he faced a problem. One of the members of the Commission was Garry Herrmann, owner of the Cincinnati Reds, and the other member was Ban Johnson, with whom Comiskey, the third member, had been feuding for years. It was impossible to go directly to Johnson, so Comiskey confided in his old friend, John Heydler, president of the National League. The story says that when Heydler took Comiskey's con-

The Faith of Fifty Million

cerns to Ban Johnson, he dismissed them with the famous one-liner, "That's the whelp of a beaten cur."[47] Seymour thinks the story is apocryphal. Based on Grabiner's diaries, Seymour thinks that Harry Grabiner, who was Comiskey's secretary and ombudsman, communicated Comiskey's concerns to Heydler, who promised to take the matter to Ban Johnson. But Heydler did not think it possible to fix a World Series, so he pocket-vetoed the matter and did not respond to Grabiner's request to put the matter before the National Commission.[48] He had reportedly dismissed Comiskey's anxiety by declaring flatly, "You can't fix a World Series, Commy."[49] What is of interest is Comiskey's seemingly sudden conviction that the Series was being thrown. Where did this conviction come from? He had heard rumors from gamblers and baseball men alike, but it might have been the conversation with Jackson, a member of his own team, that tipped the scales of his concern. After the conversation with Jackson, Comiskey might have viewed Game One with different eyes. If this were the case, Comiskey never gave Jackson credit but, as will become evident, he had good reason to follow this course of action.

Where does all of this leave Joe Jackson? A simple comparison of his actions with the conditions of Judge Landis's banishment decree is informative. Landis's pronouncement had three specific provisions and a proviso.

The three provisions:
1. No player that throws a ball game,
2. No player that undertakes or promises to throw a ball game,
3. No player that sits in a conference with a bunch of crooked players and gamblers where the ways and means of throwing games are planned and discussed,

The proviso
1. and does not promptly tell his club about it, will ever play professional baseball.

Jackson did nothing to throw any games of the 1919 Series; he never promised to throw a game, nor did he undertake to throw a ball game. He never sat in a conference with the other seven players and/or gamblers, and he never discussed the ways and means for throwing games. When he did realize that a real fix was on, he went promptly to his club and informed them about it. For this, he was banned from baseball for life! The cover story is getting threadbare. As the injustice of the case emerges, the emotional satisfaction lessens, Ken Burns's emotional archaeology notwithstanding.

It is difficult to disagree with Joe Jackson's assessment of his situation:

> Baseball failed to keep faith with me. When I got notice of my suspension three days before the 1920 season ended—it came on a rained-out day—it read that if found innocent of any wrongdoing, I would be reinstated. If found guilty, I would be banned for life. I was found innocent, and I was still banned for life.[50]

This outcome reflects the arbitrary abuse of power for which Judge Landis was known. He never allowed the facts of a case to cloud his prescient judgment. Shortly after he was named Commissioner, he clarified his intentions toward the accused conspirators:

> There is absolutely no chance for any of them to creep back into Organized Baseball. They will be and remain outlaws . . . It is sure that the guilt of some at least will be proved.[51]

As Seymour observed so aptly, "Thus a Federal judge was condemning men to the blacklist before they had been tried in a court of law and whatever the outcome of their trial."[52] Knowing Landis's predisposition toward Jackson and the others will explain why he judged him as he did, and it will be equally clear that his condemnation was not based on fact but rumor, hearsay, and blind prejudice. The man was bigoted against Jackson.

Up to this point, I have argued that Jackson played to win the World Series and that he did not participate in any of the meetings where the fix was planned. He was recruited but rejected both advances. Some questions still remain. Why did Jackson testify before the Grand Jury and condemn himself? Why did he believe that he had to testify at all? What events led up to that climactic moment?

Revelation Always Conceals
as Much as It Reveals

In order to follow the events that led to the exposure of the fix, it is important to know that there were three key moments: 1. the appearances of Cicotte, Jackson, and Williams before the Grand Jury in 1920;

The Faith of Fifty Million

2. the Chicago trial of the eight men out in 1920–1921 that led to the exoneration of all eight players; and 3. the Milwaukee trial of 1924, in which Jackson sued Comiskey for back wages. It was at this second trial that Jackson finally got to tell his side of the story.

The strange journey toward those events began on the day the Series ended. After the final game on Thursday, October 9, Lefty Williams appeared in Jackson's room carrying two envelopes.

> "Here," he asked Jackson, "do you want one of these?"
>
> "No, what is it?" Jackson answered. Williams pushed an envelope at him and Jackson said, "Go on, what is it that you got?"
>
> "Why, it's money."
>
> "I don't want your money," Jackson answered, and refused to take the envelope.
>
> Williams said the gamblers had sent Jackson's share of the payoff. He grumbled drunkenly about the amount—only $5,000 when $10,000 had been promised—but he said it was better than nothing and offered the envelope to Jackson again. Jackson refused and Williams threw the envelope down. . . . They got into a shouting match which ended when Jackson stormed out of his own room, shouting back at Williams that he was going to talk to Comiskey in the morning.[53]

The timing of the scene is important. It occurred after the Series was over. In his testimony at Jackson's 1924 trial, Lefty Williams noted bitterly, "We were supposed to lose the first two games and after the first two games we were supposed to get our money, but I never got a nickel until the last two games were played."[54] Why did Williams believe that he had to deliver the money to Jackson, who had not participated in the plot? The most obvious answer is guilt. Williams and Jackson had been friends; both were Southerners and their wives got along well. But Williams had falsely represented Jackson as participating in the fix. In the meetings where the conspirators met, Williams represented Jackson as agreeing to participate, and Gandil, who had been rebuffed on two occasions, was content to let the matter rest there. Based on Williams's assertion, he could now use Jackson's name with the gamblers and that gave him the leverage he needed. But Williams knew that he had betrayed his friend, and he felt both guilt and remorse. It was probably to assuage that guilt and to pay Jackson, after the fact, for the use of his name that he brought the envelope to the room. Donald

Gropman thinks that Williams was acting out of "remorse for having betrayed Jackson, perhaps his closest friend on the team."[55] The following excerpt from Williams's testimony at the 1924 trial reveals the magnitude of what he did. The interrogator is Jackson's attorney, Ray Cannon.

> Q: Did you yourself have any talk with Joe Jackson before or during the World Series with reference to the throwing of the Series to the Cincinnati team?
> A: No, sir.
> Q: Did Joe Jackson tell you at any time prior to or during the World Series that you could use his name in dealing with the gamblers?
> A: No, sir.
> Q: In reference to throwing games?
> A: No, sir.
> Q: Did you have any talk with him in that connection at all?
> A: No, sir.
> Q: At any time?
> A: No, sir.
> Q: To your knowledge did Joe Jackson know his name was being used by anybody for the purpose of dealing with the gamblers?
> A: No, sir.

Whatever his motivation, his attempt at making amends backfired and probably sealed Jackson's fate, certainly in the eyes of the public and probably in the mind of Judge Landis as well.

Jackson sensed the danger and difficulty of his situation. He now had an envelope with $5,000 in payoff money for deeds that he did not commit, an envelope that linked him with the conspirators after the fact. What could he do? The very thing he told Williams he would do: He went to Comiskey's office the following day, Friday, October 10. Before the Series had begun, Jackson had gone to Comiskey when all he could express were his inchoate fears; now he had proof that the fix had been real. The envelope in his hand was Exhibit A. When Jackson arrived at the waiting room in Comiskey's office at the ballpark, he went to the wooden shuttered window and knocked. Comiskey kept the shuttered window closed, and when a player knocked, someone inside the office would open it. Harry Grabiner opened the window and asked Joe what he wanted, and Jackson told him that he had some important information about the Series that he has gotten out of Williams. Grabiner was abrupt in his dismissal: "Go home, we know what you want," and he "slammed the shutter in his face."[56] Confused and bewildered, Jackson waited for more than an hour before returning to his hotel. A day or two later, Joe and Katie returned home to Savannah, Georgia, still carrying the damning envelope with them.[57]

Jackson could not have known that, when he appeared in the waiting room, Comiskey was already meeting with Chick Gandil and Happy Felsch, from whom he was learning the details of the fix. The cover-up had begun, and it would be orchestrated by Comiskey and his staff.[58] According to Grabiner's diary, which is the source of our information about Comiskey's meeting with Gandil and Felsch, Comiskey would meet with Harry Redmon on Sunday, October 12, and by the end of the meeting, Comiskey would have as much knowledge of the fix as he was likely to get. Three days after the end of the World Series then, Comiskey knew the essentials of the fix but he could not make them public. To do so would ruin his team and destroy its value. He could count on the conspirators to remain silent, and he rewarded their silence with significant raises for the 1920 season, a departure from his usual parsimony.[59] But the raises did not indicate the emergence of a kinder, gentler Comiskey or a change of policy in the way he treated his ballplayers; he was doing what needed to be done to keep the conspiracy of silence intact. Only one figure could really hurt Comiskey, because he had warned him before the Series began that it was not on the level, and he had appeared at his office with further information after the Series ended (although he had been turned away). This figure, of course, was Joe Jackson. Comiskey would have to find a way to neutralize him and keep him on the defensive. But he might have thought that would be easy to do since he was nothing more than an "ignorant millhand." What made the situation dangerous was the simple fact that the circumstances and facts that exonerated Jackson condemned Comiskey. He knew that, sooner or later, he would have to find a solution to this problem.

In order to quell rumors about the Series, Comiskey publicly denied that the Series had been fixed and offered a reward of $10,000 to anyone who could furnish proof that it had been. Gropman suggests that Comiskey also held a meeting with Hugh Fullerton after he wrote his famous column in the *New York Evening World*, just two days after the Series had ended, suggesting that the Series had been fixed. When

Comiskey discovered that Fullerton had been operating on rumor alone but had no hard facts, he made a pact with him. Each one would share with the other any information he uncovered about the Series. In this way, Comiskey could shield what he already knew while learning what Fullerton might uncover.[60] It was a cynical manipulation but it worked. Unwittingly, however, Comiskey had sealed his fate with the offer of a reward. Some of the small-time gamblers who had been involved just enough to get burned (if you will forgive the pun) found the offer tempting. The hope of collecting that reward would eventually encourage Billy Maharg to break the silence in an interview with Jimmy Isaminger of the *Philadelphia North American.*

After he returned to Savannah, Joe (through Katie, who wrote his letters for him) wrote a letter (October 27, 1919) to Comiskey requesting the World Series check that he had not yet received. In his reply (November 11, 1919), Comiskey took the opportunity to set up Jackson and keep him off balance. Comiskey accused Jackson of lacking "integrity" in the Series and offered to pay his expenses to come to Chicago and clear his name. As soon as Jackson received the letter, he shot back a response (November 15, 1919) that said in part,

> Your letter just came, and I sure am surprised to hear that my name has been connected with any scandle in the recent World Saries, as I think my playing proved that I did all I could to win . . . I will be onley to glad to come to Chicago or any place you may say and clear my name and whoever started this will have to prove his statements.[61]

Comiskey never responded to Joe's offer. Indeed, he couldn't. The risk was too great because Joe knew too much. He had called Joe's bluff, and it hadn't worked. When Comiskey sent Harry Grabiner to Savannah in February 1920 to finish contract negotiations with Jackson, Grabiner also began the negotiations by trying to put Joe on the defensive. He told him that the club had the goods on three players and knew that Jackson had discussed the fix with Williams and received $5,000 from him. Jackson responded angrily, "What's the matter with you people up there anyway, that you didn't have me come up and give you that information that I knew?"[62] When Grabiner tried to change the subject, Jackson raised the question of the money. What was he supposed to do with it? "Why, keep it," was Grabiner's reply. The reason for his reply is obvious. As long as Jackson kept the money, they could implicate him in the fix. If there is any truth to the claim that Jackson was a simple man, the evidence is here. He trusted Grabiner and Comiskey to treat him fairly and well. His simple trust was violated and betrayed. As a result of their conversation, Grabiner pressured Jackson to sign a contract under false pretenses. Grabiner assured Joe that the contract was ironclad, that is, it did not include the ten-day clause (allowing a team to release a player who was injured after ten days). He even read him the contract he was about to sign, omitting the ten-day provision that remained in the contract. When Jackson balked at signing, Grabiner used the well-worn Comiskey tactic of invoking the reserve clause. "Now you can take that or we'll kick you out of baseball. You know we can do pretty well as we please with ballplayers."[63] Chick Gandil remembered the same tactic:

> If a player objected to his miserly terms, Comiskey told him: "You can take it or leave it." Under baseball's slave laws, what could a fellow do but take it.[64]

After all the bad faith between Comiskey and his players, Jackson still took Grabiner at his word, however worthless that word turned out to be.

The worst was yet to come. After Billy Maharg, a small-time gambler and friend of Bill Burns, broke the story of the fix in an interview in the *Philadelphia North American* (September 27, 1920), Comiskey's careful cover-up operation came unravelled, and he had to switch roles. From the inquisitive owner seeking to learn the truth about the Series while secretly suppressing it, Comiskey became the wounded and betrayed owner, deeply hurt by the perfidy of his players. Of course, if he were to play this part successfully, he had to suppress any indication that he had either been warned about the scandal or been offered information about it. This meant, above all, that he had to sacrifice Joe Jackson in order to maintain his role as the wounded innocent. This necessity sealed Jackson's fate and his future.

After Maharg told his story, Cicotte cracked. Alfred Austrian, Comiskey's lawyer, coached him on what to say to the Grand Jury. Austrian told Cicotte to admit his guilt and confess his regret, especially for betraying such a "good" owner and "great" baseball man as Charles Comiskey. Austrian persuaded Cicotte that this was the only path left open to him, so Cicotte followed the script prepared for him by Austrian.

When he heard that Cicotte had gone before the Grand Jury, Jackson decided that he should follow suit. Why? The answer is not too difficult to discern. Jackson had been itching to clear his name since Comiskey, in his letter of November 11, 1919, had accused him of lacking integrity. Jackson had offered to come to Chicago to "clear my name," and now, he believed, he had a chance to do just that. Besides, Jackson had known from the time Lefty Williams showed up in his hotel room with envelope in hand that his name had been used by the conspirators. If he didn't go before the Grand Jury, then others would injure his reputation and dishonor his name. In his mind, he had little choice.

Unfortunately, the very version of events that would prove Jackson's innocence would expose Comiskey's complicity and, even more unfortunately, Jackson's purpose in going before the Grand Jury was at cross-purposes with Alfred Austrian's reasons for wanting to send Joe to the Grand Jury. Austrian was Comiskey's lawyer, and his single-minded goal was to protect his client's reputation and keep him clear of any hint of obstruction of justice. It is no insult to Joe Jackson's intelligence to say that he was no match for Alfred Austrian. Austrian coached Jackson as he had advised Cicotte: Admit his guilt, confess his remorse with a special note on how much he has hurt Comiskey. Unlike Cicotte, who was clay in the potter's hands, Joe balked; this was not the reason he wanted to go before the Grand Jury. He wanted to tell his story. Austrian tried to convince him that it wouldn't work. No one would believe the truth, he assured him. Better to admit guilt, he advised, and they would take care of him. To reinforce his point, Austrian called his old friend, Judge Charles MacDonald, who was overseeing the Grand Jury proceedings. Austrian was supporting Judge MacDonald's candidacy for baseball commissioner, and they had been friends and colleagues for twenty years. Such cronyism was part of the corruption of the legal system in Chicago that denied Jackson due process. Austrian handed Jackson the phone, and Jackson told the judge he was innocent. The judge told him that he had heard Cicotte's testimony, and he didn't believe Jackson was innocent. Jackson was shaken but Austrian had made his point. Now Austrian had the leverage he needed to coach Jackson to incriminate himself, exonerate Comiskey, corroborate what Cicotte had already told the Grand Jury, and blame Gandil, the instigator. Throughout his ordeal, Jackson acted without benefit of legal counsel. He was led to believe that Austrian was acting on his behalf when, in fact, he was acting to protect his only client, Charles Comiskey. Jackson fundamentally misunderstood his situation. After reviewing Jackson's treatment, Alan Dershowitz has written,

> Jackson received shoddy treatment. But this probably would not happen today. A modern-day Jackson would have his lawyer from the very beginning. Nor would the shenanigans employed by Comiskey's lawyer be tolerated by the bar today. But in post-World War I Chicago, corruption tainted more than the White Sox. The entire city—judiciary and all—reeked with influence-peddling and power-brokering, and among the most influential brokers was Charles Comiskey.[65]

Jackson hardly had a chance.

In light of this precarious situation, it is admirable that Jackson did as well as he did. As Gropman has argued quite successfully, Jackson managed to tell two contradictory stories to the Grand Jury.[66] He told the story he had been coached by Alfred Austrian to tell, and he also managed to tell his own story, although in a garbled and diluted version. Even as Austrian was painting him as an ignorant country boy gone bad, duped by clever gamblers, Jackson was resisting the stereotype and telling his tale of responsible action and honest ballplaying. Reading Jackson's Grand Jury testimony is like reading the Pentateuch while looking for the portions of it attributable to its reputed sources, J, E, P and D. It is a layered document. One incident will illustrate how Alfred Austrian attempted to script Jackson's testimony. As his testimony in the 1924 trial revealed, Williams received his payoff after the last game of the Series. But Austrian, in the service of emphasizing Jackson's guilt, scripts him to say he received it during the Series.

> Q: Who paid you the $5,000?
> A: Lefty Williams brought it to my room and threw it down.
> Q: When was it that this money was brought to your room . . . ?
> A: It was the second trip to Cincinnati. That night we were leaving.
> Q: That was after the fourth game?
> A: I believe it was, yes.

Austrian was unaware of the sequence of Series games. He assumed that the pattern was two games in each city, but the pattern was two games in Cincinnati, three in Chicago, two in Cincinnati, and two in

Chicago (or one in Chicago and one in Cincinnati). The Sox didn't leave for a second trip to Cincinnati until after the fifth game, not the fourth game. So the chronology was wrong on two scores. Austrian transposed an event that occurred after the final game to make it appear that it happened after the fourth game, and then he misconstrued the pattern of games played. The exchange reveals the script that Austrian (who knew little about baseball and did not follow it) prepared. It was as damning as it was inaccurate. Another piece of the testimony reveals how convincingly half-truths can condemn a person. Take, for example, the opening sequence of questions by Hartley Replogle, Assistant State's Attorney:

> Q: Did anyone pay you any money to help throw that Series in favor of Cincinnati?
> A: They did.
> Q: How much did they pay?
> A: They promised me $20,000 and paid me five.
> Q: Who promised you the $20,000?
> A: Chick Gandil.

It is true that Lefty Williams delivered money to Jackson. It is true that Gandil promised $20,000, but what is left out is that Gandil made the offer in an unsuccessful attempt to recruit Jackson and that Williams delivered the money to alleviate his guilt for using Jackson's name without his knowledge or permission. In this script, it appears as though Jackson received the money as a quid pro quo, that is, he took the money to throw the Series. The absence of time frames and the omission of critical information transforms a story about Jackson's integrity into a confession of guilt. Both of these methods and others were used throughout Jackson's testimony to corrupt the story he wanted to tell and replace it with a version of events that damned Jackson. He recounted conversations that he had held with teammates, primarily about who got how much, but the record fails to identify when the conversations occurred. Through the skillful artistry of Replogle, it appears that these conversations were held during and immediately after the Series. If they were held after Jackson had attempted to contact Comiskey and been rebuffed, then it is clear why he would not try to report these remarks. Jackson had offered to come to Chicago or any other venue of Comiskey's choosing to clear his name, and his offer had been ignored or refused. Yet, this is the script prepared by Alfred Austrian during his three-hour meeting with Jackson, a meeting for which he testified under oath that he had not kept notes. This was odd, not to say suspicious, since he kept notes of his meetings with Cicotte and Williams, both of whom he prepped for their appearances before the Grand Jury. In Burns's documentary, Gardner Stern says that the outcome of the trial of the Chicago Eight was "a travesty really." He is correct in his assessment, but it is of the wrong event. The cynical manipulation of Jackson is the true travesty of the entire affair, especially the scripting of his Grand Jury testimony.

In spite of the deck that was stacked against him, Jackson struggled to tell his story, and he succeeded so well that the foreman of the Grand Jury, Harry Brigham, testified that, "in his opinion, Jackson never confessed to any involvement in the fix at all."[67] Referring to his play, Replogle questioned Jackson as follows:

> Q: Did you make any intentional errors yourself that day?
> A: No sir, not during the whole series.
> Q: Did you bat to win?
> A: Yes.
> Q: And run the bases to win?
> A: Yes, sir.
> Q: And field the balls at (sic) the outfield to win?
> A: I did.

How odd that a conspirator who was paid $5,000 to help throw the Series could answer Replogle's questions in this fashion and elicit neither surprise nor follow-up questions. Replogle faced a major contradiction but he ignored it because, if he pursued it, he risked unearthing Joe's full story. Jackson was, by the middle of his testimony, beginning to tell his own story, thereby compromising the script Austrian had set him up to follow and threatening to expose Comiskey for what he was. Gropman summarizes Jackson's appearance before the Grand Jury very well:

> Jackson's grand jury testimony hardly constituted a confession. If there is a more enigmatic and puzzling document in the history of baseball, it has yet to come to light. . . . the most amazing aspect of his testimony is its self-contradictory nature, for Jackson told *two completely different stories* and nobody ever asked him why.[68]

It was obvious why Replogle would not ask. After the news was leaked to the public that Jackson had "confessed" to his role in the fix, the rush to judgment and condemnation would sweep away any troubling questions, unresolved issues, or mitigating circumstances.

Comiskey stepped into his new role with ease, and the media that he had cultivated through the years came to his aid. Papers carried stories that Comiskey was so deeply disturbed by the betrayal of his players that his friends feared for his health. He suspended indefinitely the eight players accused of participating in the fix even though his team was locked in a pennant race with the Cleveland Indians. In his letter to each player involved, he said,

> If you are innocent of any wrongdoing you . . . will be reinstated; if you are guilty you will be retired from organized baseball for the rest of your lives if I can accomplish it. Until there is finality to this investigation it is due to the public that I take this action, even though it costs Chicago the pennant.[69]

Comiskey's noble, self-sacrificing gesture was noted in the media. Other baseball owners made histrionic gestures. The owners of the Yankees offered to lend their team to Comiskey, and Harry Frazee, the owner of the Red Sox, suggested that each team donate players to Chicago so they could finish the season. Comiskey graciously declined the offers while making his gratitude known.

Feeding the hysteria that accompanied the announcement of the fix, officials of the Grand Jury "lifted the curtain on the proceedings and declared that Cicotte and Jackson made open confessions."[70] Just who authorized the violation of these confidential proceedings the article did not say. Its effect on Jackson was devastating. The headlines launched an intemperate rush to judgment. In the midst of these revelations, on October 4, 1920, Comiskey announced that he was giving each honest player a check for $1,500 to make up the difference between the winner's share and the loser's share from the past year's World Series. The actual difference was closer to $1,900. The Old Roman simply could not resist cheating his players even while trying to appear magnanimous. The Clean Sox dutifully responded with a public acknowledgment of Comiskey's generosity. In Boston, on September 30, the newsboys of the city put themselves on record "condemning the indicted Chicago baseball players" for striking "a murderous blow at the kids' game" while, at the same time, they passed a resolution commending Ray Schalk and Dickie Kerr "for their manly stand against the Benedict Arnolds of baseball."[71] Had there been a gallows outside the Grand Jury chambers, it is unlikely that either Cicotte or Jackson would have survived this early-twentieth-century version of frontier justice. Absent were the notions that one is innocent until proven guilty and that one deserves a fair hearing until the evidence is sifted through examination and cross-examination so that some approximation of the truth can be discovered. Instant condemnation replaced any pretense of examination and due process or seeking the truth. On the same day that the newsboys in Boston revealed their uncertain grasp of the judicial system, Hugh Fullerton wrote his damning article in the *New York Evening World* (September 30, 1920). By penning this blanket condemnation of Jackson, Fullerton showed himself to be no more mature in his understanding of justice than the newsboys of Boston. They all acted the part of hysterical fools, but Fullerton was also a vindictive fool with considerable influence. What he wrote, uninformed though it was, destroyed Jackson's reputation. It is worth quoting at length:

> There came a day when a crook spread money before this ignorant idol and he fell. For a few dollars, which perhaps seemed a fortune to him, he sold his honor, and when the inevitable came, when the truth stood revealed, Joe Jackson went before a body of men and told the story of his own infamy. While he related the sordid details to the stern faced, shocked men, there gathered outside the big stone building a group of boys. . . . A great hope and a great fear fought for mastery within each kid's heart. It couldn't be true. After an hour, a man, guarded like a felon by other men, emerged from the door. He did not swagger. He slunk along between his guardians, and the kids, with wide eyes and tightened throats, watched, and one, bolder than the others, pressed forward and said, "It ain't so, Joe, is it?" Jackson gulped back a sob, the shame of utter shame flushed his brown face. He choked an instant, "Yes Kid, I'm afraid it is" and the world of faith crashed around the heads of the kids. Their idol lay in dust, their faith destroyed. Nothing was true, nothing was honest. There was no Santa Claus. Then, and not until then, did Jackson, hurrying away to escape the sight of the faces of the kids, understand the enormity of the thing he had done.[72]

The article is an ideological production, whose purpose is to lay the blame for the entire scandal on Jackson's back. Whatever can be said about Fullerton's writing in general, this is the work of a propagandist and a political hack. It creates a scene out of his imagination and presents it as a serious eyewitness account of an actual event. This famous incident was actually invented; it was sheer fantasy. But the story also fulfilled the prophecy Fullerton had made about Jackson in 1911, and it played a leading role in changing Jackson from a ballplayer into a scapegoat.

Although his memory about how the story got started may be in question, Jackson was clear that it had never happened.

> There weren't any words passed between anybody except me and a deputy sheriff. When I came out of the building this deputy asked me where I was going, and I told him to the Southside. He asked me for a ride and we got in the car together and left. There was a big crowd hanging around the front of the building, but nobody else said anything to me. It just didn't happen, that's all. Charley Owens (of the *Chicago Daily News*) just made up a good story and wrote it. Oh, I would have said it ain't so, just like I'm saying now.[73]

In 1920, Jackson did not have a chance to say "it ain't so." He was tried, convicted, and sentenced in the press. Landis had already announced before the trial was held and its outcome known that the players would never creep back into organized baseball. Fullerton had turned a curious public into a lynch mob ready to "hang them high." It was really a travesty!

The trial itself was no less interesting than the events that had preceded it. The Grand Jury concluded its inquiry on October 20, 1920, and the players were arraigned on February 21, 1921. Noticeably absent were the gamblers. Absent too were the players' confessions. During the arraignment, Hartley Replogle informed the court that the signed confessions of Cicotte, Jackson, and Williams were missing. It should be noted that, by this time, all three players had repudiated their so-called confessions, but the prosecution was still planning to use the documents against them. They had evidently been removed from the office of the State's Attorney, during a change of administration. Maclay Hoyne, the outgoing State's Attorney, and his assistant, Henry Berger, were suspected of pilfering the confessions, and Replogle did, in fact, accuse them of doing so. As is usually the case with anything that happened in Chicago related to this event, there is another, more hidden dimension to the story. During the Grand Jury proceedings, Arnold Rothstein, on the advice of his attorney, William Fallon, had voluntarily come to testify before that body. The true purpose of his visit seems to have been to meet with Austrian to discuss matters of mutual interest. Both men evidently agreed that they shared common interests and goals, namely, to limit the investigation, exonerate the players, and return them to baseball. It is probable that out of this meeting came the plan to steal the confessions.[74] Although Ban Johnson blamed Rothstein, the confession of Jackson mysteriously reappeared in the hands of Comiskey's attorney during the 1924 trial in Milwaukee. He was unable to explain how it got there. This fact suggests very strongly that it was Austrian who orchestrated the disappearance of the confessions. Jackson's Grand Jury testimony would disappear from view for nearly sixty-five years before the law firm of Mayer, Brown & Platt donated the transcript to the Chicago Historical Society in 1988.[75]

Necessity had forced Comiskey to admit the scandal, and he was beginning to come under scrutiny and attack for his presumed role in the suspected cover-up. The operations of the Grand Jury left Comiskey even more vulnerable. *The Sporting News* accused Comiskey of protecting his investment in his players at the expense of baseball's public good.[76] Comiskey countered that his investigations had unearthed nothing more than hearsay which provided inadequate grounds for destroying "the character and reputation of men, even though they were ballplayers."[77] He was also quick to take credit for obtaining the players' confessions. His investigations, he contended against his critics, had made it possible for his attorney to procure the players' confessions of their misdeeds. Of course, it was Billy Maharg's interview that had cracked open the investigation, not Comiskey's inquiries, but Comiskey was fighting for his life. In 1929, the *Cleveland Plain Dealer* carried an article indicating that the State's Attorney in charge of the investigation of the scandal was convinced that "Comiskey should be indicted along with the players on certain evidence in his hands," a charge that Comiskey vehemently denied as an "unmitigated falsehood."[78] Whatever the truth of the story, it does indicate how precarious Comiskey's situation was.

In the absence of the players' so-called confessions, the trial was postponed. It resumed on June 27, 1921. The players were present, and the gamblers were, once again, conspicuous by their absence. Gone were Arnold Rothstein, declared innocent by no less a figure than Ban Johnson, Abe Attell, and Sport Sullivan. There were three counts to the indictment:

1. to defraud the public and Ray Schalk;
2. to commit a confidence game on Charles Nims;[79]
3. to commit a confidence game on and injure the business of Comiskey.[80]

These are hardly the issues that stir men and women to action, but the courtroom of Judge Hugo Friend, the presiding judge, was filled to capacity. Buck Weaver is said to have remarked that they should build bleachers so more folks could see the trial. One of the defense attorneys, Ben Short, saw the injustice of the situation and highlighted it at the beginning of the trial. He told the state's team that their case was weak; if they really had wanted to pursue the case,

> You'd have the real leaders of the conspiracy here—the men who made millions—and not these ball players who were reputed to be getting big salaries, but most of whom get practically nothing.[81]

The trial led to the exoneration of the players but not to the continuation of their careers. Landis would see to that.

The Scapegoat

Historian G. Edward White has noted that the scandal broke at a time baseball was struggling with its identity and aspirations. Baseball aspired to become "an American cultural icon," embodying the values of the culture as its national pastime, yet it continued to be both a sport and a business, a sport on which gamblers wagered large amounts of money and a business in which owners became rich and powerful.[82] The issues of the trial represented baseball as a sport (counts 1 and 2) and a business (count 3). But nowhere was the issue of baseball as a cultural icon at stake in the trial of 1921. Since the condemnation of the players was based on their betrayal of baseball as a cultural icon that embodies the best values of American culture, the outcome of the trial seemed unsatisfactory. It was not enough to try the players; they had to be judged, too. This dynamic led directly to Landis's pronouncement, "regardless of the verdict of juries." Baseball had been polluted and rendered unclean by the scandal. Some ritual was needed to restore the purity of the sport.

Leviticus 16 discusses the rituals associated with the Day of Atonement (Yom Kippur). Part of the ceremony involves the selection of two goats (7–10, 15–17, 20–22). One is sacrificed as a sin offering while the other is presented alive to the Lord at the tent of meeting.

> Then Aaron shall lay both his hands on the head of the live goat, and confess over it all the iniquities of the people of Israel, and all their transgressions, all their sins, putting them on the head of the goat, and sending it away into the wilderness by means of someone designated for the task. The goat shall bear on itself all their iniquities to a barren region; and the goat shall be set free in the wilderness. (Lev. 16:21–22)

The sins of the community are symbolically transferred to the scapegoat, which is then banished to the wilderness, carrying the load of sin on its head. In this way is sin removed from the community each year.

The ceremony in Leviticus 16 reflects one institutionalized form of scapegoating, but the phenomenon assumes other cultural forms as well. Speaking of the banishment of the players, David Voigt says,

> Yet the fact is that these scapegoats were denied their civil rights by the application of baseball regulations. Today such a sentence would be preposterous; its imposition in 1921 rested on a moralistic consensus of baseball people and the support of a populace unaware of the undesirable effect on civil liberties and over-aware of moralistic strictures.[83]

How would this apply specifically to Joe Jackson?

For a figure like Jackson to serve as a scapegoat, he had to meet three conditions. First, he must be seen as guilty. Austrian paved the way for this perception when he scripted Jackson to incriminate himself before the Grand Jury, and the major newspapers of the land reinforced that scripting by publishing specious excerpts as though they were Jackson's own words when, in fact, they were manufactured by the papers themselves. It is also possible that the "officials" associated with the Grand Jury who uncloaked the confidentiality of the proceedings contributed to this interpretation of Jackson as a remorseful criminal confessing his guilt. They might have fed the distorted and fabricated "testimony" to an uncritical media. Whether they knew it or not, they were fulfilling an essential role in creating a scapegoat. Jackson had to be transformed from an honest ballplayer (who played to win and notified his club when he realized that the Series was not being played on the level) into a deceitful but gullible conspirator (who wasn't smart enough to get his money up front). He was being turned into an example of the sins he represented, dishonesty in the service of greed (which is not a bad description of Comiskey!).

Only by focusing attention on the scapegoat could organized baseball avoid examining the conditions that led to the fix. The Archbishop of Recife in Brazil, Dom Helder Camara, wrote a work called *The Spiral of Violence* that speaks about this process.[84] What Camara calls "the spiral of violence" goes through three phases: 1. It begins with the daily violence spawned by systems of political oppression and economic exploitation because, in such societies, elites typically use the military to enforce their rule. 2. On occasion, the peasants or other relatively powerless groups revolt or rise up against their oppression in some specific ways. This is the second movement of the spiral of violence. 3. It generates a third movement, repressive reaction by the government. Remove the element of violence so that the spiral of violence becomes the spiral of exploitation, and Camara's model can be applied to the Black Sox scandal. The roots of the scandal lie in the everyday exploitation of ballplayers by owners. The use of the reserve clause and the ten-day clause left ballplayers helpless to negotiate a salary commensurate with the worth of their labor, and it left them without recourse if they were injured. When an owner like Comiskey ratchets up the exploitation through humiliating gestures like charging the players for cleaning their uniforms or offering less meal money than others receive, the owner may trigger the second phase of the spiral of exploitation, the revolt of the players. This happened in mid-July 1919 when the players threatened to strike, but in his characteristic fashion, Comiskey repressed the revolt, reasserting the power of the owner. But the everyday exploitation continued, and it eventually led to another revolt, the throwing of the World Series. This would in turn trigger the retributive, self-righteous action of the baseball establishment, embodied in the figure of Judge Landis, the high priest of the third phase of the spiral of exploitation.

In his study of what he calls the "weapons of the weak," James C. Scott observes what happens in a community where the powerful pretty much control the lives of the poor and the powerless. When the poor are cut off from most, if not all, publicly acknowledged and politically approved forms of appeal and redress, they turn to their own devices.

> Here I have in mind the ordinary weapons of relatively powerless groups: foot dragging, dissimulation, desertion, false compliance, pilfering, feigned ignorance, slander, arson, sabotage, and so on.[85]

The ballplayers on Comiskey's team were treated like field hands on a plantation, and they responded in kind. The more they were prevented from expressing their anger at their mistreatment, the more they turned to devious methods of undermining Comiskey's power. The scandal was a study in the relations of production. The ballplayers used the one aspect of production they could control—their labor on the ballfield—and they used their control of that labor to sabotage the World Series.

Rather than examine the causes of the fix, the owners chose to turn the players into scapegoats while directing special venom toward Jackson. The owners, supported by the legal system and the media which whipped up public opinion against the players, kept the cover story alive and diverted attention from the conditions of virtual servitude that led to the revolt. Together, they had enough power to make it stick. As Voigt has remarked, "the harried later lives of these baseball Ishmaels underscore the complete subjection of players under baseball regulations of the silver age."[86] Above all, the media kept the spotlight focused on Joe Jackson. Hugh Fullerton's "say it ain't so" fabrication was a morality fable intended to drive home the meaning of the scandal by assigning the role of betrayer to Jackson. It was an ideological production intended to blame the victim and remove the owners from public scrutiny.[87] By these means, baseball kept its oppressive and exploitive house in order while avoiding all responsibility for the scandal.

Second, the guilt of the scapegoat must be reaffirmed and the proof of his guilt must be demonstrated again and again. Jackson lived a very successful and satisfied life after he returned to the South. He was a successful businessman who owned a valet service that employed twenty-two people as well as a liquor store. Jackson summed up his situation in the *Sport Magazine* interview with Furman Bisher:

> I've been pretty lucky since I left the big leagues. No man who has done the things they accuse me of doing could have been as successful. Everything I touched seemed to turn to money, and I've

made my share down through the years. I've been blessed with a good banker, too—my wife. . . . I went back to my liquor store last July and I'm running the business now by myself. I had leased it out while I was sick. I've been doing about $50,000 to $100,000 a year business.[88]

Jackson remained a hero to the folk of Greenville and the Deep South. They thought he had gotten a raw deal. As Thomas Perry put it, "The folks who knew him best never questioned his integrity and always gave back to him the assurance that the legend would never die."[89] From the time Jackson first arrived in the big leagues with the Philadelphia Athletics, Connie Mack offered to get him a tutor so that he could learn to read and write, and his offer was echoed by almost every club for whom he played, but Jackson clung stubbornly to his illiteracy, almost as a badge of honor. It might have been his way of remembering where he came from. When he returned home after the scandal, his own received him enthusiastically and well. Joe Jackson was never abandoned in his home country.

In spite of these realities, the news media would print stories from time to time emphasizing how unhappy and unsuccessful Jackson was. In his column in the *Chicago Tribune* on the fortieth anniversary of the scandal, Joe Williams spoke about Jackson in the following way:

> A wretchedly unhappy man, Joe Jackson, up to his death, still maintained he was guiltless. Had the old .400 hitter been able to hear yesterday's TV commentator describe the 1919 Sox as "hitless wonders," he'd probably have been unhappier still.[90]

As already noted, Daniel Okrent made the same point in Ken Burns's *Baseball.* Both are wrong. Jackson lived contentedly in his later years. He could say just a year or two before his death, "I'm 61 years old now, living quietly and happily out on my little street close to Brandon Mill."[91] Just as Jackson had to be portrayed as an unhappy failure, dragging the heavy burden of his guilt to his dying day, much like Jacob Marley in *A Christmas Carol,* so he continued to be portrayed as an ignorant fool. Bob Broeg in a column written for the *St. Louis Post-Dispatch* took offense at Gropman's book because it encouraged "the rally 'round the husky hillbilly from South Carolina." The best Broeg could say in Jackson's defense was that he might have been "so dumb that he didn't know what he was doing."[92] What is important for this study is to note how quickly the media pounces on any attempt to change Jackson's status. They know that to do so would require baseball to explore the true sources of the fix that are to be found in the front offices of the Chicago baseball club, not in the players' hotel rooms. As long as Joe Jackson continues to fill the role of the scapegoat, he will be subjected to stories designed to prove his continuing unworthiness. Should his status change, his role as scapegoat would be called into question, and the cover story perpetuated by organized baseball would start to unravel.

This is one reason why major-league baseball has resisted attempts to clear his name. Both Bart Giamatti and Fay Vincent rejected overtures to reconsider the status of Jackson. Giamatti refused to inquire into the matter because "I am not going to play God with history."[93] What the normally perspicacious Giamatti failed to see is that baseball has already played God with history. Alfred Austrian rewrote history to condemn Jackson and whitewash Comiskey, and spokespersons for baseball continue to do so to this day. An example of playing God with history is found in Monte Irvin's dismissive letter to a fan (April 23, 1980). He said,

> The Shoeless Joe Jackson incident is dead forever. Baseball will never re-instate him because ignorance of the law is no excuse. Joe knew about the fix and didn't report it—that in itself was a crime.[94]

Irvin's letter is interesting on two counts. First, he condemns Jackson for not doing what he, in fact, did. Jackson notified his team when he knew the fix was on. So there was no crime. The second issue is almost humorous. What law does he refer to? Is it the "law" about promptly telling your club about a fix? If so, Irvin is holding Jackson accountable for Judge Landis's "law" propogated after the events for which Jackson was condemned. This borders on silly nonsense. But there is a more serious irony. As an African American, Monte Irvin knew what it was like to be excluded from baseball for the wrong reasons; it is a major failure of nerve, compassion, and imagination on his part that he utterly refuses even to look at the Jackson case. Evidently, prejudice comes in many forms. Fay Vincent dismissed an inquiry by noting that the events leading to Jackson's being placed on the ineligible list occurred more than seventy years ago, and "I am not prepared to reconstruct them now." Why this fear of history? One thing that makes baseball unique is its relation to history. Every ballplayer who steps to the plate stands in the shadows of all those who have come before, and every pitcher who toes the rubber stands in the midst of a "great cloud of witnesses" against whom he will be measured. Baseball is history, and baseball cannot escape history. Baseball is responsible to its history, and it is responsible for its history. Vincent's evasion of the Jackson case is a retreat from what makes baseball distinctive in American sports life. It is probable, therefore, that Vincent had another hidden agenda. In an interview in the *Philadelphia Inquirer,* Vincent argued that banishment was "the deterrent" that prevented betting on baseball games. "The fact is," he said, "nobody ever gets reinstated. So the deterrent works. You don't bet on baseball."[95] He seems to have missed the irony in his conclusion. If the deterrent worked, why is he discussing the Pete Rose case? It is almost criminally clueless to assert "so you don't bet on baseball." Has he never been to Las Vegas or heard the odds cited on Sports Center? But more to the point, Vincent is arguing that it is better to leave an innocent man on the ineligible list than to risk diluting the deterrent effect of banishment. Having made a serious mistake, baseball should cover it up beneath a theory of deterrence rather than seek justice and right a wrong from the past. It is a little bit like arguing that it is better to maintain the life sentence of a wrongly convicted innocent man than admit the mistake and free the person wrongly accused because that would risk reducing the deterrent effect of the prison sentence. It would appear that baseball has much too much at stake to reconsider the case of Joe Jackson. It is much safer to leave him as the eternal scapegoat.

Again, Scott sheds light on the refusal of organized baseball to reexamine the Jackson case:

> The struggle between rich and poor . . . is also a struggle over the appropriation of symbols, a struggle over how the past and present shall be understood and labeled, a struggle to identify causes and assess blame, a contentious effort to give partisan meaning to local history.[96]

This is why the story of Joe Jackson carries such important symbolic weight. To construct the story of the fix in a way that challenges the cover story perpetuated by organized baseball challenges baseball's control of symbols, its ability to assess blame and to discover the causes of the event.

The third condition essential to making someone into a scapegoat is perpetual banishment. After the trial and Judge Landis's pronouncement, Joe Jackson returned to the South. Since there were no major-league teams in the South, he was being banished from the big leagues. Landis would continue to pursue Jackson to thwart any attempt he might make to play organized baseball in any form, so the banishment was not a single act but a continuing vendetta. Throughout his life, Landis displayed a deep vindictiveness toward Jackson.[97] His venom was based on the three reasons he considered Jackson guilty:

1. Jackson's "confession" before the Grand Jury;
2. Jackson's acknowledgement that he kept the $5,000;
3. The absence of any notice to the team when he knew of the fix.[98]

It is now clear that none of these reasons are valid; none of them can stand the scrutiny of careful examination. Jackson's "confession" was coached by Alfred Austrian for the purpose of condemning Jackson to protect Comiskey. When Jackson's story finally emerged at the trial of 1924 in Milwaukee, it was clear that Jackson kept the $5,000 after failing in his effort to turn it over to Comiskey. Later, he kept it at the advice of Harry Grabiner. This was Jackson's biggest mistake. But the money was given after the Series was over, a Series in which Jackson clearly played to win, so it had no effect on Jackson's play or his role in the Series. Finally, Jackson did notify his club about the fix on the day the Series started. If his warning was not as clear as it could have been, that was because Jackson himself was not clear about the details, having never met with the conspirators nor knowing what their plans were. Then again, it would be harder to send a clearer danger signal than his request to be taken out of the lineup. That was an extreme request to make on the opening day of the World Series. If no one followed through to learn what was on Jackson's mind, that is not his fault. Once again, the case for Jackson's acquittal is clear.

The ideological point of the meeting between Ty Cobb and Joe Jackson in his liquor store is to reinforce how effective the banishment had been. The scapegoat remained in the wilderness. Alan Dershowitz was correct when he concluded, "Comiskey now holds an honored place in the baseball Hall of Fame while Shoeless Joe Jackson remains a scapegoat. Baseball should admit its mistake."[99] But the need for a scapegoat is strong. As René Girard has noted, the sacrifice or banishment of the scapegoat serves to protect a community from itself and keeps its violent tendencies under control rather than let them escalate out of control.[100]

Only once did Jackson return from the wilderness to the North. He traveled to Milwaukee where his attorney, Ray Cannon, sued the White Sox for $16,000 back pay and a World Series check. Because Cannon had already filed a suit on behalf of Happy Felsch and retrieved his money, he clearly thought he could perform the same service for Jackson. But Cannon did not realize that Jackson was in a category different from Felsch. Jackson was the scapegoat. At the trial, after Jackson had finally told his story without interference from Alfred Austrian, Comiskey's attorney began reading from a document that contradicted Joe's testimony. It was his Grand Jury transcript, which had suddenly reappeared for the trial. The introduction of the previously hidden transcript with its allegedly confidential information sowed sufficient confusion in the judge's mind that, after the jury decided in favor of Jackson and awarded him $16,000, he countermanded the jury's decision and held Jackson for perjury. His stay was brief, but it impressed upon him the futility of trying to clear his name. Using his political influence and the legal system, Comiskey had once again turned him into a scapegoat.

The Icon

Despite its best efforts, organized baseball has failed to maintain the cover story of the Black Sox scandal, and it continues to come unraveled as it is subjected to more intense scrutiny. Historians and novelists alike have revisited the scandal and developed different and probably more accurate readings of those events. Harry Stein's 1983 novel, *Hoopla!,* explores the scandal through the eyes of two narrators, Buck Weaver and a newspaper reporter named Luther Pond. Pond tells the cover story perpetuated by baseball, but Buck comes to see another truth, namely,

> That the very structure of organized baseball is corrupt, that in the banning of the eight players, there was a vaster, more pervasive conspiracy. The commissioner, the team owners, journalists and other players, and the American public conspired to maintain the lie around which baseball and other institutions are organized.[101]

The lie is that crooked players conspiring with greedy gamblers nearly ruined the game. The truth is that "the institutionalized abuse of players [is] responsible for the Black Sox scandal."[102] Of course, if this is true, then it necessitates a reevaluation of the scandal and a reassessment of those who were caught in it. On this point, historians agree with novelists. Historians already cited in this paper, as different from one another as Seymour, Voigt, Burk, White, Asinof, and Gropman, share a common point of view that subjects Comiskey and the powers that be to new scrutiny. They are not merely repeating the cover story.

As this reexamination occurs, Joe Jackson has once again emerged from the wilderness of obscurity to which professional baseball consigned him. This situation is directly attributable to the ground-breaking work of Donald Gropman, who argued Jackson's case in 1979, long before the current interest in the man and his fate. His work has paved the way for numerous movements to clear his name and reinstate him on the register of professional baseball players as a prelude to his being elected to the Hall of Fame. Recently, Ted Williams and Bob Feller have argued the case with organized baseball,[103] although, as the past would lead us to expect, baseball has been slow to respond. Alan Dershowitz has openly called for major-league baseball "to admit it made a mistake about Shoeless Joe Jackson,"[104] and Gropman has reminded the baseball establishment that "there is no statute of limitations—legal, intellectual or moral—on correcting an injustice."[105] As a result of his study, Gropman is convinced that baseball has wittingly or unwittingly perpetuated a lie about Jackson and, unless there is a smoking gun in the files of the commissioner, should admit its mistake and correct it. It is, however, easier to perpetuate an injustice than it is to correct it, so the challenge is a significant one.

Nowhere has the transformation of Joe Jackson been achieved more fully than in W. P. Kinsella's novel *Shoeless Joe* and the movie based on it, *Field of Dreams*. In this narrative world, Shoeless Joe has become an icon, "a symbol of the tyranny of the powerful over the powerless" and "the name Kenesaw Mountain Landis became synonymous with the devil."[106] This story evokes the reversal of values and roles needed to see the figure of Shoeless Joe Jackson through new eyes, and Ray Kinsella, the narrator, has a head start because he sees Jackson through the eyes of his father, who maintained that "Shoeless Joe was innocent, a victim of big business and crooked gamblers."[107] Shoeless Joe is a hero, but a wounded hero. When Ray asks him how it felt to be banished from baseball, he replied, "like having part of me amputated, slick and smooth and painless."[108] This is a man who loved the game enough to play for food money, even the stingy allowance offered by Comiskey. What enthralls Jackson is the game, not organized baseball, and it is the game that Ray Kinsella gives him a chance to play again when he builds his field of dreams.

In the movie, Jackson becomes a redeemer figure (a *go'el*) who intercedes with Ray to bring the other banned players with him and, in time, an all-time all-star team of others, too. But it is the reversal at the end of the cinematic story that illumines Jackson's greater meaning. All through the movie, the revelation of the whispered voice, "If you build it, he will come," was taken by Ray to mean that, if he built the field, Shoeless Joe would appear. As the film draws to a close, it is clear that the whispered revelation has another, unexpected significance. "He will come" refers finally not to Shoeless Joe but to Ray's father, John Kinsella, who was, once upon a time, a minor-league catcher, and it is Shoeless Joe, who, in some mysterious way, has arranged the meeting of father and son, reconciling the alienation between the generations. In the same way, "Ease his pain" refers, in the last analysis, not to Terence Mann but to Ray's painful estrangement from his father. The ambiguity is rich, for the phrase could refer to the pain of the son or the pain of the father, perhaps both. Shoeless Joe introduces Ray to his father just as he has introduced the outlaw seven to the field of dreams. The figure who appeared to be the beneficiary of the scheme turns out to be the hieratic mediator between realms and generations. The apotheosis of Shoeless Joe and the revelation of his deeper significance (his iconic meaning in the film) begins when he invites Terence Mann to come with the players. The invitation sparks a lively argument from Ray, who believes that, as the creator of the field, he should have been the one invited. When Joe hears this, he says solemnly, "But you're not invited." With these words, Shoeless Joe reveals that he is the bearer of a Word from beyond. Mann understands and argues with Ray: "There was a reason they chose me, just as there was a reason they chose you." The notions of election and call are clear, as is the mediating role of Shoeless Joe. But to what purpose has Mann been called? To resume his vocation as author and prophet, a vocation that he has abandoned. "Listen to me Ray, listen to me," Mann intones. "If I have the courage to go through with this—what a story it'll make. Shoeless Joe Jackson comes to

Iowa." Dumbfounded, Ray asks, "Are you gonna write about it?" With his answer, "That's what I do," Mann embraces his lost vocation. Ray can only speak a benediction, "Good. Good." Shoeless Joe then invites Terence Mann to leave the world of the living for a journey into the unknown realm beyond the rows of Iowa corn.

Jackson continues to emerge in his iconic role by bringing together John Kinsella from the realm beyond the cornfield to meet his son and play a game of catch with him. As father and son stand face to face in the darkening Iowa evening, John says of the field Ray has built, "For me, it's like a dream come true." When Ray asks John if there is a heaven, he replies, "Oh yeah, it's the place where dreams come true," and he turns to begin his trek to the rows of corn in center field. Ray calls out, "Hey . . . Dad! You want to have a catch?" Father and son stand on the field playing toss and catch, restoring the broken relationship that has separated them, seemingly forever. All of this was made possible by Shoeless Joe, who brings together the living and the dead. As the truth begins to dawn on Ray, he looks at Shoeless Joe and says, "It was you." Joe responds with the faintest trace of a smile as though hiding a great secret: "No, Ray, it was you." Ray appears to mean that it was Shoeless Joe who arranged the meeting, and Joe means that the whispered revelations, "If you build it, he will come" and "Ease his pain" really applied to Ray himself. With this reversal, Shoeless Joe has become an icon of reconciliation, bringing together those alienated from each other or their vocation.

Conclusion

If we can imagine a future different from the past, we can create it. All it takes is the courage to admit mistakes and the perseverance to atone for them. Baseball has perpetuated a cover story that condemned the innocent and the guilty alike to protect Charles Comiskey as well as its own institutional interests. The primary victim of this cover story has been Joe Jackson, whose character has been assassinated by media and organized baseball alike. Now that materials previously hidden or unavailable are open for inspection (among them Jackson's Grand Jury transcript; his testimony at the 1924 trial; Grabiner's notebooks), now that the false reports about his testimony and play in the Series can be scrutinized, now that it is evident that the verdict announced by Landis actually clears Jackson of wrongdoing, it is time for organized baseball to set its house in order by righting the wrong done to Jackson. The very words of that paragon of judgment, Judge Landis, may come back to haunt the game he mistakenly believed he was saving:

> Baseball is something more than a game to an American boy. It is his training field for life work. Destroy his faith in its squareness and honesty and you have destroyed something more; you have planted suspicion of all things in his heart.[109]

If baseball continues to cling to the cover story, it will destroy the faith of a new generation of boys who, with the benefit of hindsight and fuller information, now know that "squareness and honesty" had nothing to do with the banishment of Joe Jackson. This will lead to a corrosive suspicion of all things related to baseball. If baseball wants to stake a claim to being the national pastime, why shouldn't baseball honor due process, just treatment, honesty and full disclosure, treating people as innocent until proven guilty, protecting a person's good name and reputation rather than yielding to slander and scapegoating, admitting mistakes rather than perpetuating injustice, treating all players with dignity even if they are poor or illiterate, welcoming disclosures that enable baseball to correct past injustices? Or is the national pastime a shorthand way to speak about baseball as honoring cronyism, misuse of the justice system, bearing false witness, defaming a person's name based on hearsay and rumor, protecting the rich at the expense of the poor, management at the expense of the workers, and perpetuating error even when the truth is known? Will baseball provide a training ground for life that models justice or injustice? The word is out, and the cover story cannot overcome it.

In his study of the "weapons of the weak," Scott describes the vocation common to every villager, and one which we share.

> . . . we find ourselves in the midst of an ideological struggle, however small in scale. It is a struggle over facts and their meaning, over what has happened and who is to blame, over how the present situation is to be defined and interpreted. . . . every villager is entitled, indeed required, to become something of a historian—a historian with an axe to grind.[110]

This study has been history with an axe to grind. But then all history, whether the history of the cover story or the more recent history of the

The Faith of Fifty Million

scandal, has an axe to grind. The only questions we must answer are whose axe and for what purposes. If this exploration enables us to hew a future different from the past, then it will have served a useful purpose, a future in which Joe Jackson is released from the bondage of the scapegoat and freed to become the icon of the national pastime he is surely entitled to be. Joe Jackson has been left on base long enough; it is time for him to come home.

Albert Goodwill Spalding was a star pitcher for the Boston Red Stockings in the 1870s and went on to become a great baseball entrepreneur as club owner, President of the National League, and founder of one of the most dominant sporting goods companies in the world.

Philadelphia's Shibe Park (above) was opened on April 12, 1909, as the first ballpark built solely of steel and concrete, displaying both beauty and permanence as American ideals.

Outside Shibe Park for the opening game of the World Series on October 9, 1914.

American Presidents have thrown out the first ball on opening day since William Howard Taft began the practice on April 14, 1910. Woodrow Wilson (above) did it three times; Franklin Delano Roosevelt, (below) eight times.

Dwight Eisenhower (above) threw out the first ball on opening day seven times and John F. Kennedy, (below) three times.

Christy Mathewson was one of the game's greatest pitchers and embodied American cultural ideals as a "Christian gentleman."

Grover Cleveland Alexander, one of the game's greatest pitchers, was plagued by the limits of life and personal difficulties.

Joseph Jefferson "Shoeless Joe" Jackson hit .408 in his first full season for the Cleveland Naps in 1911. He was the only rookie ever to hit .400 but lost the batting title to Ty Cobb (.420). Jackson played for the Chicago White Sox before being banned from baseball for life after the Black Sox scandal of 1919. Note the American flag on Jackson's sleeve.

Charles "Old Roman" Comiskey was the Chicago White Sox owner who faced a precarious situation when members of his team were indicted for "fixing" the 1919 World Series with gamblers.

Joe DiMaggio, the "Yankee Clipper," was a consummate player who became a cultural icon of elegance and class.

Jackie Robinson signing a contract with Branch Rickey of the Brooklyn Dodgers.

First page of a 1946 Look *magazine article titled "A Branch Grows in Brooklyn," by Tim Cohane, showing Branch Rickey in his office.*

Young women of all ages play baseball.

While white women in the 1940s and 1950s played baseball in The All-American Girls' Professional Baseball League (AAGPBL), black women played ball in the Negro Leagues.

Julie Croteau was the first female to play college baseball.

Elijah "Pumpsie" Green, the first African American player for the Boston Red Sox, is shown here with manager Billy Jurges.

Pumpsie Green slides into second during a Boston win over the San Francisco Giants.

Part III

Baseball and the Search
for "the American Dream"

Chapter 6

Baseball's Surprising Moral Example:

Branch Rickey, Jackie Robinson, and the Racial Integration of America

Fred Glennon

The sun shines brightly on Fenway Park this warm July afternoon. My son and I sit in our seats behind third base and admire the rich green of the outfield grass, the dark red of the infield clay. The gentle breeze moves the outfield foul line flags; we glance into left field at the wall affectionately dubbed the Green Monster. It is with a reverence for the game that we sit and watch as the teams warm up in their practice uniforms. The field has become a sacred place to my son and me, and we bask in the perfect atmosphere. What a wonderful day for baseball! Although my son and I have made many pilgrimages to baseball's sacred spaces, I revere Fenway Park the most. I was born and bred a Boston Red Sox fan, while my son, who was born in Atlanta, claims the Braves as his home team. Both of us are satisfied today since our two favorite teams are playing an interleague game. We look again at the players. Although my thirteen-year-old son may not fully appreciate the import of my observation, I notice with satisfaction that nearly every ethnicity on the planet is represented in a baseball uniform. It is obvious that athletic skill and dedication to the game of baseball have overcome racial separation. But it has not always been so.

Just over fifty years ago, America's pastime was a reflection of segregated America. When historians look at the racial integration of America, they often cite professional baseball's "noble experiment," when Branch Rickey signed Jackie Robinson to play baseball for the major-league

Brooklyn Dodgers in 1946–1947. The integration of major-league base-ball came before the civil rights movement and before the historic *Brown vs. the Board of Education* ruling by the United States Supreme Court (1954), which declared racial segregation in America's schools unconstitutional. That is why in the opinion of Jules Tygiel, author of *Baseball's Great Experiment,* the noble experiment not only reflects "a saga of sport," it also "offers an opportunity to analyze the integration process in American life."[1]

While many agree that the integration of professional baseball was significant in the integration of America, few have really explored the religious and ethical components. This essay reflects my attempt to fill that void. As a baseball fan, I view the sport of baseball religiously (much to the dismay of some of my colleagues); I have taught my son to respect the rituals of the game and value the baseball field as sacred space. As a researcher and teacher of religion and ethics, I was intrigued by the question of whether religion played any part in the integration of baseball. As I explored the issue, I discovered that religion and ethics were decidedly contributing factors.

Baseball's Integration Story

The story of how baseball broke the color barrier is well known. Tygiel suggests that baseball followed the path of many professions at the turn of the twentieth century. In the opinion of the professions' gatekeepers, erecting racial and ethnic barriers to admission would elevate the status of the profession.[2] Thus, African Americans were excluded from playing major-league baseball and segregated into the Negro Leagues established for them. From the outset, such barriers appeared arbitrary to some players, fans, and citizens. Baseball officials denied there was a color barrier, of course. Judge Landis, who became baseball's first commissioner after the Black Sox scandal in Chicago, said that the only barrier to baseball was ability. If persons of color could play the game, he maintained, then they would be allowed to play. Yet, clearly, the barriers were not based on skill and were effective in keeping baseball segregated.

Segregation in baseball, and elsewhere in American society, became more troublesome with the advent of World War II. Many people openly questioned the Jim Crow laws (which were race related and led to the establishment of the separate Negro Leagues), while Americans of all races were fighting a long and bitter war to end racism in Europe. People began to clamor loudly that segregation in America, and in baseball, the sport that was becoming America's pastime, must end. If African Americans could fight for their country, then they should have opportunities elsewhere. The goal of those who wanted change was to expose the contradictions between baseball's rhetoric and its reality.

The arguments against integration lacked credibility. Many minority players who played in the Negro Leagues demonstrated their ability to compete at the major-league level. Another weak argument was that Southern ballplayers—who comprised over one third of major-league players—would protest and spring training in the South would be a problem. According to a late-1930s poll by Wendell Smith, an African American sportswriter for the *Pittsburgh Courier,* most of the players and managers in the National League had no problems with integration. Besides, the players had little power relative to the owners; if the owners chose to integrate baseball, the players had to go along if they wanted to play. Spring training was a source of revenue for southern towns. If they fought integration, the owners could train the players elsewhere. The biggest fear for the owners, however, was the impact on the box office during the regular season. It was unclear whether white fans would attend integrated baseball. Prior to World War II, there were no economic incentives to integrate. Three-fourths of all blacks lived in the South. Most major-league baseball teams were in the North. Owners didn't want to upset the northern white clientele who supported the game.[3] The only way integration would happen was if the owners of the major-league teams moved toward making it happen. Further, they would have to be motivated by justice as well as profits. Branch Rickey, president and co-owner of the Brooklyn Dodgers, decided to make the first move.

One hot August afternoon in 1945, Clyde Sukeforth, the chief scout for the Brooklyn Dodgers, brought Jackie Robinson, an African American baseball player in the Negro Leagues, to Brooklyn for a meeting with Branch Rickey. The pretense was that Rickey scouted Robinson as a possible player for the Brooklyn Brown Dodgers, a team in the new Negro League that Rickey had started. The truth was that Rickey wanted Robinson to play for the parent club, the Brooklyn Dodgers. Mr. Rickey, as everyone called him, had spent many hours investigating Robinson to see if he had the skills and the character to be the first African American to play major-league baseball, to break baseball's unwritten color barrier. His investigation was part of a larger plan to integrate baseball that, according to Arthur Mann, involved six steps:

1) The backing and sympathy of the Dodgers' directors and stock-holders, whose investment and civic standing had to be considered and protected; 2) Picking a Negro who would be the right man on the field; 3) Picking a Negro who would be the right man off the field; 4) A good reaction from press and public; 5) Backing and thorough understanding from the Negro race, to avoid misrepresentation and abuse of the project; 6) Acceptance of the player by his teammates.[4]

After a three-hour meeting, Rickey decided that Robinson was the right person and offered him a contract to play with the team's top farm club in Montreal as a prelude to joining the Dodgers. Robinson accepted.

Other owners were not happy with Rickey's decision to integrate baseball. A 1946 report written by a committee of owners who explored the race question was presented to major-league baseball owners and illustrated their displeasure. While feigning concern for the development of African American players and the demise of the old Negro Leagues, the report noted that because baseball is a business, the primary concern must be profit. The report further commented that with Jackie Robinson playing at the Triple A level, African American attendance had increased. In the minor-league cities of Newark and Baltimore, African Americans made up over 50 percent of the gate. Instead of being a cause for celebration, the committee saw this development as a cause for concern. "A situation might be presented, if Negroes participate in Major League games, in which the preponderance of Negro attendance in parks such as the Yankee Stadium, the Polo Grounds and Comiskey Park could conceivably threaten the value of the Major League franchises owned by these Clubs."[5] The report assumed that increased attendance by African Americans would cause white attendance to drop. This demonstrated that, even after integration had happened, most owners were more concerned with profits and not alienating white fans than they were with fairness or justice for African Americans.[6]

Religion and Morality
in the Integration of Baseball

Why did Branch Rickey take the surprising initiative he did? Why did Jackie Robinson agree to be the "principal actor" in what he later called "Mr. Rickey's drama" in full awareness of the potential physical and emotional abuse such a role entailed?[7] Many claim then and now that Rickey's

The Faith of Fifty Million

primary motives were pragmatic: to win games and to make money. I heard this argument most recently in a dinner conversation with an economist. There are those who suggest, however, that the motive was less important than the result. Monte Irvin (Hall of Famer and star of the Newark Black Eagles) argues that what Rickey did was far more important than why he did it. "Regardless of the motives," Irvin observes, "Rickey had the conviction to pursue it and to follow through."[8] Rickey himself admits his motives were mixed. In a letter to Arthur Mann, the magazine writer he confided in to break the news of Robinson's hiring, Rickey writes, "I don't mean to be a crusader. My only purpose is to be fair to all people and my selfish objective is to win baseball games."[9] Jackie Robinson dreamed of one day playing in the major leagues and had an unequaled competitive streak and desire to win. While these pragmatic and selfish motives undoubtedly played a role in this drama, I contend that for both Rickey, the director, and Robinson, the actor, the religious and moral convictions that shaped their characters were more significant factors in influencing the parts they played. Their nurture in the Christian faith shaped their moral convictions about the equality of all persons and the immorality of all forms of discrimination and racism. Their understanding of and commitment to the biblical injunction to "turn the other cheek" provided the "surprising example" and effective strategy to make their noble experiment work. As Robinson biographer David Falkner comments, "Turn the other cheek was . . . the point of the play. It was all in Scripture."[10]

Branch Rickey

At the time of Rickey's decision to integrate baseball, he had already earned a reputation as a devoutly religious man. In a game where many players, great and small, succumbed to excess, in drinking, spending, and the like, Rickey had "a stubborn refusal to compromise basic teachings and beliefs."[11] Exhibiting a strong Wesleyan piety, he did not use profanity or drink alcohol. He often spoke out against the problems of drinking, although he did not favor prohibition. He knew that moral persuasion, not legislation, changed people's hearts and actions. He was active in his churches in St. Louis and New York, even as a lay preacher. He was known as a man who kept his word and never broke any of his promises, including his promise to his mother that he would never set foot in a ballpark on Sundays. Rickey would not pay players too much because he thought that was sinful, and he lectured his players on the evils of sin. Carl Erskine says about Rickey, "He encouraged us to develop a spiritual life, whatever our religion—he thought the discipline that would come out of that was very important, especially in handling the pressure of pitching or playing in the big leagues. He was always counseling players to develop these disciplined lifestyles, and that stuck with a lot of us."[12] He helped to find funding for the Fellowship of Christian Athletes. Because of his religious allusions and sermon-like speeches, sportswriters nicknamed him the "Deacon." One even dubbed Rickey the "Mahatma," reflecting John Gunther's description of Gandhi as "a combination of God, your father, and a Tammany Hall leader."[13]

The source of these religious convictions can be found in his Christian upbringing. Wesley Branch Rickey belonged to a devout Methodist family (although his father was a Baptist, they joined the Methodist church). He was named after Methodism's founder, John Wesley, and he imbibed the ways of his tradition with its emphasis on personal piety and reading and studying the Bible.[14] He was taught by word and example that all persons are equal in God's eyes, and he believed it. His mother's words and example made an impact on Rickey's thoughts and actions, teaching him the importance of character and responsibility. One incident, which Rickey called a "solemn and unforgettable moment," occurred when Rickey's mother took him into her bedroom after he had done something wrong and prayed for herself for not doing her job as a mother rather than having Rickey pray for forgiveness.[15] Thoroughly chastised, Rickey learned that one person's actions affect others and that every position of authority has responsibilities attached to it.

This emphasis on a Christian's responsibilities was shaped in new directions when, as head of a YMCA in Delaware, Ohio, in the winter of 1907–08, Rickey came in contact with the teachings of the social gospel movement. In many cities and towns across the East and Midwest, reform under the heading of "Christian social responsibility" was the order of the day. This movement spoke of the importance of creating a community where all persons were treated with respect and none were denied opportunity. Rickey invited Jane Addams, Jacob Riis, and Booker T. Washington to speak at his YMCA and to share their ideas and work with his community.[16] As a result, his own Methodist convictions and beliefs, namely, that all persons were God's creatures and should be respected, combined with the social gospel movement's emphasis on Christian social responsibility to give shape to his lifelong commitment to justice and fairness.

The Faith of Fifty Million

This commitment became embodied in the cause for racial integration and equality when he became baseball coach at Ohio Wesleyan in 1903. On his team he had an African American catcher named Charlie Thomas. When the team went to South Bend, Indiana, for a game against Notre Dame, Rickey tried to register his team at a local hotel only to be told that Thomas could not stay at the hotel because he was black. After much argument, Rickey did convince the hotel clerk to let Thomas stay on a cot in Rickey's room until other accommodations could be made. Recalling the scene years later, Rickey said that when he went to his room, he found Thomas sitting on the cot, "tears welled in Charles' large, staring eyes. They spilled down his black face and splashed to the floor . . . his shoulders heaved convulsively, [as] he rubbed one great hand over the other, muttering, 'black skin . . . black skin. If I could only make 'em white. He kept rubbing and rubbing as though he would remove the blackness by sheer friction."[17]

This story has been told so many times that it has gathered almost mythic proportions. Tygiel writes, "The Charlie Thomas story, though based on fact, is vintage Rickey. The allegory is almost biblical and the sermon-like quality of the tale invites skepticism."[18] While the story may have been elaborated upon with each telling, like all good myths and stories that have moral implications, the Charlie Thomas story provided a catalyst for moral action when the time was right. This experience may have forced Rickey to ponder the problem of race and the impact of racial segregation in American life for the first time. Yet, it also triggered Rickey's passion for justice and fairness and gave birth to his own commitment to end discrimination in baseball and beyond if and when he had the chance.[19] Rickey makes this clear later when he states, "I couldn't face my God much longer knowing that His black creatures are held separate and distinct from His white creatures in the game that has given me all I own."[20] Rickey's lifelong concern about discrimination is evidenced in numerous ways. While he was the manager of the St. Louis Cardinals, Charlie Thomas, now a dentist, came to visit. Because seating was segregated in St. Louis, Rickey refused to go to the field. Instead, he spoke with Thomas in his office and vowed that one day all of this would end. Similarly, his daughter recounts a story in 1932 when Rickey, a lawyer, was helping her with a traffic violation. Rickey became interested in the police interrogation of a black suspect accused of murder: "Dad walked right over and busted right in on the grilling. He just didn't want to see the guy mistreated; he was a lawyer and he knew people had rights and he wanted to see to it that this guy had someone there for him. He wound up giving the guy his card and then, after that, hired him as a chauffeur!"[21] Such was his commitment that Dan Dodson, the New York University sociologist who was head of the Committee for Unity in New York City at the time of baseball's integration, could say without hesitation, "Rickey had a great sense of concern about the discrimination against Negroes in baseball."[22]

Jackie Robinson

When Rickey decided the time was right to integrate baseball, he chose Jackie Robinson.[23] Why Robinson? Rickey was clearly concerned that the first person had to be of a certain character. The candidate did not have to be the best black ballplayer, though he naturally needed superior skills. Instead, he had to be the most likely to maintain his competitive abilities in the face of pressure and abuse. He needed the self-control to avoid reacting to his tormentors without sacrificing his dignity. In addition to his composure on the field, the candidate had to be an exemplary individual off the field. "We could know about his playing ability in uniform," reasoned Rickey, "but what about out of uniform? . . . his associates, his character, his education, his intelligence." When Rickey had completed the portrait of the ideal path breaker, he concluded, "There were just not very many such humans."[24]

Jack Roosevelt Robinson had the education and intelligence. He had gone to junior college and to the University of California, Los Angeles (UCLA). He had played with whites on the same teams. Robinson had good baseball skills. As early as 1939, Robinson's name was put forward as one of the players in the Negro Leagues who could play at the major-league level, and Rickey's own scouts confirmed that assessment. The real issue for Rickey was character. Rickey became concerned when he found out Robinson threatened to punch out an umpire. Wendell Smith said that Robinson was not belligerent, but "he was someone who was willing to stand up for what was right."[25] Rickey knew that Robinson was proud and defiant and was willing to assert himself and his rights as an American. Such a dignified spirit was necessary to see the experiment through, but not if it led the player to lose self-control. Rickey went to California to check out Robinson's character for himself. When he returned, Rickey had concluded that Robinson was the right person. The saving grace for Robinson—and the design—was that Robinson was, in Rickey's estimation, "a Christian by inheritance and practice."[26]

As Rickey discovered, the dignity that others could not knock down developed in the context of the Christian nurture Robinson received as a child. The Rickey family had nothing on the Robinson family when it came to the importance of religion in their daily lives. Like Rickey, Robinson grew up as a Methodist. Mallie Robinson, Jackie's mother, who brought her children to California from Georgia in search of a better life after her husband deserted her, has been characterized as a strong, God-fearing woman. She refused to be broken by circumstances and found in her religious commitment and community "both spiritual sustenance and collective survival in a social order ruled by racism and poverty." She worked hard to instill key values into her children, including the importance of family unity, kindness toward others, education, and religion. Mallie Robinson believed in living according to the will of God, which was "an active, not an abstract, principle."[27] She would insist to her children, "God watches what you do; you must reap what you sow, so sow well!"[28] Her teaching influenced the consciences of her children, especially the youngest, Jackie. This explains how they kept in line even though she worked long hours as a domestic.

While Mallie Robinson's words and example influenced young Jackie, it was not until the arrival of the Reverend Karl Downs as the new minister at their Methodist church that the religion and faith that Jackie's mother tried to instill in her youngest child came home. The young minister befriended Jackie and other youth in the congregation, listened to their problems and concerns, and provided counsel and advice. Downs was able to communicate spiritually with the youngsters, including Robinson, being there with them instead of talking down to them. Under the minister's influence, Jack saw the true significance of his religion for the first time. Downs made the Bible come alive, helping Robinson to see the relevance of the biblical stories to everyday life. Downs's dedication inspired Robinson to give of himself. He became a Sunday school teacher and he never missed church, even on those Sunday mornings after athletic contests when his body would ache with pain. Participation in church life was no longer a duty but a pleasure. As Robinson would later comment, he moved from indifference as a church member to "excitement in belonging."[29]

From the religious example of his mother and the minister in his life, he developed a strong sense of his own dignity and a strong belief that segregation in America was immoral. "My mother never lost her composure. She didn't allow us to go out of our way to antagonize the whites, and she still made it perfectly clear to us and to them that she was not at all afraid of them and that she had no intention of allowing them to mistreat us."[30] Mallie Robinson stood up against the bigotry and injustice she experienced, but in ways that tried to overcome the hatred of others with love and kindness. This strategy apparently worked. For years, angry white neighbors in Pasadena tried to buy out the Robinsons. The only neighbor who had the financial means to buy them out, Clara Coppersmith, the widow next door, however, supported them apparently in response to the many chores the Robinson children, at their mother's request, did freely for her.[31] Similarly, Karl Downs brought to his ministry in Pasadena a history of advocating the dignity of all persons and courage in the face of social injustice even if it meant sacrificing comforts. Their example and encouragement reinforced Robinson's own commitment to stand up against injustice.

His courage and willingness to risk personal comforts for the cause of justice became evident in two incidents during his military career. As the morale officer of an all-black unit at Fort Riley, Kansas, Robinson listened as black soldiers complained that they were treated disrespectfully at the commissary, often being ignored and refused service. Robinson phoned a superior officer who, ignorant of Robinson's race, made racist comments about the request. Robinson got into a shouting match that was later reported to the base commander. As a result of his efforts, the African American soldiers received better treatment on the base; Robinson was transferred to Camp Hood in Texas where the commander felt that, because of the more rigid racial segregation, he could not incite more trouble. They did not know Robinson well.

At Camp Hood, Robinson was court-martialed when he refused a superior officer's order to sit in the back of a camp bus. Robinson knew that the Army had changed the rules about requiring blacks to sit in the back of buses while on the military base. Neither the bus driver nor the military police officer knew about the change when they ordered Robinson to change seats. Although Robinson was cleared of the charges, he was still released from the Army under the pretense that his sore ankle made him unfit for combat, which was where his unit was heading. Both instances, and there were others, illustrate that Robinson, like his mother and minister, would assert his dignity in the face of injustice and stand up for what he knew was right. Whether or not he also had their conviction and self-control to assert his dignity without retaliation in the face of the verbal and physical assault such a stance might invite remained to be seen.[32]

Turning the Other Cheek

During that critical three-hour marathon meeting in Brooklyn, Rickey knew that Robinson had the skills and the character the person who broke the color barrier in baseball would need. The only question left was whether or not Robinson's spirit of pride, courage, and defiance in the face of injustice, a spirit Rickey knew was critical for the experiment to succeed, could be harnessed in appropriate ways for the cause of integration of baseball (and by example, American society). Rickey told Robinson, "I know you're a good ballplayer. What I don't know is whether you have the guts." Robinson felt heat coming to his cheeks, insulted and angered by the challenge to his courage. "We can't fight our way through this, Robinson. . . . We can win only if we can convince the world . . . you're a great ballplayer and a fine gentleman." They agreed that performance on the field ought to be all that counts, but they knew for this noble experiment to work, more was required. Rickey asked, "Have you got the guts to play the game no matter what happens?" Robinson asked, "Mr. Rickey, are you looking for a Negro who is afraid to fight back?" Rickey exploded, "Robinson, I'm looking for a ballplayer with guts enough not to fight back."

Rickey then grilled Robinson, illustrating the potential verbal and physical abuse he would experience on and off the field when he played in the major leagues. At that untimely moment, Rickey handed Robinson a copy of Giovanni Papini's *Life of Christ* and asked him to read the section on nonresistance. When he finished, Robinson looked up. "Mr. Rickey," he whispered, "I've got two cheeks. That it?" Could he turn the other cheek? Given his fiery disposition in the face of injustice, Robinson was not sure he could. Yet he knew he had to do it, for himself, his family, and African Americans who would follow him. Robinson finally responded, "If you want to take this gamble, I will promise you there will be no incident."[33]

Why was this biblical injunction, "turn the other cheek," the key to the integration of baseball? We can find the answer in what Papini wrote that influenced Rickey and Robinson. Papini contends that there are three responses a person can make to violence: revenge, flight, or turning the other cheek. The first two he suggests are problematic.

Revenge just accelerates the cycle of violence. Flight is no better because, when you run, the enemy gets emboldened to become more violent. The only way, he suggests, is turning the other cheek, the path he calls nonresistance.

> Turning the other cheek means not receiving the second blow. It means cutting the chain of the inevitable wrongs at the first link. Your adversary who expected resistance or flight is humiliated before you and before himself. He was ready for anything but this. He is thrown into confusion, a confusion which is almost shame. He has the time to come to himself; your immobility cools his anger, gives him time to reflect. He cannot accuse you of fear because you are ready to receive the second blow, and you yourself show him the place to strike. Every man has an obscure respect for courage in others, especially if it is moral courage, the rarest and most difficult sort of bravery. An injured man who feels no resentment and who does not run away shows more strength of soul, more mastery of himself, more true heroism than he who in the blindness of rage rushes upon the offender to render back to him twice the evil received.[34]

Papini's point, and that of the Sermon on the Mount, is that nonviolence is not a docile or passive stance, as some surmise, but an active one. The injured person does resist, but does so without vengeance. Revengeful or violent resistance only perpetuates the cycle of hatred and alienation. "To answer blows with blows, evil deeds with evil deeds, is to meet the attacker on his own ground, to proclaim oneself as low as he."[35] Nonviolent resistance makes the absurdity of the violence evident and invites reconciliation and community.

Many people contend that Branch Rickey's motives in this drama were pragmatic. But they fail to see that his pragmatism went beyond his desire to win ball games; it encompassed his commitment to justice and fairness. Rickey recognized that the approach to the integration of baseball and society had to be the right one. It did not mean that one should do nothing, like the other teams, but that one's initiative should be transformational and effective. According to Glen Stassen, this is exactly what Jesus' statements in the Sermon on the Mount are: "transforming initiatives" that "surprise and confront the adversary's hostility, raising the possibility of a breakthrough in alienation, distrust, and oppression."[36] If Robinson returned blow for blow, the opponents of integration would use his actions to instill fear in other whites and to maintain the status quo, the injustice of segregation. The "surprising initiative" advocated in the Sermon on the Mount breaks down "the over/under relationship of oppression and hostility and initiates a relation of equality that can lead to talking and reconciliation."[37] Rickey's Methodist and social gospel roots convinced him that such transformation could not be legislated from above; it had to occur through the moral persuasion that comes through the face-to-face encounter. Rickey felt certain that, through his baseball skills, Robinson could prove he belonged in the major leagues. Rickey hoped that by turning the other cheek, Robinson could affirm his dignity as a man in the face of the inhumanity of others' hostility and demonstrate to reasonable people the absurdity of segregation. Rickey's optimism was influenced by the thesis of Columbia University Professor Frank Tannenbaum's book, *Slave and Citizen,* that "proximity" between blacks and whites would encourage more amicable race relations. Dan Dodson, the NYU sociologist in whom Rickey confided, shared this optimism. "Thus I believe there is illustrated a vital point—you don't worry about prejudices people possess too much. You create situations which bring them together for common purposes and allow them to work out their relations to each other in the best climate you can create."[38]

Turning the other cheek is no easy task. Papini saw clearly that it goes against our human nature. This was certainly true of Robinson, who had a reputation of having a "hair-trigger disposition," especially when it came to racism.[39] He admits that he was thinking such thoughts at the time of this meeting: "I was twenty-six years old, and all my life back to the age of eight when a little neighbor girl called me nigger—I had believed in payback, retaliation."[40] But Robinson also understood that he had to deny his true fighting spirit, at least for the first three years, so that the noble experiment could succeed (even though such denial would later extract a heavy emotional and physical toll from him).[41] The transforming initiative had to begin with him. As Papini writes, "Only he who has transformed his own soul can transform the souls of his brothers, and transform the world into a less grievous place for all."[42] The biblical message he learned from his mother by word and example, the way to overcome hatred is not violence but patience and love, now made sense to Robinson.

Was Robinson really transformed? There were times during that first year when Robinson wanted to retaliate. Roger Kahn, a sportswriter who later covered the Dodgers, recounts a conversation with Robinson. The time Robinson felt like quitting was after the Ben Chapman incident in Philadelphia, in which Chapman, the Philadelphia manager, repeatedly harassed Robinson with a barrage of racial slurs. Robinson said to Kahn, "All of a sudden I thought, the hell with this. This isn't me. They're making me be some crazy pacifist black freak. Hell, no. I'm going back to being myself. Right now. I'm going into the Philly dugout and grab one of those white sons of bitches and smash his . . . teeth and walk away. Walk away from this ballpark. Walk away from baseball."[43] Why didn't he? Most likely, it is because the lessons he had learned from his mother about overcoming hatred with love were more a part of him than he thought. The most striking feature of the incident with the Phillies, however, is Robinson's response to a request by Chapman to have his picture taken with Robinson in order to save his job as manager. Walter Winchell had branded Chapman as a racist and was leading a campaign to have him ousted. Chapman asked Harold Parrott, the Dodgers' traveling secretary, if Robinson would have a picture taken with him. To Parrott's surprise, Robinson quickly agreed. Not only did he agree, instead of meeting Chapman in his own dugout, he agreed to meet him halfway behind home plate. Parrott offered to go with Robinson, but Robinson replied, "No. This is something I should do alone, not as if I'm being urged."[44]

The Impact of Baseball's Surprising Moral Example

This transformation of the other was what Rickey was hoping for. He was optimistic that once this "surprising initiative" was under way, it would change the hearts and minds of players, coaches, the media, and the fans so they could see past their prejudice toward the greater good. He would quote from Alexander Pope, an eighteenth-century English poet, to say what will happen: "They don't want Negroes in baseball, but when it happens, 'We first endure, then pity, then embrace.'"[45] Nonviolent resistance, where the dignity and moral character of Jackie Robinson (and by association, all African Americans) would be affirmed in the face of racial abuse and violence, was the linchpin for overcoming racial indifference and hostility and accepting integration into America's pastime. Did such transformation occur? The simple answer is yes, but the process was not simple. Moreover, baseball's surprising moral example had an impact on society as a whole. Let me provide a few illustrations.

Impact on Baseball

Red Barber was a popular broadcaster with the Dodgers, a fan favorite. He was also southern born and bred. Rickey told Barber about his intent early in 1945 to observe his reaction. Barber's immediate response was silence. He went home and told his wife that he intended to quit, but she convinced him to wait. Barber, whose parents were Baptist and Presbyterian, was attending an Episcopal church. The pastor asked him to give a speech on "Men and Brothers" to help ease the tensions that had developed between Jews and non-Jews in the wealthy community of Scarsdale, New York. That assignment, along with what he needed to do about his job, led Barber to a crisis of conscience. "Well, when I worked out that talk I suddenly found that I wasn't nearly so interested in the relationship between Christians and Jews . . . as I was about the relationship between one white southern broadcaster and one unknown Negro ballplayer, who was coming. . . . I don't know how much help [that talk] gave to anyone who was listening, but it helped me a great deal. . . . All I had to do when he came . . . was treat him as a man, a fellow man, treat him as a ballplayer, broadcast the ball game." The event also led him to rethink his Christian convictions, especially about the command to "love one's neighbor as oneself." This did not mean you had to like other people, Barber figured, but it did mean you had to respect them and be concerned about their welfare. Barber credits Jackie Robinson with helping him to live out this conviction. "He did far more for me than I did for him."[46]

Robinson's first major-league manager, Clay Hopper of the Montreal Royals, had a similar conversion experience. Rickey's hiring of Hopper to be the manager at Montreal, after the signing of Robinson, came as a surprise. Hopper was a native of Mississippi and had racist leanings. Rickey hired Hopper for two reasons. First, he knew Hopper could develop Robinson as a player. Second, having a southern-bred manager might serve as an example for white Southerners on his team.[47] Hopper voiced his distaste for the assignment to Rickey. "Please don't do this to me. I'm white and I've lived in Mississippi all my life. If you're going to do this, you're going to force me to move my family and home out of Mississippi." Hopper did not need the money, so his decision to manage meant he was willing to try. Yet his racist attitude had not diminished. Rickey commented to Hopper during a workout that a play Robinson had made was "superhuman." Hopper responded, "Mr. Rickey, do you really think a nigger's a human being?"[48] Rickey was furious at this remark, but he later told Robinson why he restrained his anger toward Hopper. "I saw that this Mississippi-born man was sincere, that he meant what he said; that his attitude of regarding the Negro as a subhuman was part of his heritage; that here was a man who had practically nursed race prejudice at his mother's breast."[49] By year's end, however, Hopper held a different view. Robinson writes that the one incident that stood out in his mind after Montreal won the Little World Series in 1946 was when Clay Hopper came to shake his hand. "You're a great ballplayer and a fine gentleman. It's been wonderful having you on the team."[50]

Robinson's willingness to turn the other cheek proved to be the catalyst for acceptance by his teammates. When Robinson first came up to the Dodgers, some of the players started an unsuccessful petition to keep him off the team. Some asked to be traded. None of his teammates, except Pee Wee Reese, had much to do with Robinson. This began to change after the vicious verbal assault Robinson experienced at the hands of the Philadelphia Phillies, led by the manager, Ben Chapman. Chapman was extremely abusive, aiming every racial epithet imaginable at Robinson. Although fuming inside, Robinson ignored them. Finally, his teammates, who knew about the pledge Robinson had made to Rickey, could no longer tolerate the abuse. Eddie Stanky, a Dodger from Mobile, Alabama, yelled out to the Phillies, "Why don't you guys go to work on somebody who can fight back?" The hope that Rickey expressed to Harold Parrott was coming true. "Don't you see what's happening, son? . . . On this team, on any team, there are some fair-minded men of quality who will rebel against the treatment Robinson is getting, and they'll do something about it. There will be an incident, perhaps a small one, perhaps something big. But they'll be drawn closer to him and become a protective cordon around him."[51]

Acceptance by the fans was another crucial component of baseball's integration experiment. On the one hand, there would be more African American fans coming to the game to see this noble experiment. It was imperative that these fans demonstrate their own commitment to make integration work. At a 1947 meeting with African American community leaders at the Brooklyn YMCA, Rickey warned those gathered that if he brought Robinson up to the Dodgers, "the biggest threat to his success—the *one* enemy most likely to ruin that success—is the Negro people themselves!"[52] Rickey's fear was that the African American community either would use the advancement of Robinson as a symbol of race over race or would cause trouble in the stands if Robinson were unfairly treated. While we may criticize Rickey's implicit prejudice, that African Americans cause many of their own problems, we cannot ignore his insight that the behavior of African American fans played a crucial role in this drama. Rickey turned to the African American religious community for help. Churches held rallies and forums in major cities to encourage the African American community to resist any retaliation for problems. They too must turn the other cheek—practice nonviolence—in the face of verbal and physical abuse Robinson or they might receive from whites.

White fans were also important. Some feared white fans in the South would make Robinson's spring training unbearable. While he did receive verbal abuse and physical threats against his life, Robinson was aware that many white fans voiced support; town officials were the ones who had the problem with his presence. Robinson recalls one such fan: "I don't think I'll ever forget the small, shrill voice of a tiny white kid who, in the midst of a racially tense atmosphere during an early game in a Dixie town, cried out, 'Attaboy, Jackie.' It broke the tension and it made me feel I had to succeed."[53]

Tygiel contends that racial indifference on the part of whites in the North posed more of a problem for integration. Here again, Robinson's athletic skills and moral character won them over. Initial reactions to Robinson from Montreal fans were cordial. By the end of the season, in which they won the Little World Series, thousands carried Robinson on their shoulders and ran after him on the field. Sportswriter Sam Martin said of the scene, "It was probably the only day in history that a black man ran from a white mob with love instead of lynching on its mind."[54] White fans flocked to the stadiums when Robinson came to town as a Royal and, later, as a Dodger. Undoubtedly, some came hoping he would fail. Most people became admirers. Such admiration is most evident in one fan's letter. The author let Robinson know that there were "plenty of people, black and white" rooting for him. He appreciated the "guts" Robinson expressed on the field playing so well under so much pressure. Most important, he writes, "If your batting average never gets any higher than .100 and if you make an error every inning, if I can raise my boy to be half the man that you are I'll be a happy father."[55]

The approach of nonviolent resistance, taking the high moral ground in the face of threat, also had to play out at the level of management. For the experiment to succeed, Rickey had to see it through regardless of the costs and pressures. Some of those costs included the large sum of money needed to scout African American players, a disadvantage in recruitment and retention of southern ballplayers who might refuse to play with blacks, and the potential loss in revenues if white fans stayed away from the game.[56] Rickey successfully resisted pressure from players, even trading one of his stars. When, during spring training in 1946, some southern officials closed ballparks or passed ordinances that would not allow blacks and whites to play on the same field, Rickey had his teams show up anyway, forcing those towns to make the choice.[57] The following year he held spring training in Cuba, where his players got used to playing with persons of color, and southern towns experienced the economic loss of not having spring training in their communities. This combination of moral stance and economic pressure was successful. Dan Dodson notes that the very southern cities that closed parks to Robinson during his first spring training were later asking for him to come. He relates one example: "Significantly, two years later when spring training schedules were being arranged one of the large Georgia towns wanted the Dodgers to play their local club. To this Rickey responded, 'If I can bring my whole team.' 'What do you mean by that?' they asked. 'My Negro players,' responded Rickey. 'Hell, that's who we want to see play,' they responded." Fans came, players stayed, and the towns opened their doors to the Dodgers, including those players of color.[58]

Impact Beyond Baseball

The transformation Rickey sought in baseball's integration saga went beyond baseball. First, the drama transformed the director and the principal actor. Early on, Rickey claimed that, while he was committed to justice and fairness in the game he loved, he was not a crusader. He just wanted to win ball games. In truth, he was more transformed by this drama than he realized. The profit motive and desire to win lost ground to his commitment to justice. As the first to hire black players, Rickey could have cornered the market of black talent. Instead, he would not sign some players, like future Hall-of-Famer Larry Doby, in the hope that other teams would follow his lead. His role in baseball's integration and his friendship with Robinson led him to champion the cause of race relations in the broader society. He spoke more readily that his interest in racial justice was the primary motive for his actions. Looking back in 1955, he said, "I felt very deeply about that thing all my life." In a 1958 speech in Detroit, he continued to advocate a four-point scheme to end race prejudice that included the importance of proximity between blacks and whites through actions, not words, and the kind of religious moral courage evidenced by the Good Samaritan.[59] He became more vocal about racial justice and civil rights. In 1962 he wrote that the civil rights issue was "getting to be just about the only issue that interests me."[60]

Robinson was also transformed. It is true that Robinson did not stay quiet. Once the ban on retaliation was lifted after three years, Robinson was very vocal and argumentative on the field, much like any player would be. But friends and observers note that he was never confrontational, and he did not seek fights. More important, Robinson began to see beyond himself and his desire to play and win. He realized, "A life is not important except for the impact it has on other lives."[61] Robinson became a vocal advocate for integration and civil rights on and off the field. His commitment not to return evil for evil demonstrated his moral courage and gave him the moral standing in American society that provided him with a platform for speaking on civil rights throughout the country so that people would listen. Robinson spoke nonstop—at meetings, rallies, hearings, and in his newspaper columns—for full inclusion of African Americans in all segments of American society. He used his name and influence to help the NAACP raise the money it needed in its efforts to promote equality for persons of color. In light of his efforts, Robinson biographer David Falkner claims, "He was the figure who made civil rights a *popular* issue before anyone took to the streets or talked about programs, bills, or social action. Robinson was a link, and a crucial one, between despair and a movement."[62]

Baseball's surprising moral example also became a strategy for other civil rights advocates. While Cornel West may be right when he claims that Robinson's efforts reflect "the black tradition of moral struggle and political resistance," it is also true that his role in baseball's integration drama gave shape to that tradition by establishing a template.[63] Not only did Robinson's example represent "a symbol of imminent racial challenge and a direct agent of social change," it also offered civil rights advocates "a model of peaceful transition through militant confrontation, economic pressure, and moral suasion."[64] Sociologist Harry Edwards contends that the masses of black people who participated in the civil rights movement "understood the effectiveness and impact of Jackie's nonviolent disposition."[65] Robinson's example in baseball's "surprising initiative" inspired the students from SNCC (Student Nonviolent Coordinating Committee) during their lunch counter sit-ins. Like Robinson, they resisted segregation and oppression and were willing to suffer the abuse nonviolently that such resistance entailed. When other civil rights groups would not support their efforts, they came to Robinson for help (and he provided it). Hank Aaron, baseball's career home-run leader, would later call Robinson the "Dr. King of baseball." Yet one could just as easily claim that Martin Luther King Jr. was the "Jackie Robinson of the civil rights movement."[66]

Finally, baseball's integration drama transformed the consciousness of America on race issues. Baseball, America's pastime, had become symbolic of American society. Cornel West argues that an African American participating equally and with dignity on "one of the sacred spaces of American culture" marked the beginning of that transformation.[67] Jackie Robinson and the African American players who followed him into baseball, such as Roy Campanella, Don Newcombe, Joe Page, Elston Howard, Satchel Paige, and Larry Doby, appealed to the heart of America. Players, coaches, the media, and the fans started to look past color to the abilities of these players and the contributions they made to the game they loved. In the process, those who were once indifferent to race issues came to agree with Robinson's assessment of the possibilities that lay ahead. In a speech he gave in Chicago in 1957, Robinson remarks, "Certainly if such revolutionary change can be brought about in baseball, it can also be brought about in education, in transportation, and any other area of our American life."[68] In practice, segregation was still the norm in many American institutions. Few can deny, however, the change in American consciousness, and ultimately in their consciences, baseball's integration drama sparked, which "helped to usher in a new, if still troubled, age of race relations in the United States."[69]

Conclusion

Has the drama ended? Has the transformation reached its zenith in today's post–civil rights era? When I think back to the sunny July day at Fenway Park with my son, I recall that the fans, the coaches, and the management did not reflect the same diversity my son and I observed among the players. Boston is a racially diverse city, yet the faces that cheered and booed were overwhelmingly white and middle class. Where are the throngs of African American fans who came in record numbers to watch Jackie Robinson play? In 1997, baseball players were 58 percent white, 25 percent Latino, 17 percent African American, and 1 percent Asian. Little more than 5 percent of fans are African American. (Only 3 percent of St. Louis Cardinals' fans are black in a city that is 20 percent black. Few followed the battle between Mark McGwire and Sammy Sosa for the home-run title in 1998.)[70] Why are there not more African American coaches and managers? At the game at Fenway Park, one of the teams had an African American hitting instructor, but both managers were white. Do the white, wealthy baseball owners and their top advisors still believe, as Jackie Robinson charged, that the abilities of black players may make them money, but they are "lacking in the gray matter that it supposedly takes to serve as managers, officials, and executives in policy-making positions?"[71] Has the integration of baseball stopped at the players? Is another "surprising initiative" needed?

With regard to the fans, one of the unintended consequences of integration was that baseball ceased to have an institutional presence in black life.[72] As some feared, African American success in major-league baseball led to the demise of the Negro Leagues. Regardless of what one thought about those leagues, Negro League games were cultural and social events as much as sporting events in the African American community. Integration now meant that African Americans had to leave their neighborhood and go to a white setting to watch a baseball game. According to a study commissioned by the St. Louis Cardinals, many blacks didn't "feel welcome there. A night at Busch stadium was equated with a night at the opera; the stadium was seen as a white, corporate refuge."[73] As a consequence of integration, many African Americans have lost interest as spectators.

Disparities in income and wealth in many cities also exacerbate the racial divide in baseball (and in society). Baseball requires land and space. In urban settings, green real estate is expensive. Open properties that could be used for youth baseball are quickly snatched away by wealth for other uses (including the building of new baseball stadiums).[74] What fields are left are poorly maintained and often become hangouts for gangs and drug dealers. High rates of poverty in many urban black communities mean that many Little Leagues cannot find sponsorships for their teams and thus lack proper equipment and resources. As a result, many urban black youths have lost interest in baseball as players and urban high schools have a difficult time fielding teams.[75]

These economic disparities may also shed some light on the question of why there are so few African American coaches, managers, and front-office personnel. Robinson was clear that the full integration in baseball would not occur until it happened at the level of management, something he did not see at the time of his death. Thirty years later, some progress has been made (except at the level of ownership). There are a few managers, coaches, and front office personnel of color, and even an African American president of the National League. Yet in baseball, as in the rest of American society, more can and should be done. The only way this will occur, however, is through continued political and economic pressure and moral persuasion.

But do the religious and ethical resources exist among current people in baseball to address the economic barriers to full integration? We observe numerous open displays of religion in baseball. Many athletes thank God for their abilities, even for the win. Others have religious rituals to help them prepare for the game. But does this religious expression provide the moral courage and commitment to justice it will take to change the economic structures that maintain the status quo? I do not think it exists among the owners. Robinson understood early on that although baseball "poses as a sacred institution dedicated to the public good," it is actually "a big, selfish business."[76] Over the past few years, the business of baseball has become bigger and its commitment to the public good less evident. It is sad but true that the needed courage and commitment to justice are not widespread among the players either. Today's players have the financial clout and public presence to address many of the structural injustices in baseball and beyond. What they have not demonstrated thus far is the moral will to use it. Many even refuse the mantle of role model that their fame and fortune thrusts upon them. Unlike Robinson, who continued to exert his moral influence and example to provide hope for children and advocate change in society, many of these athletes no longer feel they have a moral obligation to others.

What baseball needs is a revival of the spirit that Branch Rickey and Jackie Robinson demonstrated in their willingness to stand against injustice in baseball and in society even in the face of personal and professional risk. We need owners, players, and others who understand baseball's symbolic role in American society and who will not rest until the justice and equality for which America stands are present in baseball and beyond. Like Robinson, only when "every child can have an equal opportunity," until "hatred is recognized as a disease," and until "racism and sexism . . . are conquered," can we say with confidence that we have it made![77]

1	2	3	4	5	6	7	8	9	R	H	E

Chapter 7

A Diamond Is Forever?

Women, Baseball, and a Pitch for a Radically Inclusive Community

Eleanor J. Stebner and Tracy J. Trothen

Striking similarities can be observed between the experiences of women in baseball and their experiences within the Christian church. Innumerable women follow baseball and are committed to it. As with the liturgical year, they observe the cycle of rites, from the preseason opening pitch to the countdown of the World Series. They lift up their heroes and saints, the players whom they adore and applaud, and even identify occasional antiheroes, whom they may stand and boo with equal vigor. If possible, they make pilgrimages to their sacred ballparks and bask in the pews of fandom. They stand at the invocation of the national anthem and partake in the communion of hot dogs and beer (or in case of vegetarian and temperance idealists, peanuts and soda pop). When nostalgia sets in, they may reminisce about the old days, the glory days, the primordial past of the game's great plays and players.

Yes indeed, many women—like many men—are devotees of baseball. They are often as fiercely loyal to their teams as they are to their congregations and denominations (if not more so). At a minimum, their summer lives are shaped by baseball and their social and familial communities solidified by it. Yet it is not unfair to say that baseball—like the Christian church—has not been particularly good to or accepting of women. Oh yes, women are solicited as faithful fans. Indeed, their money (or offering) is necessary to keep the business of baseball alive and well, and their commitment to car pools, fund-raisers, and other forms of support for kids' baseball is crucial. Yet their full participation has been—and continues to be—a struggle. While women may play in their own leagues, they have not been able to escalate into the so-called major leagues; full participation in such high churches may never be open to them. In such settings, a woman pitching from the mound may be as controversial as a woman preaching from the pulpit or presiding at the table. Perhaps more so.

Like the Christian church, baseball has been influenced by larger social and cultural values. As a form of popular culture, it reflects not only what people like to do and how they like to have fun, but also what people hold to be true about the nature of their world. In this sense, baseball is not just a game to be enjoyed—as a player or as a spectator—but is an extension of one's view of the universe. Without overplaying the evidence, it is easy to show how baseball has been influenced by particular understandings of normative gender roles (what it is to be male or female, masculine or feminine), the values of power and competitiveness (present from children's games through professional games), and of sexuality and race. As a team sport, baseball reflects ideals regarding community, nationhood, and the globalization (and exportation) of the so-called American Way.

This paper analyzes baseball from a feminist-theological perspective. The first part reflects on baseball and women from a historical perspective, and the second part engages in social-ethical reflections. The purpose of this paper is not to disparage the sport, but rather to emphasize the struggles women have had in defending their rights to play it and to reclaim their participation in it. As within Christianity, the contributions women have made within baseball have often been forgotten or simply regulated to the bleachers. Beyond offering an interpretation of baseball history that places women on the field, this paper highlights the ideologies of separate spheres and male privilege that have pervaded—and continue to permeate—the sport. Our study suggests that in examining baseball we may realize the need for larger cultural paradigm shifts, in the hope that women may become fully appreciated within a radically inclusive Christian community. This is to say, baseball—both as a sport and as a dominant cultural myth—needs to be liberated from the gloves of patriarchy. While many of our observations may be extended to other sports (such as basketball and, our favorite, hockey), we will stick to baseball. We may strike out. But then again, at least we got up to bat.

Historical Reflections

The origins of baseball lie in obscurity, and only well-trained, well-disciplined, and thick-skinned exegetes attempt to separate its mythical conception from its feasible beginnings. An early form of the game, called rounders (or stool ball), was played by female and male peasants in the fields of England. It became rooted in North American soil in the early 1800s and, by the 1830s, a form of it came to be played in the northeast United States and upper Canada, the latter area settled largely by American loyalists.[1] Dominant myth usually identifies baseball as first being played in 1839 in Cooperstown, New York, or, from a Canadian perspective, in 1838 in Beachville, Ontario. Baseball purists may identify the first real game as taking place in 1845 in Hoboken, New Jersey, under the inspired guidance of Alexander Cartwright. Such examples assume that baseball was founded by and originally played by men; at least in these formal contexts, such an interpretation seems accurate.

The Civil War served to spread baseball across the continent. Soldiers played it, and when they returned from the battlefields they brought the game with them. Early baseball was played in open fields (only later on sandlots and in ballparks) and involved informal team selection. Already by 1871, however, the National Association of Professional Base Ball Players was formed and the game became professionalized. Industrialization and immigration, along with the escalating urbanization of the North American landscape, proved to popularize baseball, especially among urban male immigrants. While many men simply liked to play baseball and in all likelihood expended little energy speculating as to its greater meaning, some middle- and upper-middle-class males developed ideological support for it. They argued that it was an antidote to concerns regarding the loss of male vitality within an urban environment and the capitalistic compartmentalization of life into separate segments of work and play.[2]

The response of the Christian church to baseball was initially mixed. Many Sabbatarians were deeply troubled that baseball was being played on the Lord's Day, yet games played informally did not as blatantly flaunt the Sabbath as preplanned profit-generating doubleheaders. Still, many church leaders saw baseball as a useful tool in combatting various woes within society. During the Progressive Era in the United States, baseball was upheld by both male and female reformers, who embraced it as an important way to address problems related to urban crime, poverty, and the need for socially-acceptable activities. Settlement house and YMCA leaders came to view it as a clean and relaxing form of recreation. More so, they believed that it instilled virtues necessary to the developing nation, such as the need to play by the rules, take risks, face fears, nurture patience, provide support, and, if necessary, sacrifice for one's team; in its most theoretical form, they believed baseball to be a method of extending the values of democracy.[3] Unfortunately, it was a democracy based on the active participation of men and not women; this exclusion perhaps reflected women's lack of the political ballot itself.

Given this perspective, it is not surprising that the first children's story written on baseball was authored by none other than Charles M. Sheldon. Sheldon, who was yet to pen the social gospel classic, *In His Steps,* wrote a story in 1882 titled "The Captain of the Orient Base-ball Nine." As with many children's stories, his story deals more with instilling particular morals than with plotting the peculiarities of baseball. He urges young boys to play tough but not to cheat; he shows the need of players to obey the verdict of the umpire, whether or not the call is right. Sheldon's major point, however, is that individuals have responsibility for their own moral decisions and that it is always better to be honest, even if it means losing a game.[4] Questions regarding gender (and race) are non-issues in his story.

The above discussion points to the observation that baseball—quite early in its North American formation—became a game associated with men, maleness, and masculinity. The association between baseball and Christian manliness was perhaps best incarnated by none other than baseball-player-turned-evangelist Billy Sunday (1862–1935). Although not remembered as a spectacular hitter, he was known as a quick sprinter (the first man, so legend has it, to circle the bases in fourteen seconds). Sunday preached a manly (that is, strong and athletic) Christianity. As one of his biographers proudly observed, "Sunday was a man's man" who drew men to his evangelical services: "His tabernacle audiences resemble base-ball crowds in the proportion of men present, more nearly than any other meetings of a religious nature."[5] Complementary to his manly Christianity, however, was his prescription of Christian womanhood. Sunday believed that the noble, God-given, and sole purpose of women was that of motherhood. While they were to be as courageous and brave and watchful as the mother of Moses and thereby contribute to the greatness of the United States, no proper woman would even think of playing baseball.

Women were playing, however. Neither bats nor diamonds, pitches nor catches, pop flies nor bunts, slides nor steals remained in the domain of male activity only. Students at the all-women's Vassar College, for example, had formed a baseball team by 1866. They loved the game, despite the long dresses they wore while playing it. Indeed, such young women became expert at catching the ball in their skirts. While umpires may have called such a catch trapping, it was nevertheless a creative technique adapted by women when playing baseball. Baseball and the newly opening opportunities privileged white women had to higher education were no doubt connected.[6] The question of women and baseball, however, was related to yet larger questions regarding women and sport.

Through the nineteenth century and into the twentieth century, public debate flourished regarding the acceptability and desirability of women playing sports. Was it healthy for women to exert themselves in any form of physical activity (beyond childbirth, that is)? The medical profession (perhaps more so than the Christian church) argued quite powerfully (and expertly) that women needed to be prohibited from physical activities (and higher education) because it would drain energy away from their reproductive organs and thereby threaten their ability (and usefulness) as childbearers. These kind of arguments, combined with the lack of leisure time for most working women, lead some scholars to suggest that for most women within western society, the development of sport as a leisure activity has excluded them.[7]

Women played baseball not only in safe and secluded college settings, however. As early as the 1860s, games between men and so-called ladies were organized by keen businessmen as a way to draw crowds and make money. Women players were usually recruited not for their throwing and batting abilities, but for their perceived femininity and attractiveness. Other women's teams were formed and referred to as Bloomer Girls. Such teams included women and some select men, and they barnstormed around the continent, challenging various men's teams. Perhaps the most famous of these bloomer teams was called the Blondes and the Brunettes who, in 1875, gained fame for their hair color more than for their playing abilities.[8] The moral reputation (and the class standing) of such women was considered questionable, not only because they played baseball but because they wore pants. The association between women's dress codes and feasible physical activities cannot be overstated. Dress codes for women were restrictive and negatively affected their abilities to be physically active, whether playing baseball or riding bicycles, an activity that was also deemed unwomanly, unhealthy, and immoral for nineteenth-century women.[9]

For women growing up in environs that lacked numerous social outlets, all this moralizing about baseball was laughable in its shocking seriousness; baseball was simply an activity they enjoyed. It did not threaten their morals or their understandings of themselves as women. It was harmless fun. Many girls—as did many boys—grew up playing baseball; they often played it together and they even played it at church socials. Perhaps too much, then, can be made of baseball and how it was related to women. The fact remains, however, that voices within dominant culture attempted to define baseball as out of bounds to women and used religious, social, and physiological arguments to support their position. Godly women would not play it; they would not exert themselves in sport or even sweat in public. Good women were to be passive, and while baseball itself requires the ability to be passive, this was not the form of passiveness upheld for women.

The ideology of separate spheres for women and men, combined with the prescriptive so-called cult of true womanhood, made playing baseball a rebellious—if not a revolutionary—act. Barbara Welter's now classic identification of true womanhood as including purity, piety, submissiveness, and devotion to domesticity clearly marked women as outsiders to the game. The rise of sports journalism (staffed by men) helped spread the message: If only women would listen! Women who refused to docilely accept such categories and who, at least in their younger years, participated in physical activities that were in theory appropriate only for men were called pejorative names. The most common name was *tomboy,* a word that originated in the Middle Ages but which, in the late nineteenth and early twentieth centuries, became used more and more in an attempt to keep women in their place and off the field.[10]

While debate continued as to the acceptability of women playing baseball, women were recruited as fans almost from the beginning. Male promoters of baseball believed the presence of women to be desirable; their presence would not only make the sport more popular and therefore more profitable, but would also make the sport more socially acceptable (and decrease the cursing heard during ball games). Men and women fans initially sat in separate sections at ballparks. Ladies Day, first introduced in 1883 in a game played between the Athletics and the Orioles, was an attempt to "encourage American women to come out to the park, free of charge, [and] to look in on the game that had stolen the hearts of their menfolk."[11] The building of women's bathroom facilities made such marketing plans feasible. Freely admitting women on such designated days proved too costly to retain, but the practice did help popularize the game among women.

Promoters then realized that baseball might be the ideal outing for dating couples. The recruitment of heterosexual couples to baseball games was solidified by the practice of announcing marriage engagements during "lulls in the action."[12] (Similar practices continue today.) The presence of women and men at ballparks became a way to support a new ideal within North American culture, that of male and female togetherness in the pursuit of leisure activities. Such togetherness, however, did not extend to racial integration, and baseball involving African American players—and the social outlets that it provided—developed through the Negro Leagues. The recruitment of women as fans, however, was based on the premise that women would be more interested in the male players—or their male companions—than in the game itself.[13]

Between the World Wars, a number of developments affected the participation of women playing ball. First, the formation of industrial teams became a popular practice. Women no longer needed to attend college to play organized baseball or play on lowly bloomer teams; they could now play in formally acceptable settings. Women's company teams became popular and organized competitions. Employers sponsored teams because they knew women wanted them and because they believed that such activities would positively influence their female employees' productivity and sense of loyalty to their firm. Second, baseball began to be replaced by softball, a game officially named in 1932. Softball was similar to baseball, but considered easier and therefore more appropriate for women. The ball was larger and the bases closer; it was believed to require less skill and be less dangerous.[14] Softball became more popular than baseball at the grassroots level and drew more spectators than minor- or major-league baseball. Yet even women who played softball faced an "image problem," as scholar Gai Ingham Berlage observed, and were often the target of a trinitarian slur that represented them as being "masculine, physical freaks or lesbians."[15]

World War II and the exit of many professional baseball players from the competitive diamonds of North America to the warring fields and bombing skies of Europe and Asia opened opportunities for women to play in a professional league. The All-American Girls' Professional Baseball League (AAGPBL) was first formed in 1943 and folded in 1954.[16] It was the brainchild of millionaire Philip K. Wrigley, whose purpose—other than making money and keeping Wrigley Field occupied—was to provide entertainment and boost patriotism.

The league initially involved four teams playing out of the Midwest: the Rockford (Illinois) Peaches, the South Bend (Indiana) Blue Sox, the Racine (Wisconsin) Belles, and the Kenosha (Wisconsin) Comets. At its height, it was composed of fourteen teams, including teams named the Milwaukee (Wisconsin) Chicks and the Fort Wayne (Indiana) Daisies. More than five hundred women played in the league, and hundreds of thousands of fans watched them. Players were usually in their late teens or early twenties and single, although some were older, married, and mothers. All were white women; a few black women played ball in the Negro Leagues rather than in the AAGPBL. Toni Stone was the first woman in the Negro Leagues when, in 1953, she played with the Indianapolis Clowns and, in 1954, with the Kansas City Monarchs.[17] While black women born in the United States were not allowed to try out for the league, white women born in Canada and Cuba were considered All-American enough to be recruited and included as players. The majority of players hailed from the middle part of the continent; as one Canadian quipped, women from Saskatchewan were especially well represented because there was little else to do in Saskatchewan but play baseball and chase grasshoppers. As the AAGPBL victory song put it: "We've got Canadians, Irishmen and Swedes, we're all for one, we're one for all."[18]

The women in the league were good ballplayers, and as former player Annabelle Lee said, they "lived, ate and drank baseball." Yet Wrigley believed that the league would succeed and be profitable only if the players were seen as wholesomely feminine. To this end, players submitted themselves to hours of baseball practice—under the tutelage of male coaches and male managers—took lessons in etiquette, and were answerable to female chaperones. They wore uniforms with skirts (ah, but skirts no shorter than six inches above the kneecap), and were not allowed to sport "boyish bobs" or smoke and drink in public. They were required to attend charm school, where they learned appropriate beauty routines and what supplies to keep in their survival beauty kits (which were to include everything from medium rouge to hair remover). They were groomed in what to wear, and how to talk and walk. The concern of management was to create a feminine product, both on and off the field. Rule number one in the players' *Rules of Conduct* manual stated, "Always appear in feminine attire when not actively engaged in practice or playing ball."

And point number ten in the *Charm School Guide* stated, "In a final summing up, be neat and presentable in your appearance and dress, be clean and wholesome in appearance, be polite and considerate in your daily contact, avoid noisy, rough and raucous talk and actions and be in all respects a truly All American girl."[19]

The requirements placed on the players of the AAGPBL, of course, reflected middle-class understandings regarding women during the 1940s and 1950s. Some of the players appreciated learning how to apply makeup and how to dress to enhance their physical appearance, while others found the requirements restrictive. Like many young people, they both obeyed and disobeyed the rules. Player Faye "Fanny" Dancer (portrayed by Madonna in the movie *A League of Their Own*) said that "rules are only made to be broken."[20] One of the most popular players in the league, Dancer was known for her beer-drinking party style and her fun-loving attitude with fans. She loved to play practical jokes on her chaperones and was known to have replaced the white filling of Oreo cookies with toothpaste. Yet Dancer was not only an energetic character who pushed the prescriptive gender and social rules of the league, she was also an excellent player who played professional ball for seven years and retired in 1950 only because of injuries.[21]

Historians suggest various reasons for the folding of the AAGPBL, none of which include their inability to play good ball or their corresponding lack of feminine makeup. The return of the boys from military engagements (WWII and Korea) and the resurgence of the male major leagues certainly affected the number of fans in attendance. The decision of the league to decentralize their administration led to managerial competition rather than cooperation. Larger societal factors were also at play. Gender propaganda in the post–World War II decades pushed women off the field and out of the factories, and insisted that women support the nuclear household and their assigned role as homemaker. The rise of television and its coverage of only male games, and the entrenchment of sports journalism, which again focused almost exclusively on male teams, also contributed to the league's decline.

In his book *Creating the National Pastime,* scholar G. Edward White writes that the AAGPBL, "however great its intrinsic interest, cannot fairly be made part of the story of baseball's emergence as the quintessentially American sport."[22] He considers the league but a blip in the baseball world, one that served the purpose of "clowning" and thereby showed the separateness of real (that is, white men's) baseball from

Eleanor J. Stebner and Tracy J. Trothen

women's (and black) baseball. The players in the AAGPBL would have wholeheartedly disagreed. They played real baseball and they played it well. They were professionals and played ball despite the cultural constraints of their era. White's exclusion of their game—indeed, his exclusion of all women (except women fans) from his study of organized baseball—is highly suspect. He admits the irony of arguing for the emergence of a national pastime based on the exclusion of over half of the national population, yet does so because he claims that the exclusion of women was not "patently sexist." "Organized Baseball courted female fans," he writes. "[T]he exclusion of female participants, for most of its twentieth-century history, was treated as simply confirming the principle that certain physical skills were required to play the game, and women as a class lacked these skills." Such scholarly reflections make one wonder if something indeed is rotten in the state of baseball and in its being uplifted as a national pastime.

While women's exclusion from professional baseball is significant in showing the struggles women face as athletes, professional baseball was not the beginning and is not the final word on the game. Little League baseball was formed in 1939 and in 1973 admitted girls. Title IX of the Education Amendments of 1972 theoretically provided an equality of opportunity in law for women in sports by requiring the funding of women's sports in college and university settings. Girls and women continue to play baseball and softball, and international competitions involving teams from around the world are common. The 2001 Women's World Series, for example, was held in Toronto and featured teams from Japan and Australia. While the Colorado Silver Bullets, a professional women's team organized in 1993 and disbanded in 1997, shows that women are not yet able to make a living as ballplayers, they keep trying. One is tempted to ask why. The answer may be quite easy: Some women simply love the game. And perhaps—despite the many and various attempts made to prevent them from playing it—women will eventually persevere. In doing so, they may also change ingrained social and religious understanding of what it is to be female in North America.

Social-Ethical Reflections

The "baseball world pays off on works rather than faith and on merit rather than grace." So reflected Robert McAfee Brown in 1958.[23] He was and is quite accurate, but his statement is based on certain assumptions.

Within the dominant paradigm truth is constructed according to what is defined as normative. While the value—salvific or otherwise—of works and merit continue to be recognized where white men are concerned, for others, including women, this is not as often the case. Also, when discussing baseball, a professional athletic context is commonly assumed. Yet many people—men and women, boys and girls—play baseball and only a few are professionals and gear their efforts toward the so-called World Series. A related assumption is that it is somehow best to be a pro and that the pros—who are all male—play better ball and are icons to be emulated.

Our use of language often serves to camouflage the ethical. The meaning of terms such as "better ball" and the "baseball world" need to be deconstructed so that the hidden values and ethical claims can be named. Equally important is the reconstruction of a vision of baseball that values women's works and merit, together with faith and grace. Such a radically inclusive vision first must be imagined, dreamed, and experienced in concrete moments of realized eschatology if it is to gain more pervasive life. We are convinced that such experiences of baseball do indeed exist, but that we must continue to deepen our communal imagination of experiences of sport so that they become more consistent with such a vision. Similarly, we must continue to resist paradigms that perpetuate exclusivity and other dualistic notions.

The deconstruction and reconstruction of baseball—as a sport that holds emancipatory potential—must include the naming, examining, and reconceptualizing of camouflaged ethical claims. To this end, gender norms and embodiment, power, and community are discussed.

Gender Norms and Embodiment

The dominant patriarchal paradigm that shapes baseball for both spectators and players is neither hegemonic nor desirable. The common assumption, for instance, that "throwing like a girl" is an insult and something to be overcome if one wants to be a real baseball player or, for that matter, a real man (which is clearly preferable to being a real woman, particularly in the world of high-ticket sport) is indicative of the persistence of both dominant gender norms and our dominant social value system. These assumptions clearly did not end with Billy Sunday's contention that women were called to motherhood and not baseball. Even this example, however, is a socially constructed belief that is sexist and based on an erroneous understanding of kinetics. As Michael A.

Messner points out, "[t]hrowing 'like a man' is an unnatural act, an act that (like most 'masculine' behavior) must be learned."[24]

Numerous feminist thinkers have pointed out the relationship between sport and the perpetuation and enforcement of gender stereotypes.[25] The nineteenth-century North American social prohibition against women sweating in public may have passed, but, nonetheless, it remains clear that women are expected to participate only in certain sports—sports defined as less masculine—and only at less economically valued levels. Even debatable is the claim that women simply are not as physically able as men to play baseball.[26]

Men and boys, likewise, are charged with the preservation of heralded gender norms. As sociologist Nancy Shinabarger has observed, "by its very definition in American culture [sport] embodies idealized masculine traits of competitiveness, aggression and loyalty."[27] When a male embodies these traits, he is seen as a fine example of masculinity. However, when he competes with regard for the other, is loyal and gentle in his play, or is not highly skilled, he is labeled feminine, wimpish, unmanly. He may even be ostracized from the "real" male community. Similarly, when women dare to break these stereotypes, they are seen as deviant or unnatural. "In virtue of presenting herself as 'female' and 'athlete,' the woman in sport questions the isomorphism between sport and male identity."[28] Surely, any successful women athletes, including ballplayers, must be lesbian or unduly masculine. Not only are these stereotypes meant to be insulting to women athletes, they are indicative of a widespread hate and fear towards non-normative women and, in particular, lesbian women.

Sexuality and spirituality are entwined; how we love, experience passion, and live as embodied beings reflect and inform our relationships with the divine mystery and vice versa. The incarnation of Christ affirms these claims. Jesus the Christ as fully human and fully divine exemplifies the connectedness of the spirit to the body; the fuller one's humanity in its embodiment, the more fully incarnate and closer to the Divine one becomes.

Such a pantheistic conceptualization of divinity is predicated on the belief that we are called to exalt our embodied selves and one another as holy, living temples of the Spirit. Just as surely as the Holy One is mystery that transcends and deepens that which we can grasp in this world, God is also immanent in our embodied selves. This then is the meaning of ecstasy and the life energy of eros; we find and know the meanings of these God-inspired gifts through—and not in spite of—our embodiment and the embodiment of others. We come to know God through our sensualities. Some of us feel closest to the Spirit and most embodied when we play baseball and feel the exertion of our muscles and the sweat roll down our backs; when we lean into the next pitch or reach for the ground ball.[29]

Women have often been denied the experience of God within the body and have been associated with sex and sin. Men, on the other hand, have been associated with—but not reduced to—the higher realms of spirit and rational thought. This split has limited and diminished humanity and has been particularly harmful to women. Women have been told to deny their bodies or view them as corrupt or in need of protection (and therefore women have not been able to play baseball or any other too physically demanding sport). Men's bodies have not been directly associated with sin or evil, and therefore, they could play baseball. Baseball, however, is not essentially dependent on violence, the abuse of power, or the sacrifice of the body and can, in fact, be redemptive for women and men. When the love of the game is the motivating force behind playing the game, our spirits and bodies can be reconnected. For women, this means learning to love our embodied selves in a cultural context that tells us relentlessly to despise our bodies, carry a survival beauty kit, and not to resist when our bodies are violated.

Playing baseball can foster a greater love for and awareness of our embodied selves. The historic concern that women would be diverted from their prescribed call to heterosexual marriage and motherhood through participating in baseball is—as the moral conservatives feared—well founded. Women who play baseball may be less apt to compromise their embodied selves and more apt to live authentically. Not all women are the same: Not all women are heterosexual, not all women want to be in a monogamous or long-term relationship, not all women are lesbian, not all women choose (or can choose) motherhood. Sport can help women to better appreciate their bodies, to recognize and honor difference, and to live more fully as "incarnate spirits achieving wonders."[30]

It is not sufficient to protest that women can do whatever men can do. It is not useful to say that we too can be just as competitive, aggressive, and loyal. While this claim may well be true, it does not serve to reconstruct sport in ways that are redemptive and dedicated to a vision of a radically inclusive community. Rather, it merely perpetuates the status quo conception of the "kingdom."

Eleanor J. Stebner and Tracy J. Trothen

In upholding these socially prescribed gender norms, including the denigration of women's bodies and sexualities and ideals of baseball, we make idols of social constructions that limit personhood and reduce the divine mystery to a holiness that exists only in socially dictated immanent ways. Such a forced pantheism is blasphemous. Feminist theologian and historian Denise Lardner Carmody puts it well: "The prime danger of sports . . . is their congruence with mammon, forgetfulness, and a tiny or superficial soul."[31] We do not believe that this must be nor always is so; no hegemony is complete.

Power

Power has long been associated with might and with the utilitarian notion that might is right; the ends justify the means. In baseball, winning counts. Fans and players participate in the lust for winning and the pain of losing. And, of course, winning is equated with the greatest number of runs. Rarely does one encounter teams who celebrate a win not because of the number of runs but because they have played a good game, one in which both teams were honored, all were encouraged and supported, and all players put forward their best effort to play the game as well as possible. Dominant sociocultural values argue instead for a dualistic view in which one team wins and one team loses. No one wants to lose. Everyone wants to win. Indeed, players are urged to win at any cost, within the rules of the game.

Patterns of domination are systemic and, in the case of professional ball, begin with men against men. Sport encourages extreme competitiveness, aggression, and disdain of femininity. Too often organized male sport also encourages the depersonalization of the enemy—the opposing team—in order to win. As theologian Shirl J. Hoffman reflects, "competition, even between the most amiable opponents, often becomes a rite of unholy unction, a sacrament in which aggression is vented, old scores settled, number one taken care of, and where the discourteous act looms as the principal liturgical gesture."[32]

If this type of power is the foundation of baseball, then surely faith communities must agree that baseball is antithetical to our calling to relationships based on love and radical justice, in which none are free until all are free. This requires a form of power that is life-giving and without prejudice, rather than death-dealing and based on a win-lose paradigm. To embrace a reliance on grace as well as on works demands a form of letting go that engages our best and allows the Spirit to move.

In many ways similar to our understanding of organized Christianity, we do not believe that baseball is essentially sexist and dependent on a form of power that breeds domination. Many features of baseball can call us into deeper relationships with self, community, and divine mystery. Thirty years ago George Gmelch examined the tendency of professional ballplayers (male, by definition) to use ritual and other forms of magic. In response to the question of why, he pointed out the limited amount of control or power attached to most baseball positions. The success of hitters is determined not only by the player's ability to hit, but also by the skill of the pitcher and the fielders. The pitcher is most dependent "upon the proficiency of his teammates, the inefficiency of the opposition and the supernatural (luck)."[33] Fielders have the greatest amount of control over the play. The most highly skilled ballplayers are aware of these limitations and their dependence on their teammates. Furthermore, the quality of the game as a whole is dependent on both teams.

Both boys and girls need to be taught more about the roles of chance and interdependence upon which the game—the community—depends. Yet this chance (or luck or magic) tends to be interpreted differently for males and females. Nancy Shinabargar notes the findings of Roberta S. Bennett and her colleagues: "[w]hen girls do engage in organized athletic activities, success is attributed to 'luck'; failure to a lack of 'skill.' . . . Success for boys is attributed to 'skill'; failure is attributed to 'bad luck.'"[34]

Research such as that conducted by Carol Gilligan shows that girls tend to be socialized to share and cooperate whereas boys are encouraged to be competitive and aggressive and to suppress tender emotions.[35] Baseball can be countercultural and redemptive by creating opportunities to combine these socialized qualities; it can foster interdependence and strength. What must go is the "painful dichotomy between winners and losers. It has been all too like the other dynamics of a culture pivoted on aggression, power, individualism, and satisfying the luxuries desired by the strong while ignoring the needs of the weak or the gentle."[36] The emphasis instead must be on the team and on the necessity of relying on others and, of course, on fair play and fun.

Sociologists Susan Birrel and Diana M. Richter conducted a qualitative study of four self-identified feminist women's softball teams in one community. Several issues were articulated by most of the members of these ball communities regarding the relationship of softball to their feminist commitments. Two of these areas directly pertained to models of power. As already discussed, winning cannot be defined as the ultimate good. "The most clearly voiced sentiments from these feminists were their refusal to elevate winning to the principle of ultimate worth, their refusal to subvert the process of play to the product of winning, and their insistence on measuring the value of the activity for themselves against the joy of playing."[37] Connected to this commitment was the appreciation expressed by several players for the many fans who cheered for every good play regardless of the team. Second, the "structure of the game was challenged only in one area—coaching." The concern was that when the decision-making power rests in one person's hands—namely, the coach's—conditions are created for power to be used without accountability to the community. One solution was to rotate coaches, so that several women on the team would take turns coaching. Coaches were also encouraged to consult with the team members rather than making all decisions unilaterally.

If we believe in a male God who coaches (rules) from above and who is the paradigmatic manifestation of all that is male—namely, competitive, aggressive, emotionally stoic, loyal, dominating, and so on—then we sacrifice the claim that women and children are also made in God's image. All major institutional religions—including that professed within Christian churches—favor male deity images. This exaltation of maleness is linked to our collective understandings of what it means to be male. First and foremost, it means not to be female or, in dominant baseball parlance, not to "throw like a girl."

Community

Baseball loses its redemptive quality when it emphasizes extreme individualism that thrives at the expense of self and the other, that asserts my rights over and against yours, and that buys into the systemic oppressions characteristic of our North American cultures. The idea of God as trinitarian, dynamic, and incarnate compels us to uplift community and to seek freedom that does not assert one's needs over another's. Baseball can and sometimes does provide such a community. Birrel and Richter's study shows one example of self-identified feminist women's softball teams who chose to practice a model of the game that fosters communal competition and well-being. The tendency is to assume that competition precludes mutuality, and that somehow one dampens or compromises the other. Competition is commonly cutthroat and fierce; it need not be so. The ugliness of competition can stop people from enjoying baseball.

Cutthroat competition is not the only manifestation of an extreme individualism in baseball; hero worship—and the corresponding obscene salaries allotted to such so-called heroes—is another. Instead of seeing each player worthy of appreciation, we elevate one or two members on a team and focus our attention and adoration on these few individuals; we place all our hopes on them, as if one or two excellent players can win a game on their own. The qualities of these heroes seemingly have less to do with character, values, or commitments and more to do with their abilities to score the most runs and/or rack up the most outs. Value is reduced to statistics and confined to the individual; community as a locus of salvation is denied or simply forgotten.

Systemic oppressions also limit and distort the redemptive and salvific dimensions of baseball. People are excluded often because of gender, class, race, sexual orientation, age, and weight. Teams only want the "best" players, as defined by dominant sociocultural norms. We need only to remember the AAGPBL was composed only of white women, as if African American women were not all-American enough—therefore not good enough—to play. Women who do not conform to dominant norms continue to be excluded from sport for many reasons. Different skill levels certainly exist among men and women, but skill itself can become a form of exclusion. Birrel and Richter write, "When outcome is privileged over the process of play, those whose skill levels are less developed are often disenfranchised from sport."[38]

There is no room for these exclusive and divisive norms within an eschatological vision of a radically inclusive community. The proposal of a countercultural model often is met with bewilderment and opposition. An old *Peanuts* cartoon created by Charles Schulz demonstrates this point. A new baseball season is about to begin and Charlie Brown is contemplating the meaning of this tradition. As he walks onto the pitcher's mound he reflects appreciatively on his long anticipation of this moment. Lucy agrees that walking onto the mound generates strong feelings, but where Charlie Brown experiences a feeling of newness and a "feeling of being part of a great tradition," Lucy experiences a surge of power. This power—in keeping with Lucy's character—is a power that is expressed with a snarl. She lusts after winning and desires no less than to grind her opponent into the dust. She simply does not understand or share Charlie Brown's association of connectedness and newness with baseball.[39]

As Schulz makes clear, women neither automatically nor essentially embrace a communal model of baseball (or anything else). The redemption of baseball and its players, however, may be a more pressing concern for the disenfranchised, including women. Women and other marginalized groups are expected to want to change the status quo. The deliberate consideration of alternative models is one possible way of addressing one's disenfranchisement.

It is not sufficient to get more women playing ball or to long for the day when women can play professional baseball just as men do.[40] An eschatological vision of a radically inclusive community requires not simply a liberal feminist adjustment to baseball as it is, but a remodeling and a re-creating of the sport.

Conclusion

"Batter up! Hear that call! The time has come for one and all to play ball." So shouted the AAGPBL players in their victory song. Theirs was a song of resistance and insistence that women, too, can play great ball. They may not have realized that victory was not limited to the number of runs scored nor to major-league pennants. Yet they knew something of the thrill of being and becoming "incarnate spirits achieving wonders." Though they fell short of re-creating the sport in fully just ways, they upheld a vision of baseball as a radically inclusive community. Like the Christian church, however, it remains a cheer of promise and hope, not one of reality.

Part IV

The Lure of the Elysian Fields

1	2	3	4	5	6	7	**8**	9	R	H	E

Chapter 8

The Coming of Elijah:
Baseball as Metaphor

William R. Herzog II

Prologue

This essay is a concoction of fact, fiction, fantasy, memory, and whimsy, all of which are employed in an effort to provide a glimpse of that most elusive quality we call truth. I will not try to separate these elements in the elixir that follows, for they are inextricable. It is my hope that you will enjoy the magical potion.

Part I

A Pilgrimage Remembered

The alarm clock on the bedside stand was set for 4:30 A.M., but when it finally announced the beginning of a new day, I had been awake for at least half an hour, lying in bed, listening as the still quiet sounds of a fading Vermont night slowly gave way to the livelier melodies of waking birds subtly disclosing the nearness of the coming dawn, all the while anxiously wondering when the alarm would finally go off. The moment it did, I sprang out of bed and began getting dressed. My restless excitement was due to the fact that today, another hot August day, was the day my father and I would take our yearly trip to Fenway Park to see the Red Sox play.

I no longer remember when my father and I started making our annual pilgrimage to Fenway Park but, by the summer of '59, when I was fifteen years old, it was already an established custom. My father and I would ride to Boston with the village veterinarian, Doc Miller, his son, Robert, who lived in Chester on the other side of the state, and his grandson, Daryl, who was a bit younger than I but a true baseball lover and a card-carrying member of that long-suffering society known to the world as Red Sox fans.

We always left early in the morning, no later than 5:30 A.M., because we had to pick up Robert and Daryl, because the trip was in the era long before interstate highways, and because we wanted to get to Fenway early enough to get good tickets on the first-base side and watch batting practice. In the late 1950s, getting tickets was no problem but getting them in just the right place was a bit more difficult, particularly for a group of five.

By the time I came down to the kitchen for breakfast, my mother was already fixing sandwiches for our picnic lunch. It was a regular ceremony. Every year we stopped for lunch at the same roadside rest area just west of Fitchburg, Massachusetts, because it was shaded by a lovely stand of pine trees and gave us room to stretch and play a bit of toss and catch. Like every kid who has ever attended a baseball game, Daryl and I brought our gloves just in case a foul ball was hit in our direction. Mom always packed tuna fish sandwiches, lemonade, a thermos of coffee for the adults, chocolate chip cookies, and other assorted goodies. It was a movable feast.

The trip to Boston was always filled with conversation about the state of the Red Sox. By early August 1959, it was clear that the Sox were going nowhere. Even the great Ted Williams was hitting below .300 for the first time in his career, a threatening intimation of mortality that presaged the end of a long and brilliant career. The late 1950s were a bleak period in Red Sox history, a time between the times. The Shekinah glory of the great teams of the late 1940s and early 1950s had, at first, faded and then departed the temple that was Fenway Park, leaving only the memory of their legendary feats and defeats lingering amidst the malaise of Second Division finishes. The surprising miracle of 1967 was still too far in the future to be glimpsed even by the great prophets of this exile.

So, quite naturally, our conversation centered on the reasons for the Red Sox's decline. The conversation would go something like this. I don't always note who said what because the conversation was like a litany in which anyone could take any part. In this liturgy of quiet despair, there were no parts designated clergy and laity; all Red Sox fans were part of an encompassing priesthood of all believers, and all participated accordingly, as the "spirit of Bean Town" moved us.

"The Red Sox may not be going anywhere," I argued, "but at least they got rid of Pinky Higgins. He was a do-nothing manager, born to mediocrity and who managed accordingly."

Doc disagreed. "You younger fellas don't appreciate a manager like Pinky. He's a throwback to the old days when managers managed by their instincts, like John McGraw or Joe McCarthy. Besides, the Red Sox haven't improved much since Billy Jurges took over. They're still in last place."

"That's because Pinky ruined the young players they brought up. He never gave the younger players a chance to prove themselves because he wanted to play veterans."

Robert chimed in: "Granted, he didn't do much for the confidence of the younger players but they also are part of the problem. Take Don Buddin. He's found more ways to lose ball games in the infield than the rest of the team put together. Bootin' Buddin, isn't that what they call him? Didn't I hear his license plate reads E-6?" That well-worn quip still drew appreciative chuckles from the pilgrims on their way to the shrine in the fens.

Daryl and I conceded that Buddin had created novel and entertaining ways to throw away ball games and keep the opponents' rallies going strong but, we noted, he was an example of how the Red Sox had mismanaged their talent. They brought him along too fast while keeping Gene Stephens on the bench too long. He was little better than Ted Williams's valet. And the young arms they wasted through poor instruction and bad decisions were too numerous to mention. Just look at Maurice McDermott or Frank Baumann. In the general discussion that followed, we all agreed that the Red Sox had wasted more good young talent than most other teams even had.

My father had his own slant. "The problem with the Red Sox is Yawkey," he said. "He runs the team like a country club, not a baseball club. Look at the salaries he pays the players whether they win or lose. They're not hungry, and they don't care." To tell the truth, my father was a lifelong Yankees fan who approved of the parsimonious habits of Yankees' management. It was only once a year that he entered the secret cabal of Red Sox analysts, so we all humored him.

"Country club or not," I argued, "you can't win with Vic Wertz at first and Pete Runnels at second. They can't cover ten feet of ground between them, and the last I heard, the bases were still ninety feet apart."

William R. Herzog II

"But they do hit," Doc responded. "They do hit the ball."

"Yeah," Robert noted, "and they lose 8–6 and 11–10." And so the conversation continued all the way to the picnic site and beyond, right up to the sacred approaches to Fenway Park itself. The conversation was an indispensable part of the trip; it got us in the mood for the game itself which would, no doubt, confirm our fears and justify our suspicions.

We got tickets for the Red Sox doubleheader with the Kansas City A's, a team locked in an intense struggle with the Sox to see who would occupy the cellar in the American League. We always tried to go to a doubleheader even though we couldn't stay for all of the second game. When you get only one trip to Boston a summer, it was worth seeing even a part of the second game.

I went to see Ted Williams play. He was the final, fading link to the glory years following World War II. In previous years, he had never let me down. He usually would hit a home run, or, failing that, a double or a couple of singles and some RBIs. But Ted Williams was not himself in 1959, and he held true to form in the first game of the doubleheader in which an unknown stole the show. A kid named Pumpsie Green played second base and batted in the leadoff position. He led off the first inning with a triple high off the Green Monster. It was his second triple in the last four games; he had speed, something I hadn't seen on the Red Sox in years. Runnels singled him home, and the Red Sox had a 1–0 lead.

But he did small things, too. He laid down a sacrifice bunt to advance runners whom Runnels redeemed by singling home. He turned a double play and fielded well. Tom Brewer shut down the Kansas City bats, and with two innings of hitless relief from Mike Fornieles, won the game 4–1, raising his record to 8–7. Brewer was another one of those young pitchers whose promise exceeded his fulfillment. What surprised me was the rookie Green's power. After hitting the triple, he sent A's center fielder Bill Tuttle up against the wall in the deepest part of the outfield, where, with a great catch, he robbed him of what would have been another extra base hit.

The second game was a slugfest. We left in the bottom of the sixth, just after the A's had scored six runs in the top of the inning. On the car radio, we listened to the Red Sox rally for two in the bottom of the seventh and one in the eighth before losing 8–6. When the game ended, Robert looked around at all of us in the car with the smug expression of a prophet whose prediction had just come true. In the second game,

Green, batting third instead of his usual leadoff spot, singled and scored a run. He was 1–3 in each game of the doubleheader.

For the first time in my memory, Ted Williams had not been at the center of the action. Batting cleanup, he was 1–3 in the first game, a single that didn't figure in the scoring. I went home, vaguely disappointed, even a bit dispirited, because I could see that the end was in sight for "the Kid," and I couldn't imagine watching the Red Sox play without him. As darkness settled in, I tried to doze for a bit, but every time I closed my eyes, I saw Pumpsie Green laying down a bunt or hitting one off the Green Monster. But I worried about the fading career of the greatest hitter I had ever seen far more than I wondered about the fledgling career being born before my eyes. Surrounded by the darkening August evening, I finally fell asleep while visions of Ted Williams and Pumpsie Green danced in my head.

Part II

A Pilgrimage Revisited:
The Coming of Elijah

About twenty years later on another clear and beautiful summer day, I was seated in the lecture hall at Tantur, an ecumenical institute in the Holy Land located in the West Bank on the road between Bethlehem and Jerusalem. It was, in fact, close enough to Bethlehem to offer a view of the Church of the Nativity and Manger Square in the distance. I was listening to a lecture by Rabbi Pinchas Peli, of blessed memory, on the Passover Seder. It was part of a study seminar organized by the seminary where I served as Professor of New Testament.

At the moment, Rabbi Peli was remembering the first Passover when he was old enough to ask the momentous question, "Why is this night different from every other night of the year?" On that same evening, after the family sat down to dinner, his father indicated the empty chair at the end of the table and reminded those present that it was placed there in case the great prophet Elijah should return to celebrate the Passover with them. Following the custom of the family, the father then asked the youngest child—in this case it was Pinchas—to go to the door to see if perchance Elijah were waiting outside. The young boy raced to the door, fully expecting to meet Elijah face to face, but when he threw open the door, Elijah was nowhere to be seen. Instead, Pinchas found himself staring into the vacant darkness of a star-filled night, straining to catch the slightest hint of a movement indicating that Elijah might be passing through the neighborhood. But, alas, Elijah was not there, leaving Pinchas crestfallen and disappointed that Elijah would not sit at the table with them that evening to share the Passover meal. The chair would remain vacant for another year.

Through the years, Rabbi Peli participated in the ceremony over and over again, first as a son and then as a father of his own children, and each time the outcome was the same. Elijah was always expected but never appeared. In time, the rabbi explained how he had come to realize that the absence of Elijah was not nearly as important as the promise of his coming. The hope for the coming of Elijah was able to overcome the disillusionment and disenchantment that occurred each time he failed to appear. So he continued the custom of opening the door to welcome Elijah even though he knew that Elijah would not be there.

While he was relating his discovery, a voice whispered in my ear, "But you have seen the coming of Elijah." I was seated at the last row of tables in the lecture hall and thought a seminar member was playing a practical joke on me, but when I turned around to catch the culprit, I saw only the cool emptiness at the back of the lecture hall. I turned my attention back to the lecturer, who was now walking us through the Passover Seder, glancing every now and then at my companions on either side. They were transfixed by the lecture and obviously had heard nothing. I settled back in my chair to enjoy the remainder of the lecture, pondering the empty chair and the invitation to Elijah. In the midst of my reverie, the voice spoke again, ever so quietly yet so clearly I could hear every letter of every word: "But you have seen the coming of Elijah."

How? I wondered to myself, accepting for the moment, without protest, the truth of the words spoken to me. How? When? Quite naturally, my thoughts turned to the incident in the Gospel of Mark when Jesus and three of his disciples were returning from the mount of transfiguration. As they descended the mountain, the disciples asked Jesus, "Why do the scribes say that Elijah must come first?" (Mark 9:11), a reference no doubt to a current interpretation of the prophecy of Malachi, "Lo, I will send you the prophet Elijah before the great and terrible day of the LORD comes. He will turn the hearts of parents to their children and the hearts of children to their parents, so that I will not come and strike the land with a curse" (4:5–6).

Jesus responded to the disciples' inquiry by saying, "I tell you that Elijah has come, and they did to him whatever they pleased, as it is written about him" (Mark 9:13). It was Jesus' way of identifying John the Baptist with Elijah, a startling reinterpretation of the Elijah tradition. It was an identification that Mark probably found in the Jesus tradition and made his own. Indeed, it quite likely influenced Mark's early description of John the baptizer. Mark 1:6 clearly alludes to Elijah. John the Baptist appeared in the wilderness "clothed with camel's hair, with a leather belt around his waist, and he ate locusts and wild honey" (cf. 2 Kings 1:8).

But not even Mark's attempts to clarify Jesus' comments to the disciples could mask the great discrepancy between the Elijah whose coming was anticipated as a harbinger of the messianic age and the Baptist whose coming stirred a few to repentance. John might be thought of as Elijah, but he was an Elijah quite different from the great prophet who was swept into heaven in a fiery chariot. The reason was clear. John the Baptist never fulfilled the lofty expectations associated with Elijah in the prophetic or rabbinic traditions. Yet, Mark portrays John as an Elijah who turns the Elijah expectations on their head, reversing the triumphal Elijah into the marginal Elijah, the powerhouse prophet who confronted the powers that be in the house of Ahab and Jezebel into the wilderness prophet who challenged the corruption of the house of Herod and Herodias, the one who would usher in the great and terrible day of the Lord into the messenger who made the paths straight and declared humbly that "one who is more powerful than I is coming after me; I am not worthy to stoop down and untie the thong of his sandals" (Mark 1:7–8). As both Jesus and Mark knew, and as I was about to discover, the fulfillment of prophecy usually changes its form.

If I have seen John, I thought to myself, then I suppose I have seen Elijah, just as Mark intended. The more I thought about it, the more reasonable it seemed. Just as John upends the Elijah legend, so Jesus transforms messianic expectation. Jesus no more fulfilled the portfolio of messiah than John fulfilled the role of Elijah. Yet, John could be conceived as Elijah, the forerunner for the kind of messiah Jesus was proclaimed to be, the Suffering Servant messiah. As John reinterpreted the Elijah myth, so Jesus redefined the messiah myth. This is why their identities are so often intertwined in the Gospel of Mark. It was beginning to make sense.

I was becoming reasonably certain that I had solved the mystery of the voice until the voice spoke a final time: "But *you* have seen the coming of Elijah." This time, as the voice spoke, I saw an image of my father, who had died more than a decade earlier, as clearly as though he were sitting in the same room with me. He looked younger than I had ever seen him, except in family pictures of him as a young man, and he was smiling and happy. It lasted only for a moment, but evanescent as the vision was, I knew I had seen it clearly and could remember every detail, much like a vivid dream that awakens you out of a deep sleep.

At first, I was simply startled by what I had seen because, by the time I was old enough to notice, my father was a man old beyond his years, beaten down by failure and ill health, a man who had almost lost the capacity for happiness, except when he watched a baseball game or listened to one on the radio. Then and only then did he seem content with his life. But the man in my vision was young and happy, joyful and smiling, unlike the man I had known as my father.

He must be in heaven, I thought to myself, and then I remembered what I had seen. He wasn't in heaven but someplace better—a baseball park! It figured. My father's idea of heaven would be to watch the 1927 Yankees play the angels, and I don't mean the ones from California. There, he could watch Lou Gehrig, forever freed from the disease that bears his name, continue his endless streak of consecutive games without losing his power, his youth, or his health, and as he watched his beloved Gehrig, he would say to himself, "Today I consider myself the luckiest man on the face of the firmament." He might even grudgingly watch the Babe, though he was sure that Ruth's greatness had overshadowed The Iron Horse and kept him from getting the recognition he deserved. But there he could watch the Babe, no longer haunted by the debilitating cancer that consumed his energy, cracked his voice, and wasted his life, swing from the heels and swat another home run, breaking into that mincing gait for which he will forever be remembered, leaving in the dust the ludicrous pretenders to his throne like Maris or Aaron.

The memory of that image was fading but not before I realized that my father was not just in *any* baseball park. He was in Fenway Park, in the grandstand behind the Red Sox dugout, which was our favorite place to sit because I played first base as my father had before me. As I placed him in the grandstand, remembering his laughing, happy demeanor, I also realized that he was gesturing to me, pointing out toward the field. Mentally I surveyed the field I had seen in that intense image, looking first at the batter's box. When I did, I saw "the Kid" filled with the brash and boyish enthusiasm of a nineteen-year-old rookie just discovering his prowess as a hitter. He stood there perfectly poised, balanced and waiting to unleash his picture perfect swing. It was one for the Brearly Collection.

But as I studied that image over and over again, I knew that my father was not pointing at the batter's box but gesturing toward the infield as though sharing a secret or a punch line to a joke, and then it faded, and I was back in the coolness of the lecture hall at Tantur at the edge of Bethlehem, surrounded by the shepherds' fields where the angels had so long ago announced the birth of the messiah and the beginning of another new day.

Part III

Baseball as Metaphor, or
"But You Have Seen the Coming of Elijah"

Almost twenty years later, I was working on materials to be presented in another lecture hall for a course called "Baseball as Metaphor." One week of the intensive summer school course was devoted to a study of the events surrounding 1947, when Jackie Robinson broke the modern color barrier in baseball. It was during the preparation for this course that I finally solved the mystery, and I learned, many years after the fact, how I had indeed seen the coming of Elijah.

I had been dimly aware of the fact that the Red Sox were uncommonly slow to integrate their team. In 1945, in response to criticism and mounting pressure from the African American community, General Manager Eddie Collins wrote, "I have been connected with the Red Sox for twelve years and during that time we have never had a single request for a try out by a colored applicant."[1] That same year, Wendell Smith arranged a try out for three Negro players: Jackie Robinson, then in his first season with the Kansas City Monarchs; Sam Jethroe, a speedy outfielder with the Cleveland Buckeyes; and Marvin Williams, a second baseman for the Philadelphia Stars. All three players were in their mid-twenties, and two were established stars in the Negro Leagues. Never a team to do things gracefully, the Red Sox at first refused to try out the players when they showed up on April 14. The Red Sox repeated their refusal on April 15, thus making a sham of Collins's disingenuous remarks. It took media pressure to force the team to arrange a try out on April 16, 1945, but it was a charade. One sportswriter present for the event remembers hearing an anonymous voice cry out, "Get those niggers off the field."[2] One version of the event attributes the remark to Collins, another to manager Joe Cronin. Even if neither said it, the remark summarized the Red Sox's attitude toward the entire affair. Although the team promised to contact the players, they never did.

Nor was this the only time the Red Sox missed an opportunity to sign a significant black player. According to Al Hirshberg, the Red Sox could have signed Willie Mays when he was playing with the Birmingham Black Barons.[3] The Birmingham Barons were a Red Sox farm club who rented their facilities to the Black Barons in return for the right of first refusal on any Black Barons players. When the Sox sent scout Larry Woodall, a Texan, to look over Mays, he refused to stay in town an extra day to see Mays play. No white man should have to wait to see a black man play ball, he believed, and rain had forced postponement of the game in which Mays was scheduled to appear. Another of the Red Sox so-called "superscouts" refused to attend a tournament where a number of black prospects were showcasing their ability. "How long is this nigger tournament going to last?" he asked, before declaring, "I'm not hanging around here three days to watch a bunch of black kids."[4] A number of prospects were signed by other major-league teams whose scouts were more interested in talent than skin color.

When black athletes broke the color barrier, Joe Cronin conceded that Jackie Robinson, Larry Doby, and Satchel Paige were "certainly a source of honor to their race," but suggested that they were the exceptions who proved the rule. Even after black athletes won the National League Rookie of the Year honors in six of the seven years following Robinson's debut season and Minnie Minoso and Luke Easter captured the same award in back-to-back seasons (1951, 1952) in the American League, the Red Sox did nothing. By 1954, the year of the Supreme Court decision in *Brown v. the Board of Education,* all but three major-league teams had recruited black ballplayers. In a fit of enthusiasm, sportswriter Harold Rosenthal found the pace of change revolutionary. "From open rebellion to universal acceptance in just seven seasons is a staggering thought," he wrote, employing a bit of hyperbole, because as Jules Tygiel noted, "Acceptance was not yet universal. The Philadelphia Phillies, Detroit Tigers, and Boston Red Sox remained as vestiges of the Jim Crow era."[5] Even the Cardinals who had been long-standing holdouts had signed their first black prospect and were on the way to becoming a team that modeled the success that could be achieved when black and white talent were blended.[6]

Nor was the prospect of change promising. In 1950, the Red Sox had signed Lorenzo "Piper" Davis and assigned him to their Class A farm team in Scranton, Pennsylvania. As part of their agreement with the Birmingham Black Barons, from whom they had purchased Davis's contract, the Red Sox paid the Barons $7,500 and promised to match that figure if Davis stayed with the organization past May 15. By May 13, Davis was leading his team in batting (hitting .333), home runs, RBIs, and stolen bases. When he was summoned to the office of Scranton's general manager, he thought he was being promoted to the Red Sox's Triple A club in Louisville. Instead, he was told that he was being released for "economic reasons."[7]

Some thought that the Red Sox's refusal to integrate traced directly to their owner, Tom Yawkey, while others traced the refusal to the racist scouts they employed, while others traced the stubbornness to middle management, especially the Red Sox's general managers and field managers. By the mid-1950s, the Red Sox were managed by Mike "Pinky" Higgins, who is reputed to have declared, "There'll be no niggers on this ball club as long as I have anything to say about it."[8] In this atmosphere, it is nothing short of miraculous that any black player could have been signed at all.

By 1959, every other major-league club had brought African American ballplayers to their teams. Only the Red Sox remained lily white. In February 1959, the Red Sox invited E. Jerry "Pumpsie" Green to spring training in Scottsdale, Arizona. The Red Sox had purchased Green's contract in 1953 and assigned him first to their Class A farm club in Albany in the Eastern League and then to their Double A farm team in Oklahoma City in the Texas League. Green remembers that he could not travel with the Oklahoma City team when they played the club in Shreveport, Louisiana, because Louisiana law prohibited blacks from playing on white teams. "When the team went to Shreveport, I didn't go, because they didn't allow blacks to play in Louisiana," he remembered, "so I had a three- or four-day vacation. In truth, I never thought about it. . . . When you went south that time of year it was nine hundred degrees, and if they wanted to give me three days off, well, okay, fine."[9] After establishing himself in each setting, Green was promoted to the Red Sox's Triple A farm club in Minneapolis. By the spring of 1959, they felt he was ready for an invitation to spring training with the big club.

Green's spring training experience began much as Jackie Robinson's had begun twelve years earlier. He was denied lodging at the Safari Hotel in Scottsdale, Arizona, where the Red Sox made their spring training headquarters. *The New York Times* (February 22, 1959) carried a brief notice of the incident. The Safari Hotel, like other hotels in Scottsdale, was segregated and refused to lodge Pumpsie Green. As usual, the Red

Sox colluded with the racist practice. Jack Mahoney, the team publicist, "insisted that only the normal seasonal tourist jam had been responsible" and noted that Green would be placed in a plush hotel in Phoenix, although he declined to specify just where the hotel might be.[10] Yet, in spite of its troubled beginning, the 1959 spring training season was good for Green, who hit over .400 and fielded well. However, his batting average faded during a barnstorming tour through Texas, prompting manager Pinky Higgins to send him back to the minors for more seasoning.[11]

When the Red Sox arrived in Boston in April, the African American community was in an uproar. The NAACP accused the Red Sox of racist hiring practices and sought an investigation of the team's employment record. The group named Green as the latest case of unfair labor practices, a charge that the team's general manager, Bucky Harris, vigorously denied. "The charge that the decision to option Pumpsie Green to Minneapolis was prompted by bias has no foundation in fact. . . . The truth is that Pumpsie Green was optioned to give him an opportunity to play regularly and to develop his profession" (*New York Times,* April 13, 1959). But Harris's denials could not prevent the NAACP from demanding a hearing before the Massachusetts Commission Against Discrimination. From April 12, 1959, the day when the charges surfaced in the papers, until June 4, 1959, when the Red Sox were cleared of charges by the commission, Pumpsie Green was a cause celebre in absentia. The commission found that the Red Sox had acted in good faith and would continue to do so.[12]

On July 4, 1959, the man who had vowed that "there'll be no niggers on this ball club as long as I have anything to say about it" was replaced as manager, and Billy Jurges was appointed for the remainder of the season. This may have prepared the way for the coming of E. Jerry "Pumpsie" Green. With the Red Sox mired in the basement of the American League, the team may have thought it had nothing to lose, so on July 21, 1959, they called Pumpsie Green up to the big club. He joined the team in Chicago, and on Tuesday, July 21, 1959, Pumpsie Green entered the game in the eighth inning as a pinch runner and played the ninth inning at shortstop. The box score shows that he ran for Vic Wertz, who had in turn pinch-hit for Don Buddin in the eighth inning. The Red Sox lost 2–1. The next day, July 22, 1959, Pumpsie Green debuted at second base, the first African American ever to start a game for the Boston Red Sox, and the experiment begun by Branch Rickey and Jackie Robinson was complete. The final major-league club was integrated. Green

The Faith of Fifty Million

grounded out twice, flied to center field, and walked. After drawing a walk, he stole second base, showing the quickness and speed for which another African American baseball pioneer, the laces of whose spikes he was unworthy to untie, was known. He handled three chances in the field "flawlessly." The Red Sox lost. Green was then consigned to the bench because Pete Runnels, whom he had replaced, recovered from an illness, and he didn't appear in a game until later in the road trip at Cleveland. It was there that he began to play regularly.

On July 28, 1959, he pinch-hit for Ike Delock in the seventh inning of the first game of a doubleheader and flied out before starting the second game, in which he was 1 for 2 as a leadoff batter, stole a base, scored one run, and laid down a sacrifice bunt in helping the Red Sox to a rare 8–4 win. This began a string of fourteen games, in which Pumpsie Green became the starting second baseman. On July 29, as the leadoff hitter, he was 1 for 2, drew a walk, and scored a run in the Red Sox 4–1 victory over Cleveland. The following day he went 0 for 4 with a sacrifice fly while turning a double play in the Sox's 4–3 loss to Cleveland. At the end of the Cleveland series, Pumpsie had fielded well, shown good speed, bunting ability, and a willingness to sacrifice himself to advance runners, but his hitting remained a question mark. He was 2 for 13, leaving him with a .154 batting average.[13]

The series in Detroit changed all that. On July 31, he was the key to the Red Sox victory over the Tigers, getting three hits and scoring three runs. His three hits included a triple and two singles. In each of the next two games, he went 1 for 4, played errorless ball, and raised his batting average to .280 (7 for 25). He was showing promise. Not surprisingly, when the team arrived in Boston at 1 A.M. on the morning of August 4, 1959, just a few hours before I woke up on that exciting morning, the press was there to greet the team's newest member. In his typically unassuming way, Pumpsie still remembers his reception: "We were stepping off the plane, and I saw the bright lights and cameras. I thought that was the way it was in the majors. . . . I didn't know they were there to see me. . . . The reporters did what they usually do, asked a lot of questions. I was so surprised."[14]

Green's debut at Fenway Park occurred on Tuesday, August 4, 1959, in a doubleheader against Kansas City. He went 1 for 3 in each game, hitting a triple off the Green Monster in the first game and narrowly missing a double off the center-field wall. He scored a run in the first game, batting from the leadoff position, and another run in the second game, batting third. In the first game he sacrificed a runner along, and he participated in turning two double plays. The Sox split the double-header. Green remembered his first game at Fenway. "I was lucky . . . to be facing a guy I had faced in the minor leagues, John Tsitouris. We were playing Kansas City . . . and I hit the ball all over the ballpark. First time up, I tripled high off the Monster . . . and I hit another shot up against the left-center-field wall, and Bill Tuttle ran and leaned up against the wall and caught it."[15]

The next day, August 5, he went 2 for 4 and scored three runs in a 17–6 rout of Kansas City. For the second day in a row he caught a line drive and doubled a runner off first, killing potential rallies. The next day, he went 0 for 4 in a 4–3 Red Sox win over Kansas City. During the home stand, which included a series with Detroit and a makeup game with the Yankees, Green batted .364, raising his cumulative batting average to .328.

After his initial appearances, Pumpsie disappeared from the Red Sox lineup for a week, and his first two appearances thereafter were in pinch-hitting roles, for a total of nine days out of the lineup. When he returned on August 21, he played well on a road trip through the Midwest, hitting .260 and lowering his cumulative batting average to .306. Batting leadoff, he continued to score runs regularly, and his fielding was a bright spot for the team. From July 21 through August 27, Pumpsie Green had been a solid contributor to the team.

After August 27, his performance tailed off at the plate, and his batting average dipped to a final .233. He continued to field well, and with the exception of one three-game stretch against Washington when he made three errors in three days, he was a defensive asset, especially adept at turning the double play. By the end of the season, he was on the bench as the Red Sox tried out other rookies and combinations of veterans in order to assess their future.

The following year, 1960, he played in 133 games and hit .242, and in 1961, he played in 88 games before illness forced his removal from the lineup. He never returned as a regular after that. Pinky Higgins was back as manager and consigned Green to the bench. Unfortunately, his tenure as manager nearly coincided with Green's stay with the team. When Higgins was fired for the last time, the Red Sox traded Green to the Mets, where he played his final year of major-league ball in 1963.

Green had a way of contributing in small ways that didn't show up in the box scores. For example, take Ted Williams's final game as a Red

Sox, on September 28, 1960. Everyone remembers that "the Splendid Splinter" hit a home run in his final at bat in a storybook finish to a Hall of Fame career. Number 521. At the time, the Sox were trailing the Orioles 4–2, and Williams's solo shot made it 4–3. Had his bat had the final word, Ted's last game would have been a loss. But trailing 4–3 in the bottom of the ninth, the Sox rallied. Marlin Coughtry, an eminently forgettable second baseman whose fielding made Don Buddin look like Ozzie Smith, singled, and Vic Wertz, pinch-hitting for Mike Fornieles, doubled off the Green Monster in left. With runners at second and third, Pumpsie Green came to the plate and drew a walk. That brought Willie Tasby, a speedy black outfielder, to the plate. Tasby hit a perfect double-play ball to third baseman Brooks Robinson, who whipped the relay to second baseman Billy Klaus. But Klaus threw wildly to first, letting in the two runs that won the game. Who was the speedy runner, breaking for second at the crack of the bat, who got there in time to force Klaus to hurry his throw to first? Pumpsie Green! He did what every ballplayer is supposed to do. He never gave up even though it looked like a certain rally-killing double play. He ran hard and slid straight for Klaus. Ninety-nine times out of a hundred, it is a futile attempt to influence an inevitable outcome. But one time in a hundred, if you're lucky, it might make a difference, so a true professional hustles on every play, just as Pumpsie Green did on that cold and dark September day in Fenway Park. His hustle turned Ted Williams's farewell game into a victory celebration. Ted Williams retired on a winning note. The box score shows only that Green was 0 for 3, no runs, no RBIs. John Updike has written a memorable account of that day, titled "Hub Fans Bid Kid Adieu," but he utterly missed the contribution of Pumpsie Green. But for those who have eyes to see, it is all there between the lines.[16]

What writers have not missed is perhaps the most bizarre incident from his brief career with the Red Sox.[17] It all began on the hot summer afternoon of July 27, 1962, after a galling loss to the Yankees, when Gene Conley and Pumpsie Green left the team bus, caught in a horrendous Bronx traffic jam, to find a restroom and a beer. By the time they had had a few beers and returned to catch the bus, it was long gone, and the team was on a plane to Washington. Since it was just before the All-Star break, and Conley wasn't scheduled to start until after the All-Star game, he decided to go AWOL, and at least for a day, Pumpsie joined him. They went to Toots Shor's, had a few beers, checked back into the team hotel, drank a few more beers, and discussed their future. Conley was frustrated because he believed that a victory over the Yankees that day would have placed him on the American League All-Star team, but his loss precluded that happy outcome and reminded him that he was entering the final phase of his baseball career. Arm trouble and persistent pain were the early signals of his coming demise.

In the midst of their conversations, Conley proposed that they buy tickets to Jerusalem and go to Israel. Pumpsie decided that he had had enough and returned to the Red Sox but Conley got his ticket, reappeared at Toots Shor's, and announced, "Hey, I'm gonna go to Jerusalem. I'm going to Bethlehem. I'm going to the Promised Land. I'm gonna get everything straightened out between me and my Savior."[18] Word got out, and by the time Pumpsie returned to the Red Sox locker room, he found himself the center of attention, answering questions like whether he and Conley really planned to go to Israel. He was puzzled by the whole affair. The Red Sox did not take kindly to the caper, and although Conley got out of the embarrassment with a fine later refunded to him, they sent Pumpsie back to Louisville. He was traded away the next year.

When he was traded away, *The Sporting News* (December 22, 1962) carried an article on the transaction titled, "Weiss Sees Greener Pastures for Pumpsie." From the Mets point of view, Green was the major figure in the deal with the Sox, which sent Felix Mantilla to the Bosox for Green, Tracy Stallard, and a third player to be named later. Weiss had traded for Green on the advice of Johnny Murphy, whom the Mets had hired away from the Red Sox to direct their minor-league operations. Murphy had recommended that the Mets trade for Green who was "apparently in disfavor with Boston," presumably for his caper with Gene Conley. Weiss noted, "I was prompted to take Green not only because I was confident he had not been able to develop his potential at Fenway Park, but because he can play anywhere in the infield except at first base, and he is a switch hitter." In addition to Murphy's recommendation, Weiss had heard from a Mets scout who had remembered that when Gene Mauch, then managing the Red Sox Triple A team in Minneapolis, was being projected as the next manager of the Red Sox, he said, "If I go up, I would like to have Green go with me." Mauch was considered to be an astute judge of baseball ability.

All of this intrigued me. The episode with Conley had connected Pumpsie with the Holy Land. Finally I decided to look up his lifetime record in *The Baseball Encyclopedia*. It was time to turn to the Bible of baseball for some answers. As usual, after finding Pumpsie Green's entry,

I first perused his lifetime record and then happened to glance back at what was recorded first: his name. When I read it, the pieces came together and all the cosmic tumblers fell into place. I had vaguely wondered what the E. stood for in E. Jerry Green, and I had noticed that *The New York Times* sometimes listed him as E. Green and sometimes as J. Green in the box scores. Finally, there it was:

Green, Elijah Jerry
"Pumpsie"

As the import of the name registered, I heard that still, small voice speaking its quiet, crystal-clear words once again: "But you have seen the coming of Elijah." I was waiting expectantly for what followed, and once again, I saw the image of my father. In the moment he stood before me (was I awake or dreaming?), I could see that my father was laughing the way one does when sharing a happy secret, and he was gesturing, touching his chest and then extending his hand to me. I didn't need to read his lips to know what he was saying. "We have seen the coming of Elijah, you and I, together."

Indeed we had! The day we went to Fenway Park to see the Sox play the A's, August 4, 1959, turned out to be an historic day, for when Elijah Jerry "Pumpsie" Green came out of the dugout and crossed the first base line on his way to his position at second base, he filled the last empty chair at the table of integrated major-league baseball clubs. At the head of the table, of course, in the seat of honor was Jackie Robinson, and seated on his right and left were the likes of Larry Doby, Roy Campanella, Satchel Paige (the patriarch of patriarchs), Don Newcombe, Luke Easter, Monte Irvin, Willie Mays, Sam Jethroe, Joe Black, Connie Johnson, Minnie Minoso, Elston Howard, Hank Thompson, Junior Gilliam, Bob Trice, Gene Baker, Carlos Paula, Chuck Harmon, Curt Roberts, Tom Alston, Brooks Lawrence, Ernie Banks, Vic Power, Hank Aaron, Chico Fernandez, and Ossie Virgil, to mention just a few of the saints who belong to this great cloud of witnesses.

Yet, for many years, one chair had remained empty at that table, and it bore the name of the Boston Red Sox. Until Elijah came and took the empty chair reserved for him and fulfilled the promise.

Many have followed the coming of Elijah in Boston, for the coming of Elijah "Pumpsie" Green prepared the way in the wilderness for such future stars as George Scott, Reggie Smith, Luis Tiant, Cecil Cooper, Tony

Armas, Mike Torrez, Jim Rice, Dennis "Oil Can" Boyd, Ellis Burks, and Mike Greenwell and, because of Pumpsie, the Red Sox no longer hesitated to bring aging black stars on the downside of their careers to strengthen their club, including the likes of Orlando Cepeda, Ferguson Jenkins, Bob Watson, Tony Perez, and Don Baylor. Perhaps most important, the Red Sox have brought their share of ordinary black major leaguers (if any major leaguer can be considered ordinary, it can only be in the sense that an ordinary angel is considered a run-of-the-mill angel) to their club, like Willie Tasby, Earl Wilson, Jose Tartabull, Diego Segui, Carlos Quintana, and Tony Pena. All because of the coming of Elijah, Elijah Jerry Green.

It is not given to human beings to witness the fulfillment of prophecy, and when we do, we usually fail to understand what we have seen because the fulfillment of prophecy changes its form. It is so different from our expectation. It was like that when John appeared in the wilderness of Judea by the Jordan. Most didn't see Elijah at all. And it was like that on a hot August day in Fenway Park in 1959 when Pumpsie appeared at second base. I didn't know then that I had seen the coming of Elijah; indeed, not until thirty-five years later would I understand what I had seen. Now that you have seen what I saw, what my father and I saw, I hope you can now join us in saying that you, too, have seen the coming of Elijah.

1	2	3	4	5	6	7	8	**9**	R	H	E

Chapter 9

Baseball: A Spiritual Reminiscence

Tex Sample

I was the best player on the worst teams and the worst player on the best ones, at least those I was able to make. While this leaves a lot of teams in between, it nevertheless suggests the ambiguity of my relationship to baseball, a tie I never expect to understand fully and never expect to get over. You see, I love the game. I played baseball and then softball for forty-six seasons, from the time I was ten through my fifty-fifth year. It has a grip on my life that I regard as amazingly constructive and yet it may be as destructive as anything I ever loved.

In 1945 when I first began to play baseball, it was just something we did because football was out of season. My first love was football, and I had dreams of becoming Johnny Lujack, the great quarterback of the Notre Dame football team. It would be much later before I was told that Notre Dame was a "Cath'lik college" and that "we" didn't go to those kinds of schools, only one of a growing list of my disappointments in athletics. Still, when I went out for the high school football team in the eighth grade, I was too embarrassed to tell them I wanted to be a quarterback, so I went out for linebacker instead, a position for which I was equally inept. Within a month I was having terrible pains in my lower back. When I went to the bone doctor, he told me I had spondylolystheses—or something like that—which meant I had a vertebrae congenitally out of place and that I had to "quit football, have an operation," and "become a semi-invalid the rest of my life." He put a brace on my back to wear "until summer when you are out of school and can have the operation." I asked him what would happen if I did not have the operation, and he told me I would one day step off a curb and be paralyzed for the rest of my life. Well, I never had the operation, and I never was paralyzed either. Long before Foucault I learned that the sciences, and especially medicine, were inexact disciplines and operated in a regime of knowing that was not universally true or without error.

That first summer with the back brace I began to sneak out to play baseball. I "knew" baseball wouldn't hurt me, and it never did, at least not that way. I discovered that I played well with my friends. I had an arm, I could hit, and while I couldn't run fast, I could catch almost anything I could touch. In that "universe" I was a baseball player.

All of the passion I had poured into football suddenly found expression in baseball. The entire walls of my room were covered with pictures of the Yankees. My great hero was Lou Gehrig, not Babe Ruth. Somehow I connected my spondylolystheses with his amyotrophic lateral sclerosis. In my boyhood fantasies I fought as brave a fight as he, but I envisioned myself coming to bat in the World Series and hitting the winning home run only to have my back come apart in that instant and to live from then on in paralysis. The fantasy was wonderful because I could have all the acclaim of such heroics without having to live as a paraplegic.

I remember, too, that there was something about that Sears Roebuck authentic "Ted Williams glove." The leather molded to my hand, and I had the "best pocket" of any kid in town. I still remember that first year throwing a ball back and forth in the parking lot behind the 13 Taxi Company—a twelve-foot-square concrete block building that served as the command center for a fleet of four cars of which my Dad was "owner and operator." Though I had no words for such things I do remember a kind of spell that came over me as I caught and then threw back that ball. It was a mesmerizing experience. I never lost my love of "warming up," and that ritualized liturgy of tossing a baseball with another player even yet has more power for me than any range of practices promoted by the increasing array of gurus both Christian and otherwise who flock around middle-class life. Watching the arc of the ball move through the air and folding itself into the swallowing wrap of the glove of my coreligionist, or seeing it come toward me in that geometric curve through space, that beautiful loft, and the feel of something so precisely smack into the socket of your own grasp. I never cease to be struck that something could so move through space and come to rest at a place of such "perfect" fit. Indeed, life hardly ever seems so complete as that except in sexual love and mystical experience.

So my love of baseball came on the rebound. As composed as such a love is of hurt and hope, it is nonetheless a powerful passion. From then on I worked out at baseball all year round. Anytime I could find anyone who would play pitch and catch or hit fly balls or get together enough people for batting practice, I did it. I threw balls at the cabstand wall so I could "practice" picking up grounders on the sidewalk in front. This was one more case where an extraordinary amount of practice was wasted. Throughout all my playing days the only place I was effective in picking up ground balls was in the outfield, never at shortstop.

Still, there was a fateful moment in this love on the rebound. John B. Perkins owned the furniture store next to the cabstand. With his retroactive permission I drew a strike zone on the alley-side wall of his building; measured off sixty feet, six inches to the other side of the back lot; scraped up enough gravel for a mound next to the Almand's cleaners; and started to pelt that wall with three rubber-coated baseballs I had bought for 49 cents each at the Western Auto Store. My Uncle Paul, who owned the local fish market and would later distinguish himself as the fire chief of the Brookhaven Fire Department, walked out back to watch me pitch.

"Boy, do you want to be a pitcher?" he asked.

"Worse than anything in the world," I answered.

"Well, there ain't but two things you gotta do. You gotta want to bad enough, and you gotta work hard enough."

"Is that true, Uncle Paul, is that really true?" I asked desperately because I never knew anyone—ANYONE—who wanted to play big-league ball as badly as I did, and in all the years I played in public school and college and semi-pro leagues, I never knew anyone who practiced more or harder or longer than I did.

"Shore it's true. You can do anything you want to if you work hard enough and want to bad enough. Hell, look at Babe Ruth. If he could do it, you can."

This assurance from my Uncle Paul helped at the time. But later as I thought about it, I knew that Babe Ruth was one of the most naturally gifted baseball players of all time. He was a great pitcher and held longtime records for his World Series feats on the mound, and, of course, his power hitting was epoch making. All of this Ruth did while engaging in mammoth debauchery and legendary night revelry with an inexhaustible capacity for food, drink, and sex. No amount of practice on my part could have matched Ruth in any of those categories, much less his enormous success in baseball while living out the seemingly contradictory combination of such things. Much later, my Uncle Paul put a shotgun to his chest in further contradiction to such assurances.

That day with my Uncle Paul seems unusually important. Surely the culture put the winner ethic in me before that. I must have known by then that trying harder and working longer were key to making it to the top. Yet, I strangely remember a shift after that, which I certainly don't blame on my Uncle Paul, but from then on baseball was something I no longer only played. It took on a reality consumed with becoming the best, with making it to the top, and, even worse, I came to have some persistent feeling that when I failed, it was my fault. No, it was worse than that. I had the sense that baseball became the arena in which I determined my worth as a human being. Worse even than that, in that social world it became the place where you prove you have balls. My failures, which were inevitable, then became testimonies to my own inadequacies and my lack of courage or the ability to deliver in the clutch, or to "get up" for the big game.

I started a game one night on the Fourth of July in Manchester, New Hampshire. While warming up, I thought I was ready. Seldom did I have as much stuff as I did that night on the sideline. The fastball moved, the curve broke, and I was hitting spots where the catcher held his glove. When I took the mound in the first, I threw eight straight balls and walked two batters. I threw my first strike to the third hitter, just one before I walked him. When I got three balls on the fourth batter, their cleanup hitter, I said to myself, "I must not, I will not walk him, no matter what." I threw the ball waist high right down the middle of the plate. The last time I saw that ball it was headed over the light tower in right center field. Anything that goes that high and that far ought to be in the NASA program. Somehow I got out of the first inning with the score "only" 4 to 0. In the second inning when they scored two more runs and I walked the bases loaded without getting anybody out, they pulled me from the game.

I experience such moments as being gutted. It feels as though there's nothing below your rib cage and your testicles seem to be creaming into a vacuous nothing. You are afraid to breathe deep, feeling as though your breath will become urine only to display your loss of control and to disclose your cowardice and impotence. It is the most demeaning and emasculating thing I have ever known. When you are afraid in a game, when you do question your ability, when you are exhausted, such things become a secondary response to more primary emotions, but they take on a powerful "reality." That is, if fear, hurt, and sadness, for example, are primary emotions, and anger is a secondary way to cover these emotions and deny them, then baseball can be constructed around anger. Motivation is then based in your fundamental being and you play the game in rage. It does not take a genius to see the ways that competition and baseball, masculinity and sexuality, and baseballs, bats, and genitals constitute forms of life with extensive cultural and psychic consequences. Let me say, too, that it is not necessary to reduce baseball to these dynamics alone to make the case that these things are a significant and major dimension of the way the game is played in America.

The plain fact of the matter is that I never had the talent to play baseball at a professional or even at a top collegiate level, but somehow my limitations never came into play in the equations with which I thought about my relations to the game. For me it was a failure of being, a failure to be a man. Once I lost a game 3 to 0 in which I had pitched twelve innings. I pitched well that day. We just never got any runs. It's hard to win a game if you don't score. Yet, I blamed no one but myself for that loss. I should have hit a home run in the ninth inning. I should never have given up three runs in the twelfth inning. I also made two errors in the game in part because I was exhausted but unwilling to tell the coach he should take me out. I could not be satisfied that I had pitched eleven innings of shutout ball. All I knew was that we had lost, and it was my fault. I just didn't have what it took. On days like that, baseball becomes not something one plays but a field where you attempt to prove your capacity as a man. It is not a game but a nut cutting. I left the field that day with that gutted, empty, impotent feeling. I could not enjoy the eleven innings I pitched well. All I could do was rehearse over and over again the series of events that led to their three runs. Seeing reports in the newspaper the next day was not so much like reading my obituary but rather like reading some inappropriate account of my castration. Some days dying seemed better.

I don't mean to suggest that there were no wonderful moments. There are those times when baseball has a transcendent character. To see a fastball move in on a hitter and "jump" as he swings and then bury itself into the catcher's mitt. To be in the groove and to throw strike after strike, to be able to do, seemingly at will, whatever you want to do with a pitch. In the outfield to go after a long drive hit directly over your head so that you are running "full tilt" with your back to the plate, and at the last moment to jump, fully extended, and catch the ball in the webbing of the glove. To then tumble to the ground but come up throwing and fire a strike to second base. To hit a ball right—when you hit it supremely right, you can hardly tell you make contact because the head of the bat just seems to go right through the ball—and then to watch that ball take off in a long drive bending away from the outfielder and past him. Then to hear, "It's gone! Home run!" Something happens in events like that that seems to make the whole world come together. No sport puts a player alone with a ball the way baseball does. So that when the play comes to you, it is you and the ball. It is a Rocky Mountain high. It can be so thoroughly real—in the sense that absolutely nothing else seems to matter, at least in that ecstatic, transcendent moment.

It can also be so terrifying that you wonder if you can move. I'm sure that the truly good players see such moments as *kairoi,* as instants filled with chances and opportunities to make the good catch, or as a runner to take the extra base, or to make the outfield a stage and the moves with the ball a dance of grace and artistry. But for those of us with much less talent, so many of those moments are filled with what might have been. It is no matter of a few times; it is the dominant character of one's memories of games, a serial tradition of failure. In any time of memory about baseball, I can "live through" twenty or twenty-five moments in which I had the opportunity to make the good play, but did not: missing a routine throw, or as a catcher losing my grip on the ball in a collision at home plate, or striking out with the bases loaded in a game-decisive moment, or as a pitcher walking home the winning run. I can be so lost in the compulsive, riveting reverie of such that I am brought to self-consciousness only by the twitching of my body in an attempt to redo, to redeem the action.

It simply became difficult to play baseball. I suppose that's it. The longer I was in the game, the less I could play it. It was no longer a game; it was an acid test of manliness, often "warfare," winning and domination. It was the place where you kicked ass or got yours kicked. It was supposed to be a game, but it took on the seriousness of war. I suppose that's a way of saying it is American.

In this connection, I am struck most today by how violent the language has become in sport, baseball included. The language is that of a fight when it is not one of war. The talk is not simply about winning; it is about humiliating your opponent. It is about whipping the other team, about making them look bad, about dominating them, about kicking their ass. With that the push is, of course, to be number one, to make it to the top, to be the winner. Here the problem is that "kicking butt" is not intrinsic to baseball. Playing is.

At this point it is too easy to take this in the direction of winning and works righteousness and to suggest instead that we receive our worth through God's grace and that the direction of life needs to be toward wholeness and not toward winning and domination. It is also too easy to move into a critique of American culture and to work with those big abstractions. In my experience all that, even while it is true, doesn't do much good. At least, it never helped me. Besides, I see too many athletes today who use faith to secure competitive advantage, and if you think Jerry Falwell is a bad theologian, take a look at some of these evangelical ballplayers.

We need something "less" basic. When I married Peggy, I was a virgin of enormous naïveté, but I brought to our relationship all the determination and will of my baseball construction of desire. I mean, sexual love was something that one achieved, and I intended to be a winner. I had read all the sex manuals; I had the techniques correctly abstracted in my mind. It was like baseball. It requires determination and will. In the outfield you get a running start at a line drive hit in front of you, catch it in full stride, and release the ball with all your momentum going toward the plate.

This is not the way to make love.

I have come to believe it is not the way to play baseball either. I don't mean you never make such a throw home. Such a throw can be one of the wonderful moments of the game. I mean, rather, that I played too much with my will, whatever in hell that is. I was so determined to win, to do it right, that I missed too many opportunities to play out of my desire or, when I did so, I played out of a distorted desire. I tried too hard to prove too much and missed the chance to play. I channeled too much of my passion into determination and overwhelmed the aesthetic flows of the game.

My point here is not that there is some essentialist kind of desire that naturally flows into baseball and other performances. All desire, so far as I can tell, is socially located and mediated, and expressions of desire in art forms like baseball require skills. Moreover, I am making no claim that I would have played better, though it is hard to believe that I could not have played a little better since I was as bad as I was. But I would have played differently. My love of the game would not have been so consumed in extrinsic efforts to prove my manhood or to be a winner. Winning would not be eliminated, but had I enjoyed the dance more, the end of the ball would have taken a different turn.

In speaking this way, I do not mean to suggest that this is something I never experienced. I remember coming in to relieve a game in the old Northeast League, a semi-pro group of town teams along the Merrimack River in Massachusetts. That afternoon is luminous in my memory. We were playing Newburyport, the best hitting team in the league. But that afternoon the strike zone was as big as a barn door. I could pitch down and in, out and away, up and in, and waste a pitch off the corner. The fastball jumped and the curveball broke like a darting dragonfly. I was in that zone where you don't think about your manhood or winning. There is only you and the ball and the catcher. The batter is almost insignificant to the action. Your windup is like some pirouette in slow motion, and your skin, muscle, and bone are connected to reality. You can feel the ball like some extension of your hand, except that your hand participates in some larger ecology, some enormous capsule that envelopes you and everything around you. At times the field seems to be only some surface resting in some infinite void of things, an emptiness filled with the trace of balls flying through space, of bats swinging, players running, and of the graceful beauty of the human body doing something well. You don't wonder where the pitch will go. It is flying along some mystic plane moving to a destiny undeterred by finitude or self-doubt. You become the beneficiary of some seemingly inexhaustible flow of energy. This is no longer war; this is aesthetics. This is no longer willed determination; this is desire moving in the forms of life of baseball and ballet.

We lost. While I gave up a scratch single in the four or five innings I pitched and shut them out, their three-run lead, which I inherited, held up, as I remember. But that day the losing was irrelevant. I could have cared less. In the face of such ecstatic experience I did not give a damn. I know now that even failure on a canvas of such excess is part of a larger thing of beauty.

I have a half-dozen memories like that in forty-six seasons of playing ball. I know those moments "in the zone" don't last, and I don't for a minute think that all of sport can be like that, at least not for more than a fleeting time. What I do believe is that at other times I could have played ball on an entirely different basis than I did. I do not mean that I would have somehow overcome my limited skills, not that I could not improve, but that it would never be enough. Still, my skills were sufficient to play the game. I missed so much because I thought I had to dominate it in order to prove something finally external to baseball itself. I wish I had played out of my desire, aesthetically formed, rather than out of my will and determination shaped so thoroughly by commitments extrinsic to the game.

Comments like these have significance far beyond my personal experience alone. I am not the only person who played ball in these extrinsic ways or found such frustrations. As I grew older I had occasion to get to know and play with people who were professional baseball players, and a few big leaguers. I found experiences quite close to my own. One time a former major-league pitcher heard me give a lecture in which I talked of my frustrations with baseball. He said, "Tex, you need to understand that we all top out." He said that he played five years in the "Bigs" and that he felt very much the way I did. He said, "I just topped out a little later than you." The comment did not help, but it did remind me of something I have known a long time. Talk with deep honesty to a man who played ball in this country and he will tell you finally of his own sense of failure. There are those who boast of their talent and blame loss on teammates or circumstances, but in all my experience, if you get them into the closet of their athletic lives, you find self-blame. Even ol' Joe DiMaggio required as a condition of his appearance at an event that he be introduced as "baseball's greatest living player." If he really thought so, then why did he need it said? Somewhere in all that talent is the gutted, emasculated emptiness of what is arguably baseball's most graceful player.

Perhaps I want too much. Perhaps I have baseball and art confused. I do know that competition is basic to baseball. I would hate to play against someone who did not want to win. I can't stand it when someone lets me win. That, too, is demeaning. Yet, baseball is not war; it is not a struggle over dignity; it is not the ultimate stage upon which the reason for life is lived out. More than that, the best part of baseball is playing it. I occasionally hear big leaguers say before an important game that they just have to "get out there and have fun." It is a far wiser thing to say than to be preoccupied with kicking ass. The focus on domination is distractive. Turning baseball into a life-and-death struggle destroys it as a game, and it is the love of the game that makes it so right. Too much intentionality takes you out of the flow. The fun is not in domination; it is in making the plays and working with a team.

I suppose I learned from Augustine how important the ordering of desire is. When the flows of desire get diverted into idolatries of domination and the religion of winning, when eros is corrupted into proving masculinity, then a field of play becomes an arena of perdition. Baseball is not ultimate, but it flows into a larger realm of yearning. How I wish now I had known to let it be finite, to let it be a game, to let it be like tossing a ball behind the 13 Taxi Company.

I never expect to get over many of the stinging memories of the game. In 1957 I picked up a routine bunt down the first base line and threw it past the first baseman and into right-field foul territory. The runner ran all the way home. It cost us the game. I have thrown that ball over and over again, thousands of times.

Yet, I owe baseball. It drove me to find a different place to live my life. It made me search for an arena where my talent and my desire more nearly came together. It made me look for what I could do. I learned that I do have competence, that I do have gifts and graces, and that these can be enormous repositories of energy. I have passion about my work. Life does not have to be "pushing a truck with a rope," an endless straining against a challenge for which you do not have ability. I found a vocation in teaching that is more like water skiing, where the energy is so much there and the interest so real and the payoffs rich and profoundly rewarding, and where you do not so much push as "hang on."

It too has its moments. A student sees something never engaged before, or, better yet, discovers the call and vocation of her life. Or someone transforms before your very eyes and becomes the person he has never been before but was always meant to be. Or a former student becomes a competent, sensitive professional making a significant contribution to the faith and the community. Or students who were initially your "enemies" become your lifelong friends. Then things take on a rightness, not unlike the arc of a ball settling so perfectly in the pocket of that Sears Roebuck authentic Ted Williams baseball glove.

1	2	3	4	5	6	7	8	9	R	H	E

Conclusion

The Faith of Fifty Million:
A Kingdom on Earth?

Christopher H. Evans   *William R. Herzog II*

In Game Six of the 1956 World Series, the Brooklyn Dodgers experienced the last *kairos* moment in the history of their franchise. They were facing their arch rivals, the New York Yankees, for the seventh time in World Series play. The score was tied in the bottom of the eleventh inning, when Jackie Robinson came to bat for Brooklyn. With one out and runners on first and second, Robinson lined a hard shot to left field. Playing left field for the Yankees was Enos "Country" Slaughter, another player like Robinson who was in the twilight of his career. Nine years earlier, Slaughter had intentionally spiked Robinson, in one of the most overt acts of racism committed against Robinson during his rookie year in the major leagues. Now, Robinson had revenge. Slaughter, playing too shallow to make a play, watched the ball fly over his head and carom off the left-field wall. Junior Gilliam, a young African-American ballplayer, scored the winning run from second base. That game played at Brooklyn's legendary Ebbets Field was the last great moment of triumph not only for the Brooklyn Dodgers, but for Jackie Robinson. The next day, the Dodgers' ace pitcher, Don Newcombe, one of the first African American players to break into the major leagues, was pounded by Yankee bats. The Dodgers lost the game, 9–0, and the Series, 4 games to 3. For Brooklyn, the pain of that defeat was amplified by the fact that Jackie Robinson, in what turned out to be his last major league at bat, struck out for the game's final out.[1] A year later, the Dodgers played their last game at Ebbets Field and left Brooklyn for Los Angeles.

If you happen to be a Yankee fan, the above story is an account of triumph over adversity. Brooklyn had the momentum going into the seventh game. They were playing at home and they had won Game Six in dramatic fashion. But the Yankees showing their customary big-game clutch and poise came through to win the Series. If, however, you are like the majority of Americans who actively root against the New York Yankees, then the 1956 World Series is just another example of the fact that the Yankees always seem to win. In fact, a quick review of Yankee-Dodger World Series confrontations might make the theologically inclined argue that the least worthy of the two clubs won the majority of times. After all, the Dodgers were not only the first team to integrate, but by the mid-1950s they had become a symbol of America's future as a multicultural, pluralistic society. In addition to African Americans, the Dodgers included Caucasians and Hispanics on their roster. Their fans, far more than other major-league cities, reflected that diversity.

The Yankees, on the other hand, were a symbol of white America's resistance to change. They were not only one of the last major-league franchises to integrate (catcher Elston Howard was the only African American on the Yankees' roster for the 1956 series), but their fan reputation, unlike the diverse ethnic and social-class constituencies that graced Brooklyn, resided with white upper-middle-class America (even though Yankee Stadium was in a section of the Bronx whose residents had little in common with the fans in the stands or the players on the field). At a time when Americans from a variety of backgrounds were being galvanized by the civil rights movement, the Yankees were a symbol of America's Anglo past, a symbol of white recalcitrance in the face of the pluralistic society that America was becoming. Although the Dodgers did beat the Yankees in the 1955 World Series, the fact remains that in 1941, 1947, 1949, 1952, 1953, and 1956 the Dodgers, a symbol of America's future, failed to defeat the Yankees, a symbol of America's past. When one considers that the Yankees are still the most winning (and wealthiest) franchise in the major leagues and that the site of Ebbets Field now contains a low-income housing project, one would be hard-pressed to argue against the logic that the Yankees were the stronger team. At the same time, the Yankee dominance of the Dodgers, given the character of the two teams, just doesn't seem fair. Brooklyn may have been the more "virtuous" of the two franchises, in relation to larger events taking place in America at the time. The fact remains, however, that they still lost, both on and off the playing field.

On October 21, 1975, in Game Six of the World Series between the Cincinnati Reds and the Boston Red Sox, Carlton Fisk hit the game-winning home run in the bottom of the twelfth inning to give Boston a dramatic come-from-behind victory. Since that fateful night, the image of Fisk waving the ball fair has stuck in the minds of many baseball devotees, and the joy that the memory of that event evokes for Red Sox fans is one of pure ecstasy. To this day, many Red Sox fans will note with pride where they were that night and how they reacted when Fisk hit that shot. Not unlike Babe Ruth's "called shot" in the 1932 World Series (when "the Babe" allegedly pointed in the direction of left field before hitting a mammoth home run in Wrigley Field, Chicago), that Game Six has generated an "I was there" response from more persons than could have ever possibly fit into the confines of Fenway Park.

Yet what is overlooked in the retelling of that historic Game Six is that the Red Sox lost Game Seven (a game where they blew a 3–0 lead in the sixth inning), and the Series, adding to their plagued postseason legacy of chronic failure. No matter how much Red Sox fans gloat over the Fisk home run, the Red Sox have not won a World Series since 1918, when Babe Ruth was one of their star players (as a pitcher and hitter). For Red Sox fans, the reality of Fisk's home run rests side by side with an image from another famous Game Six—that of Red Sox first baseman Bill Buckner allowing a lazy ground ball to roll harmlessly through his legs, ultimately costing the Red Sox the 1986 World Series to the New York Mets.

What do these accounts suggest about the relationship between faith and the national pastime? Commentators who wax poetically about the virtues of baseball will point to what they believe are its intrinsic qualities of greatness—the fact that the game reflects a uniqueness that metaphorically and literally can open our souls to a vision of paradise. Yet, what the accounts of the Dodgers and Red Sox suggest, and what many of the chapters in this book suggest, is that baseball is just as likely to break our hearts as give us ecstacy. For many who passionately follow a sports team, who play a sport, or who love someone who plays a sport, we are amazed at how difficult it can be to absorb a loss—even with the passing of years that pain still lingers (ask any Red Sox fan about the 1986 World Series). To say "It's only a game" is little solace when we as a culture are so passionate about winning—no matter the context or the cost.

What this book reveals is that baseball, far from giving us a new heaven and a new earth, individually or socially, produces results on the playing field that seldom seem fair. The common argument that baseball honors all individuals equally (it is a game played on "a level playing field") can be offset by the argument that baseball has nothing to do with social equality; it has to do with which team has the greatest talent, money, and zeal to win. What this book shows is that baseball in American culture, both individually and socially, is often about losing—a fact that cannot be overturned by faith in a just God. The failures of "Kid" Scissons and Tex Sample on the pitcher's mound, like the failure of Santiago in *The Old Man and the Sea,* reflect the fact that God does not reward us for our hard work, or our faith in God's righteousness. The overwhelming evidence that points to the innocence of Joe Jackson does not negate the fact that he continues to be branded a baseball heretic, barred from entering the Elysian Fields of Cooperstown. In baseball, as in life, faith that our good works (and our suffering) somehow will offer the promise of a better future guarantees us nothing but disappointment. Perhaps the only theological moral we can draw from the examples of the Brooklyn Dodgers and the Boston Red Sox is that "God allows rain to fall upon the just and the unjust" (but it rains harder on teams with less talent), and nothing we do, or try to do, can stop that.

What we are suggesting is not that our good works are in vain, but that it is ridiculous to believe that God cares about the outcome of a sporting event. Success on the diamond has never been the mark of God's imparted or imputed righteousness. Success is based on the fact that those who win have the greatest material resources (talent and money) and have the best luck. And from a larger theological perspective, that's the way it should be. When we look at the range of large-scale problems in our society and upon our globe—poverty, genocide, political violence, to name only a few—and consider the disproportionate amount of wealth that exists in the United States in relation to the rest of the world, it stretches the imagination to argue that the world's salvation depends on whether God roots for the Yankees or the Red Sox. To believe that there is a larger plan to what takes place on the baseball diamond, or to believe that God grants divine favor to any specific individual or team, is not only nonsensical, but a form of the worst marriage between pseudo-faith and self-centeredness. The very fact that so many contemporary athletes see God's hand as the primary reason why they hit a home run, or make an impossible catch, goes to show that Augustine and other theologians

The Faith of Fifty Million

were right to suggest that the essence of our "fallen nature" is personal selfishness. Perhaps the pattern of athletes invoking the deity every time they win is just another illustration of the doctrine of original sin.

Yet on another level this book suggests that baseball has been at times a transcendent symbol in American culture. Throughout its history, baseball has lived with the uneasy tension that it was a symbol of national unity, at the same time that the game's practices often contradicted that mythology. Unlike with other popular sports, Americans return to baseball because it is grounded in a clear tradition that affirms our nation's unity through diversity. Many times, this faith in the national pastime has resulted in idolatry. But at other moments, baseball has manifested itself as a sport that really does espouse what it allegedly stands for: fairness. Americans have seen baseball as a transcendent symbol that reminds those who tarry in the present that the future will somehow be better than the past. In effect, what baseball has offered the nation is a faith that through the national pastime anything is possible—and in the sport's better moments, like 1947, that faith has been justified.

More than any sport in American history, baseball has shown Americans that the prophet's proclamation, "Behold I am doing a new thing, do you not see it?" is not just an eschatological plea to be saved out of the world, but a prophetic hope that the future will be better than the past. In a sport born out of the myth that it was "a game invented by boys to be played by men," baseball holds out hope that fairness in life, as on the diamond, will ultimately prevail, where the inequalities of our time will give way to a new era that reflects biblical themes of peace, justice, and the mutuality of all persons.

There is no doubt that actual realizations of this prophetic hope occur rarely in baseball—and in history generally. But such rarity does not diminish the fact that this prophetic spirit is real and has been actualized from time to time. When hope becomes a reality, for an individual or for a community, it is a transformative event. The fact that baseball can serve as an enduring symbol of hope is one reason why the sport still carries the label of the American national pastime, even as other sports, one could argue, have achieved more popularity. The sport reminds us that just as the game and the nation have had to deal with multitudes of Ben Chapmans, it also has had a few visionaries like Branch Rickey and Jackie Robinson: persons who serve as signs of things to come, in baseball and in the nation. Baseball historically has served not as a passage to the promised land, but as a way to see grace through the unexpected—when sinners become saints and saints become sinners. Yet all of these persons contribute to a legacy that goes beyond lifetime earned run averages or slugging percentages—or even about the number of wins and losses one achieves.

Much of the Christian theological tradition has spoken of how God's presence has been manifested through ordinary human channels. These channels are "means of grace," objects that in some mysterious way become signs and symbols of a hidden, divine mystery. Perhaps baseball, too, has served Americans in this fashion. Perhaps seeing baseball as a means of grace is the best way to view the relationship between faith and the national game. Even though the Dodgers left Brooklyn for the California suburbs and even though the Red Sox still have not won a World Series, there is something about the memory of the past and the unknown possibilities of the future that give us hope that God will do "a new thing" that we are not expecting. To view baseball as "a means of grace" sheds light on how the game reflects genuine *kairos* moments in America. As the story of Jackie Robinson makes clear, the ultimate question is not about winning or losing; it is how we go about playing the game.

This book highlights that baseball's greatest moral failures often came at times when it took itself too seriously as a "divinely ordained" American sport. At the same time, when baseball has been able to awaken itself to its own fear of the future, then it has reflected something transcendent. For whether a means of grace be understood as bread and wine, or a bat and a ball, it enables us to cast away our fear of the unknown and momentarily see signs of hope for a better future. Such a perspective resists the romanticism that wants to view the game as a bridge to world peace or global reconciliation. By the same token, it leaves open the possibility that something big can, and will, happen when we least expect it. Sometimes the greatest act of faith is being open to the possibility that miracles can and do happen at anytime in our world—and in the ballpark. (And if you don't believe in miracles, take a look at Bill Mazeroski's home run in Game Seven of the 1960 World Series in the bottom of the ninth inning to lift the lowly Pittsburgh Pirates over the mighty Yankees.) What baseball can teach us, like Christianity, is that if we keep our eyes open, we might witness the fall of the mighty and the rising up of the weak. We may not see the final outcome of that transformation in our lifetimes, but the signs are there.

If you are a Red Sox fan you will forever wish that Bill Buckner fielded that ground ball in the World Series, and if you are like most Americans, you hope that the Yankees will lose (or put more positively, that other teams will find ways to beat them). But the chances are that in the immediate future the Red Sox will continue to lose and the Yankees will continue to win. For those who love the game, we hope, and perhaps we even pray, that for just one moment the impossible will become possible, and that we can experience through a game the awe that comes through encountering the sacred. To connect faith and the national pastime is not to argue that baseball is something more than a game; it is to affirm that baseball is a game.

And in the eyes of God that is all that is required.

Endnotes

Introduction

1. F. Scott Fitzgerald, *The Great Gatsby* (New York: Charles Scribner's Sons, 1925), 74. The title of this volume of essays is taken from Nick's comment about playing with "the faith of fifty million people."
2. The reference here, of course, is to Babe Ruth, who is popularly portrayed as "the savior" who redeemed baseball from the shame of the Black Sox scandal and returned the game to a central place in American life.
3. For classic interpretations of the Protestant experience in American Christianity, see Sidney E. Mead, *The Lively Experiment: The Shaping of Christianity in America* (New York: Harper & Row, 1963); Sydney Ahlstrom, *A Religious History of the American People* (New Haven, Conn.: Yale University Press, 1972), and Robert T. Handy, *A Christian America: Protestant Hopes and Historical Realities* (2d ed., New York: Oxford University Press, 1984).
4. Geoffrey C. Ward and Ken Burns, *Baseball: An Illustrated History* (New York: Alfred A. Knopf, 1994), 384.
5. The years leading up to Jackie Robinson's integration of the major leagues in 1947 were marked by numerous successes of African Americans to integrate a variety of amateur and professional sports. One thinks especially of Jack Johnson and Joe Lewis in professional boxing and Jessie Owens in amateur track and field. Additionally, small numbers of African Americans played professional football in the American Professional Football Association (APFA) and its successor, the National Football League (NFL), during the 1920s and 1930s (and Jackie Robinson himself was a star college running back for UCLA in the late 1930s). Professional basketball, still in its nascent stages prior to World War II, followed a pattern of team segregation similar to major-league baseball. Clearly, the integration of Robinson into professional baseball opened up greater opportunities for African Americans in other professional sports. See Arthur R. Ashe Jr., *A Hard Road to Glory: A History of the African-American Athlete, 1919–1945* (New York: Amistad, 1988).
6. Jacques Barzun, *God's Country and Mine: A Declaration of Love Spiced with a Few Harsh Words* (Boston: Little, Brown & Co., 1954), 159.

Chapter 1

1. A. Bartlett Giamatti, *Take Time for Paradise: Americans and Their Games* (New York: Summit Books, 1989), 83.

2. G. Edward White, *Creating the National Pastime: Baseball Transforms Itself, 1903–1953* (Princeton, N.J.: Princeton University Press, 1996), 319.
3. Ibid., 8.
4. In this paper, I use G. Edward White's definition of "organized baseball" to refer "to the established, 'official' major and minor professional leagues . . ." (chiefly the National League founded in 1876 and the American League founded in 1901). It does not include the so-called "outlaw" baseball leagues not recognized by major-league moguls, nor the Negro Leagues, which became the primary outlet for African American baseball players who were excluded for sixty years from playing in organized baseball. See White, 5.
5. Robert N. Bellah, "Civil Religion in America," in *American Civil Religion,* ed. Donald G. Jones and Russell E. Richey (New York: Harper & Row, 1974), 40–41.
6. See, for example, Bob Costas, *Fair Ball: A Fan's Case for Baseball* (New York: Broadway Books, 2000).
7. See Henry Warner Bowden, *Church History in the Age of Science: Historiographical Patterns in the United States, 1876–1918* (Chapel Hill: University of North Carolina Press, 1971), 31–68.
8. Cited in Albert G. Spalding, *America's National Game: Historical Facts Concerning the Beginning, Evolution, Development and Popularity of Base Ball,* with an Introduction by Benjamin G. Rader (Lincoln and London: University of Nebraska Press, 1992), 64.
9. *The Sporting News,* April 30, 1908. (Editions of the sport journals, *The Sporting News* and *Sporting Life,* are from the National Baseball Hall of Fame Library, Cooperstown, New York.)
10. Warren Goldstein, *Playing for Keeps: A History of Early Baseball* (Ithaca, N.Y.: Cornell University Press, 1989), 43–44.
11. Henry Chadwick, *The Game of Baseball: How to Learn It, How to Play It, and How to Teach It* (New York: George Munro & Co., Publishers, 1868), 9.
12. Charles C. Alexander, *Our Game: An American Baseball History* (New York: Henry Holt, 1991), 9.
13. Ibid.
14. Goldstein, 101–102.
15. Ibid., 102.
16. See, for example, G. Edward White, 190–93.
17. John Montgomery Ward, *Base-Ball: How to Become a Player* (Philadelphia: Athletic Publishing Co., 1888), 21.
18. Ibid., 23.
19. Benjamin G. Rader, *Baseball: A History of America's Game* (Urbana and Chicago: University of Illinois Press, 1992), 84.
20. Peter Levine, *A. G. Spalding and the Rise of Baseball* (New York: Oxford University Press, 1985), xv. After his retirement, Spalding made an unsuccessful run in California for the U.S. Senate, largely campaigning on his legacy as a baseball entrepreneur.

21. Both *The Sporting News* and *Sporting Life* magazines gave extensive summaries of the Spalding tour. See also Levine and Rader.
22. Benjamin G. Rader, "Introduction," in Albert G. Spalding, *America's National Game*, xiii.
23. Spalding, xiv.
24. *The Sporting News*, December 2, 1905.
25. Levine, 114.
26. Spalding, 19.
27. Ironically, around the same time that the Hall of Fame opened, a librarian named Robert Henderson produced a documented study into baseball's origins that showed how the game derived from rounders. See Rader, 84. Abner Doubleday never lived in Cooperstown, and during the time he supposedly invented the game, he was a cadet at the United States Military Academy at West Point.
28. Levine, 97.
29. Martin E. Marty, "Two Kinds of Civil Religion," in *American Civil Religion*, 151.
30. Spalding, 4.
31. Ibid., 5.
32. Ibid., 11.
33. *The Sporting News*, October 4, 1945. Sadly, the perspective of Larry MacPhail in the 1940s continues to be expressed in subtle, and not so subtle, ways by the establishment of organized baseball. In 1987, Al Campanis, a vice-president for the Los Angeles Dodgers and former teammate of Jackie Robinson, stated on national television that he felt African Americans lacked "some of the necessities" to succeed as club managers and owners. See Geoffrey C. Ward and Ken Burns, *Baseball: An Illustrated History* (New York: Alfred A. Knopf, 1994), 452.
34. Spalding, 281.
35. *Sporting Life*, March 14, 1908.
36. Spalding, 256.
37. *The Sporting News*, August 4, 1921.
38. Levine, 107.
39. Ibid., 108.
40. Marty, "Two Kinds of Civil Religion."
41. Spalding, 14.
42. There are many aspects of how baseball's civil religion gets manifested ritually in America: the custom since the early twentieth century for the President of the United States to throw out the first pitch on opening day of the first game of the season and the playing of the national anthem before each ball game being two examples. For further discussion on the role of sports as American ritual religion, see Joseph L. Price, ed. *From Season to Season: Sports as American Religion* (Macon, GA: Mercer University Press, 2001).
43. Marty, 148.
44. White, 316–30.

Chapter 2

1. David Chidester, "The Church of Baseball, the Fetish of Coca-Cola, and the Potlatch of Rock 'n' Roll: Theoretical Models for the Study of Religion in American Popular Culture," in *The Journal of the American Academy of Religion* 64 (Fall 1996): 748.

2. Perhaps the classic statement that traces the influence of the kingdom-of-God doctrine in the United States is H. Richard Niebuhr's *The Kingdom of God in America* (original publication, Harper & Row, 1937), 164.

3. Warren Goldstein, *Playing for Keeps: A History of Early Baseball* (Ithaca, N.Y.: Cornell University Press, 1989); see also my chapter, "Baseball as Civil Religion," in this volume.

4. See Steven A. Riess, *Touching Base: Professional Baseball and American Culture in the Progressive Era* (Westport, Conn.: Greenwood Press, 1980); Harold Seymour, "Baseball: Badge of Americanism," in *Cooperstown Symposium on Baseball and American Culture,* ed. Alvin L. Hall (Westport, Conn.: Meckler, 1990), 1–22; Bruce Kuklick, *To Everything a Season: Shibe Park and Urban Philadelphia, 1909–1976* (Princeton, N.J.: Princeton University Press, 1991), and G. Edward White, *Creating the National Pastime: Baseball Transforms Itself, 1903–1953* (Princeton, N.J.: Princeton University Press, 1996).

5. Washington Gladden, *The Church and the Kingdom* (New York: Fleming H. Revell Co., 1894), 8.

6. Ibid.

7. See Herbert Gutman, "Protestantism and the American Labor Movement: The Christian Spirit in the Gilded Age," in *The American Historical Review* 72 (October 1966): 100–101.

8. G. Edward White, 10–46.

9. Walter Rauschenbusch, *Christianity and the Social Crisis,* rev. ed. (Westminster/John Knox Press, 1991), 377. Rauschenbusch's extensive family correspondence, housed at the American Baptist Historical Society in Rochester, New York, makes it evident that he was at least a casual baseball fan. His lecturing itinerary took him throughout the United States, and he often found relief by going to professional baseball games. One letter from Cleveland in 1912 captures a whimsical tone that periodically emerged in Rauschenbusch's correspondence: "Saw a ball-game, big ball, thin bats, fat players, lots of fun." Letter Walter Rauschenbusch to his family, June 15, 1912, Rauschenbusch papers, Box 143.

10. Kuklick, 25.

11. Riess, 222.

12. Susan Curtis, *A Consuming Faith: The Social Gospel and Modern American Culture* (Baltimore: Johns Hopkins University Press, 1991). Curtis's biographical sketches of major social-gospel figures like Washington Gladden and Shailer Mathews shows how recreational activities like baseball were perceived to promote moral character and Christian virtue.

13. Curtis, 243–54. See also Eleanor J. Stebner and Tracy J. Trothen's chapter in this volume.

14. Peter Levine, *A. G. Spalding and the Rise of Baseball: The Promise of American Sport* (New York: Oxford University Press, 1985), 98.

15. Washington Gladden, *Applied Christianity: Moral Aspects of Social Questions* (Boston: Houghton Mifflin Co., 1886), 262.

16. Curtis, 48–59; Shailer Mathews, *New Faith for Old* (New York: Macmillan Co., 1936), 19–20.

17. Mathewson continues to fascinate contemporary fiction and nonfiction writers, as an enduring symbol of baseball's goodness and purity. In addition to Donald McKim's essay in this volume, see Eric Rolfe Greenberg, *The Celebrant* (Lincoln: University of Nebraska Press, 1983).

18. Albert G. Spalding, *America's National Game* (repr., Lincoln and London: University of Nebraska Press, 1992), 9.

19. See Paul T. Phillips, *A Kingdom on Earth: Anglo-American Social Christianity, 1880–1940* (University Park: Penn State University Press, 1996), 120–21. Clifford Putney, *Muscular Christianity: Manhood and Sports in Protestant America* (Cambridge, MA: Harvard University Press, 2001).

20. Henry Frederick Cope, *The School in the Modern Church* (New York: George H. Doran Co., 1919), 94; Curtis, 24–25.

21. Gladden, *The Church and Modern Life* (Boston: Houghton Mifflin Co., 1908), 220; Curtis, 46–47.

22. Curtis, 24.

23. Riess, 25.

24. Ibid., 230.

25. *Baseball: A Film by Ken Burns* (Florentine Films, 1994), "Inning Three."

26. See, for example, A. Bartlett Giamatti, *Take Time for Paradise: Americans and Their Games* (New York: Summit Books, 1989) and Doris Kearns Goodwin, *Wait Till Next Year* (New York: Simon & Schuster, 1998).

27. John Thorn, "Why Baseball?" in Geoffrey C. Ward and Ken Burns, *Baseball: An Illustrated History* (New York: Alfred A. Knopf, 1994), 61.

28. David Heim, "Picking Up the Signs," *The Christian Century,* 7 December 1994, 1149.

29. Kuklick, 193.

30. Thorn, 60.

31. Niebuhr, 193. As I have argued elsewhere, however, one needs to be careful in applying Niebuhr's critique blindly to every theological movement that has been tagged "liberal." Indeed although many "liberals" associated with the social-gospel movement did possess an optimistic, progressive view toward social progress, their outlook on questions of sin and evil was often more incisive than later critics gave them credit. See, for example, the essays in my edited compilation, *The Social Gospel Today* (Louisville, Ky.: Westminster John Knox Press, 2001).

32. W. P. Kinsella, *The Iowa Baseball Confederacy* (New York: Ballantine Books, 1986).

33. *Iowa Baseball Confederacy,* 166.

34. Ibid., 178.

35. Ibid., 254–55.
36. Kinsella, *Shoeless Joe* (New York: Ballantine Books, 1982).
37. *Shoeless Joe,* 193.
38. Ibid.
39. *Shoeless Joe,* 213.
40. Thorn, 58.

Chapter 3

1. Ray Robinson, *Matty, An American Hero: Christy Mathewson of the New York Giants* (New York: Oxford University Press, 1993), 41. On McGraw, see also Donald Honig, *Baseball America: The Heroes of the Game and the Times of Their Glory* (New York: Galahad Books, 1993), who writes that "the flinty soul of John McGraw melted before the radiance of his ace," 33. On McGraw's twenty-fifth anniversary with the Giants, *The Sporting News* called him "the little fighter of baseball" and said he was still a "dynamo of relentless action, a foe of the quitter and loser." See Richard C. Crepeau, *Baseball: America's Diamond Mind* (Lincoln: University of Nebraska Press, 2000), 129.

2 The last line on Mathewson's plaque in the Hall of Fame reads: "Matty was master of them all." Matty's pitching exploits can be traced in Ronald A. Mayer, *Christy Mathewson: A Game by Game Profile of a Legendary Pitcher* (Jefferson, N.C.: McFarland & Co., 1993) as well as in numerous baseball statistical works. Sources for baseball statistics include John Thorn, ed., *Total Baseball,* 7th ed. (New York: Total Sports, 2001) and on the Internet: http://www.baseball1.com; http://www.mlb.com/NASApp/mlb/mlb/stats/mlb_stats_entry.jsp; http://www.baseball-almanac.com; http://www.sportsline.com/u/baseball/mlb/players/index.html; http://www.bballsports.com. Cf. http://www.retrosheet.org. For baseball links and baseball pages on the World Wide Web see http://advocacy-net.com/bballmks.htm; http://www.baseball-links.com; and http://members.tripod.com/baseballstats/links.html.

3. Robinson, *Matty,* 57. Other theories are that since it was not common for ballplayers to be over six feet tall in those days, Matty was regarded as huge and, as one sportswriter said, "Hey, he's a big six, isn't he, the biggest six you ever saw." Thus, the nickname "Big Six." Another theory was that Matty was nicknamed after a "peerless car" made by the Matheson Motor Co. in Wilkes Barre, Pennsylvania. It was called "Big Six." Yet it is unclear whether the car was named for Matty or Matty was named for the car. Fred Lieb speculated that "Big Six" also could have referred to a famous typographical union in New York. See Fred Lieb, *Baseball as I Have Known It,* repr. (Lincoln: University of Nebraska Press, 1996), 145. An early home baseball game from around 1910 was called "Big Six: Christy Mathewson Indoor Baseball Game." See *The Barry Halper Collection of Baseball Memorabilia,* 2 vols. (New York: Barry Halper Enterprises, 1999), 1:426 (Item #1187).

4. This was the term used by manager McGraw in describing Matty's stel-

lar performance in the 1905 World Series against the Philadelphia Athletics, in which he pitched three complete games in six days, allowed fourteen hits, one walk, and no runs in twenty-seven innings. He struck out eighteen batters. He was, said McGraw, "pretty much the perfect type of pitching machine." See Joseph Durso, "Baseball and the American Dream," in *The Sporting News*, 1986.

5. Robinson, *Matty*, 163–64. Robinson notes, "Such were the social mores of postbellum Texas."

6. Robinson, *Matty*, 176.

7. Among other baseball men in the Chemical Warfare Service (CWS) were Ty Cobb, Branch Rickey, and George Sisler.

8. See Robinson, *Matty*, 192–93.

9. Robinson, *Matty*, 193–94. Matty's brother Henry had died of tuberculosis in 1917; his other brother, Nicholas, committed suicide in the Mathewson barn in 1909. Matty found his brother's body. See Robinson, *Matty*, 112–13, 181.

10. On Fullerton, see Steve Klein, "The Lone Horseman of Baseball's Apocalypse," at http://www.blueear.com/archives/issue_8/apocalypse.txt. Cf. Robinson, *Matty*, 198–202. On the Black Sox scandal, see below, William R. Herzog II, "From Scapegoat to Icon: The Strange Journey of Shoeless Joe Jackson." Matty had picked Cincinnati to win the Series. Robinson notes that after the scandal, Matty continued to show "broad tolerance for the alleged sins of those eight Black Sox. 'There is such a thing as condemning the acts of these men and still forgiving the individuals,' he said. 'I don't think Kid Gleason and the rest of the White Sox wanted to see their former comrades sent to the penitentiary for violating the trust placed in them by the fans. They would not have been human if they did. Even a judge must dislike sentencing a man to jail, unless he is a most hardened criminal.'" *Matty*, 201–02.

11. Robinson, *Matty*, 203.

12. See Lieb's account of this game and his efforts in *Baseball as I Have Known It*, chap. 12.

13. A checkerboard once belonging to Mathewson was part of the Barry Halper Collection of Baseball Memorabilia auctioned by Sotheby's in New York City on September 23–29, 1999. It was signed by Mathewson with the date May 24, 1924. With it was a photograph of Mathewson playing checkers with his father in 1922 (Lot 749). The items sold for $10,925. Other Mathewson memorabilia appeared among the items (see lots 352, 371, 372, 376, 410, 445, 464, 472, 526, 738, 739, 749, 1187, 1281, 1282, etc.). See *The Barry Halper Collection of Baseball Memorabilia*, 2 vols. (New York: Barry Halper Enterprises, 1999).

14. Robinson, *Matty*, 215.

15. Ibid. Honig writes, "It was as if the baseball season had sustained him, for when it was done the last props of life fell away, and the forty-five-year-old master of the fadeaway knew they were going." *Baseball America*, 152–53.

16. See the picture of Goose Goslin at bat in the 1925 Series with the arm-band on his left arm in Lawrence S. Ritter, *The Glory of Their Times: The Story of the Early Days of Baseball Told by the Men Who Played It* (repr., New York: William Morrow & Co., 1985), 286–87.
17. Honig, *Baseball America*, 152.
18. Cited in Robinson, *Matty*, 217.
19. See these and other laudations in Robinson, *Matty*, 217. Some articles about Matty that appeared during the days of his fame can be found at http://www.leaptoad.com/raindelay/matty/.
20. See Crepeau, *America's Diamond Mind*, 127. Mayor Curley was the Irish-Amercan politico who was the model for Edwin O'Connor's *The Last Hurrah*.
21. A contemporary Christian devotional Web site tells of a reported incident when Matty was on third base and a squeeze play was called. Dust enveloped the plate when Matty slid home so that the umpire could not see for certain what happened. After a conference it was agreed that Matty himself should make the decision. Matty announced, "He got me." When asked later why he had not called himself safe, "the great athlete, with great pride, said, 'I am a church elder.'" The devotional on "Dedication" continued: "Christy Mathewson was dedicated enough in his service to God that, when tempted to compromise his integrity, he resisted and was truthful, earning him one of the most honorable reputations in baseball history." See http://www.heartlight.org/timely_truths/dedication.html.
22. See Crepeau, *America's Diamond Mind*, 127.
23. Honig, *Baseball America*, 26.
24. Crepeau, *America's Diamond Mind*, 127. This is confirmed by Lieb, who wrote: "There was a legend that Matty didn't drink or smoke. He did take an occasional drink and he smoked cigarettes, but he was not a chain smoker. He did swear on occasion and he loved to gamble. He was good at card games of any sort and usually won—he was smarter, had a quicker mind, and knew cards and percentages better than most of them. He studied opposing card players much as he studied batsmen when he was pitching, and this gave him a decided advantage." *Baseball as I Have Known It*, 145. Matty's face was used to advertise "Tuxedo—The Perfect Tobacco." See Robinson, *Matty*, 218, and *The Baseball Anthology: 125 Years of Stories, Poems, Articles, Photographs, Drawings, Interviews, Cartoons, and Other Memorabilia*, ed. Joseph Wallace (New York: Harry N. Abrams, 1994), 106, where the advertisment is reproduced.
25. See Robinson, *Matty*, 183–84. After the game, Matty and McGraw were hauled before a magistrate because of a complaint by the Sabbath Society. The magistrate dismissed the case and praised the two managers for providing the opportunity for people to use their Sunday for good entertainment while they might not otherwise have been able to do so had the game not been played.
26. Ritter, *The Glory of Their Times*, 176.
27. Ibid., 96. Sportswriter John Kieran of *The New York Times* said of Matty

without qualification: "He was the greatest I ever saw. He was the greatest anybody ever saw. Let them name all the others. I don't care how good they were, Matty was better." Robinson, *Matty,* 219.

28. Robinson, *Matty,* 222. Mathewson's grave may be viewed at http://www.findagrave.com/pictures/1577.html. See also the account of a visit there in Dave D'Antonio, *Invincible Summer: Traveling America in Search of Yesterday's Baseball Greats* (South Bend, Ind.: Diamond Communications, 1997), chap. 23.

29. See Eric Rolfe Greenberg, *The Celebrant* (New York: Penguin Books, 1986). W. P. Kinsella called this "Simply the best baseball novel ever written."

30. See the "Matty Web Site" at http://www.matty.org for Frierson's work, performance schedule, reviews, photos, products etc. Its phone is 1-800-75-MATTY. Frierson's inspiration came from Matty's 1912 book, *Pitching in a Pinch: Or, Base Ball from the Inside.* Frierson has also begun The Mathewson Foundation with this mission statement:

> The Mathewson Foundation is a not-for-profit educational organization established to support research, provide education (directly, through training and, indirectly, through scholarships), develop media and promote events which will encourage young people to identify their own unique combinations of talents and to nurture the important character traits exemplified in the life of Christy Mathewson. The Foundation is committed especially to identifying and supporting individuals who combine athletic abilities, academic talents and fine arts interests within the framework of a strong personal faith.

> Cf. http://tbcatalog.totalsports.net/Matty.htm, among other reviews of Frierson's stage performance. In 1996, it was an off-Broadway play. See the Matty Web Site for reviews of Frierson's stage performance ("Matty Reviews"). Frierson performed in Matty's hometown of Factoryville, Pennsylvania during the "Christy Mathewson Day 2000." See http://mrudolf.tripod.com/mattyday. Mathewson's image now is represented by CMG Worldwide (see http://www.cmgww.com/baseball/mathew/mathew.html).

31. Cited along with other Mathewson quotations at http://www.baseball-almanac.com/quomath.shtml.

32. Honig, *Baseball America,* 85. He goes on to note: "Named for a sitting president, he was later to have a future president portray him on the screen in a movie based on his life (*The Winning Team,* starring Ronald Reagan, made in 1952, two years after Alex's death)."

33. See the biographies of Alexander by Jack Kavanagh, *Ol' Pete: The Grover Cleveland Alexander Story* (South Bend, Ind.: Diamond Communications, 1996) and *Grover Cleveland Alexander. Baseball Legends* (New York: Chelsea House Publishers, 1990).

34. Honig, *Baseball America,* 86–87. Alexander faced Mathewson three

times and won all three games. Alex was the first to admit, however, that by then Matty was past his prime.

35. By the 1930s, most major-league teams had a pitching machine used in spring training. Most of these machines were called "Ol' Pete" after Alexander. See Lloyd Johnson, *Baseball's Book of Firsts* (Philadelphia: Running Press Books, 1998), 119. Sportswriter Grantland Rice said, "Alex could throw a ball into a tin cup. I have never seen such control." See Jonathan Fraser Light, *The Cultural Encyclopedia of Baseball* (Jefferson, N.C.: McFarland & Co., 1997), 190.

36. Honig, *Baseball America,* 92.

37. Ibid. Cf. Kavanagh, *Ol' Pete,* 71, and *Grover Cleveland Alexander,* 30.

38. Honig, *Baseball America,* 93.

39. Quoted in Kavanagh, *Ol' Pete,* 72 from an interview in *Baseball Magazine.*

40. Kavanagh, *Grover Cleveland Alexander,* 31. According to Kavanagh, "Ol' Pete knew he had a problem with alcohol. The trauma of front-line service had changed him from a cold-beer-after-the game casual drinker to one who would hide bottles of booze and drink to ward off epilepsy. It was his opinion that an alcoholic edge held the sneak attacks of his ailment at bay." *Ol' Pete,* 92. Kavanagh believes that Hans Lobart's story told to Lawrence Ritter (*The Glory of Their Times,* 195), describing how he and teammates on the Phillies used to help Alex through his epileptic seizures before he went to the war, is concocted. He argues that the army would not have inducted a known epileptic and also that in the small town of St. Paul, neighbors would have known of Alexander's epilepsy had it been present then. Kavanagh also believes that Cubs owner Charlie Weeghman would have told the draft board of Alex's condition since he was so valuable to the Cubs. *Ol' Pete,* 71.

41. Bob Farrell, Alexander's longtime catcher with the Cubs, told Lawrence Ritter: "I don't believe Alex was much of a drinker before he went into the army. After he got back from the war, though, he had a real problem" (*The Glory of Their Times,* 252). Likewise, Specs Torporcer, Alexander's fellow Cardinal pitcher, who believed Alexander was "The Greatest Pitcher of All Time" (the title of his article in *Blue Book Magazine* in July 1952), wrote of Alexander that "Once, when he was in a rare confidential mood, he told me that he had started drinking heavily while on overseas duty in the first World War. True or not, it was evident he hoped it might have been otherwise. . . . The effect of excessive alcohol upon his nervous system caused him to be grumpy and irritable at times, and, on occasion, he would vent sarcasm at players he thought were softies. That is about all that can be said against him." See Kavanagh, *Ol' Pete,* 115.

42. Honig, *Baseball America,* 155.

43. Hornsby was quoted as saying: "I'm no Sunday School teacher. I don't care what Alexander does off the field. He always looked like a great pitcher to me. At $4,000 he's the greatest bargain I ever saw." See Geoffrey C. Ward and Ken Burns, *Baseball: An Illustrated History* (New York: Alfred A. Knopf, 1994), 176.

44. Donald Honig, *The October Heroes: World Series Games Remembered by the Men Who Played Them*, (repr., Lincoln: University of Nebraska Press, 1996), 84. Charles C. Alexander relates an account via Flint Rhem, who was in the bull pen with Alexander and reported in 1961 that Alex had been dozing with a pint of whiskey in his pocket: "Seeing Hornsby's signal, Alexander grinned, 'staggered a little, handed me the pint, hitched up his britches and walked straight as he could to the mound.' Hornsby walked out beyond the infield to meet Alexander and explain the situation: two out, bases loaded, Lazzeri up. 'Do you feel all right?' Hornsby asked. 'Sure, I feel fine,' said Alexander. 'Three on, eh. Well, there's no place to put Lazzeri, is there? I'll just have to give him nothin' but a lot of hell, won't I?'" *Rogers Hornsby: A Biography* (New York: Henry Holt, 1995), 119. Another account quotes Hornsby as saying: "I looked into his eyes and saw that they were bloodshot, but they weren't foggy. I gave him the ball and told him to get Lazzeri." See Mark Vancil and Peter Hirdt, *All Century Team* (Chicago: Rare Air Media, 1999), 73.

45. Honig, *Baseball America*, 158.

46. In Honig, *The October Heroes*, 84.

47. Honig writes: "Grover Cleveland Alexander linked his name forever with that of Tony Lazzeri, who went on to a long, hard-hitting career but who was destined to be remembered for having passed through the shadow of Grover Cleveland Alexander for one enduring moment. (The linkage has its somber side: Lazzeri, too, was epileptic, falling to his death down a flight of stairs during a seizure in 1946. Baseball can flip its ironies in uncanny ways)." *Baseball America*, 159. On the game, see Kavanagh, *Ol' Pete*, chap. 14 and *Grover Cleveland Alexander*, chap. 6, and also the account by Les Bell, who was playing third base for the Cardinals, in Donald Honig, *The October Heroes*, 83–84 (also recounted in *Baseball America*, 157–58).

48. Honig writes: "It was the most classic of confrontations, a generational one, an endless human theme replayed over and over in every walk of life but most dramatically and poignantly in the arenas where athletes compete, where almost inevitably the young seize their destiny. But not this time." *Baseball America*, 156.

49. Paul Dickson, *Baseball's Greatest Quotations* (New York: HarperCollins, 1991), 8.

50. Ruth said, "Just to see old Pete out there on the mound, with that cocky little undersize cap pulled down over one ear, chewing away at his tobacco and pitching baseballs as easy as pitching hay is enough to take the heart out of a fellow." Kavanagh, *Ol' Pete*, 105.

51. Cardinal catcher Bob O'Farrell told Ritter: "When he struck out Lazzeri he'd been out on a drunk the night before and was still feeling the effects" and that when the call went out for him in the seventh inning, "Alex is tight asleep in the bullpen, sleeping off the night before. . . ." *The Glory of Their Times*, 252.

52. Honig, *The October Heroes*, 97, 100–101.

53. Kavanagh, *Ol' Pete*, 109. In his account of the strikeout, Torporcer made no reference to Alexander not having kept the promise he made to manager Hornsby the night before not to get drunk. Cf. *Ol' Pete*, 115–16.

54. Yankee pitcher George Pipgras told Donald Honig that when the two posed for a pre-game opening picture, "I put out my hand for him to shake and he reached for it and, I swear, missed it by a foot, he was so drunk; either that or he had a wicked hangover." See Donald Honig, *Baseball When the Grass Was Real: Baseball from the Twenties to the Forties Told by the Men Who Played It,* (repr., Lincoln: University of Nebraska Press, 1993), 128.

55. Kavanagh, *Ol' Pete,* 128. The Cardinals said Alexander was suffering from lumbago and baseball writers were discreet.

56. See McKechnie's account of his suspension of Alexander and his accounts of Alexander's struggles with alcohol in Lieb, *Baseball as I Have Known It,* 188–90.

57. See Kavanagh, *Ol' Pete,* 147–53 who cites a letter from National League President Ford Frick to Baseball Commissioner Kenesaw Mountain Landis which concluded with a P.S. that said, "I think it is not a question of what we can do for Alexander, but is there anything we can do about him?"

58. Ibid., 152.

59. Ibid., 153.

60. See the letter from Branch Rickey to Cardinal Publicity Director Ed Staples in Kavanagh, *Ol' Pete,* 157–60.

61. Those chosen ahead of him were Ty Cobb, Babe Ruth, Honus Wagner, Walter Johnson, and Christy Mathewson. Fred Lieb wrote in *The Sporting News* about Alexander's appearance at the opening of the Hall of Fame in 1939 when he was inducted:

> One of the most pleasing things in the entire Cooperstown show was the fine appearance of old Grover Cleveland Alexander. After his glorious diamond career, Pete, as he was known affectionately to his mates, seemed in danger of slipping from the standard of genteel respectability maintained by his fellow immortals, but Alex took hold of himself in time and no member of the famous 11 received a greater hand than the former Philly, Cub and Cardinal mound ace.

See *Middle Innings: A Documentary History of Baseball, 1900–1948,* ed. and comp. Dean A. Sullivan (Lincoln: University of Nebraska Press, 1998), 177.

62. Lieb, *Baseball as I Have Known It,* 186. Lieb said of Alex: "No pensions . . . an improvident person. . . . I was face-to-face with a human tragedy."

63. Al Laney described Alexander's work in the *New York Herald Tribune* and concluded by describing New York's Forty-Second Street in its tawdriness and by saying that "Old Pete, ex-hero, has a job in one of its

gaudiest places, sharing time with sword swallowers, dancing girls, hypnotists and performing fleas." Kavanagh, *Ol' Pete*, 162.

64. Ibid., 167.
65. Ibid., 169.
66. Ibid., 169.
67. Honig, *Baseball America*, 271.
68. Kavanagh, *Ol' Pete*, 169.
69. Alexander's grave can be viewed at http://www.findagrave.com/pictures/1812.html. D'Antonio writes: "The plot was unremarkable: a war veteran's off-white headstone, synthetic flowers, two red plastic bats, and a plastic ball. A bronze plaque noted his 1938 enshrinement into the Hall. It covered his date of death, which had been incorrectly engraved. If you can add insult to death, the town had done so, just as it added insult to his final years of life." *Invincible Summer*, 16.
70. Kavanagh, *Ol' Pete*, 170.
71. Lieb, *Baseball When the Grass Was Green*, 186.
72. Kavanagh, *Ol' Pete*, 170.
73. D'Antonio, *Invincible Summer*, 14.
74. See http://www.eonline.com/Facts/Movies/0,60,25422,00.html.
75. Kavanagh, *Grover Cleveland Alexander*, 57.
76. Hal Erickson from *All Movie Guide* at http://video.barnesandnoble.com. See "The Winning Team." One critic's headlines read "The Winning Team Fouls Out on Facts."
77. Robinson, *Matty*, 5.
78. Ibid., 7.
79. Ibid., 42.
80. Ibid., 215. Jane said of her husband, "I believe that he gave his life for his country, just as many boys like Eddie Grant, who was killed in action overseas." *Matty*, 216. Jane lived on in Lewisburg and accepted Matty's plaque when he was inducted into the Hall of Fame in 1939. After 1955 she attended the induction ceremonies for the next twelve years and became "baseball's most celebrated and gracious widow," attracting more attention than the widows of Babe Ruth and Lou Gehrig. She always wore Matty's Phi Gamma Delta fraternity pin when she visited the Hall. She died at 87 on May 29, 1967 in Lewisburg.
81. Kavanagh, *Ol' Pete*, 164.
82. Amy always watched *The Winning Team* on television reruns, always insisting that the actor who played her husband (Ronald Reagan) was not as handsome as Alex! With funds from her consulting fee for the movie, Amy paid for a monument to be erected on the Alexander plot after a February 1952 article in *The Sporting News* decried the fact that Alexander's grave was marked only by a small white cross and identification plate supplied by the mortuary. It was to be erected by May 31, 1952: the thirty-fourth anniversary of their first marriage. Amy died in December 1979 in a Los Angeles retirement home at age 87 (the same age as Jane Mathewson when she died) after a period as

a semi-invalid. She too died alone. Near her body was a baseball from the 1926 World Series. See Kavanagh, *Grover Cleveland Alexander*, 57, and *Ol' Pete*, 171.

83. Wendy Farley, *Tragic Vision and Divine Compassion: A Contemporary Theodicy* (Louisville, Ky.: Westminster John Knox Press, 1990), 30.

84. Lieb, *Baseball When the Grass Was Green*, 186.

85. Farley, *Tragic Vision and Divine Compassion*, 33–34.

86. Ibid., 23.

87. One feature of a heroic life is "imitation": "The excellencies manifested in a heroic life evoke the greatest possible compliment: the desire to imitate, to acquire and manifest a similar greatness." See Brian S. Hook and R. R. Reno, *Heroism and the Christian Life: Reclaiming Excellence* (Louisville, Ky.: Westminster John Knox Press, 2000), 6–7.

88. "Eddie Frierson's Notes on Christy Mathewson and 'Matty'" at http://www.matty.org.

89. One may also note that in Christian theology, a particular view of the death of Jesus Christ (atonement) views Christ's death as being an example of suffering love which his followers are to imitate. "Salvation" comes through this recognition of this love of God found in Christ which, in turn, causes humans to turn to God and to other people in love.

90. Kavanagh, *Ol' Pete*, 170.

91. Honig, *Baseball America*, 155.

92. Kavanagh, *Ol' Pete*, 103. According to Amy Alexander, Cardinal manager Rogers Hornsby told her years later, "The biggest mistake we made, Amy, was in not denying the story from the start. At the time it made good reading, so we let it go." Kavanagh also quotes Alex as always having blamed Hornsby for not making it clear that he was not drunk when he fanned Lazzeri and completed the game. Hornsby was quoted as saying of Alex: "He could pitch better drunk than any other man sober," 168. Hornsby's biography relates the story of Alex's hangover. See Charles C. Alexander, *Rogers Hornsby*, 119–20 citing the 1961 recollection of pitcher Flint Rhem who in 1930 disappeared in the midst of a pennant race with the Dodgers and emerged later saying he'd been kidnapped by gangsters and made to drink bootleg alcohol. See *Ol' Pete*, 110. Cf. Ward and Burns, *Baseball: An Illustrated History*, who write: "Alexander had been out celebrating his second series victory and now sat in the bull pen, nursing a hangover," 176.

93. Robinson, *Matty*, 206.

94. Ibid., 215.

95. Again, Ol' Pete is in contrast to Mathewson who is buried with his wife, Jane, and son, John Christopher. Christy Jr. had his own set of life tragedies and died on August 16, 1950 (just a few months before Alexander) as a result of a gas explosion at his home near San Antonio, Texas. He was forty-four. See Robinson, *Matty*, 224–25.

Alexander is now honored in St. Paul with the Grover Cleveland Alexander Ballpark and by "Grover Cleveland Alexander Days," held each year on the weekend following July 4 and which were "developed as a way to honor a local hero." The "tourism" segment of the St. Paul Web site describes these as "a three-day celebration [that] includes a talent show, sporting activities, sidewalk sale, car show, street dance, sidewalk vendors, children's games and a variety of other activities, provided at low or no-cost so that families may enjoy a fun time in St. Paul." Families now may celebrate in St. Paul and honor a hero whose own family life was less than celebratory. See http://www.esu10.org/~stpaul/grover.htm. Alexander joins Dazzy Vance, Sam Crawford, Bob Gibson, and Richie Ashburn in St. Paul's "Museum of Nebraska Baseball Greats." A likeness of Alex for children to color is found in the Kids! Stuff section of the Nebraska history Web site: http://www.nebraskahistory.org/oversite/kidstuff/alexandr.htm.

96. Cited by Bob Broeg in the Foreword to Kavanagh, *Ol' Pete*, xv. In this respect, again we see contrasts between Alexander and Mathewson. Matty's character as a multidimensional hero is celebrated by a one-man stage play that still runs while Alexander's "heroism" is limited to his baseball exploits alone.

97. See the comments on Alexander in Joseph Wallace, Neil Hamilton, and Marty Appel, *Baseball: 100 Classic Moments in the History of the Game* (New York: Dorling Kindersley, 2000). After extolling Alexander's greatness, the authors note: "Yet Alexander's prickly personality and well-publicized off-the-field exploits—including an ongoing battle with alcoholism—kept the fans at a distance. It also contributed to his being traded several times in his career, rare for such a great talent at that time. In fact, today he might be remembered more for his failings than for his successes, if not for his spectacular performance with the St. Louis Cardinals during the 1926 World Series, when no one expected anything from him." 62.

98. George F. Will, "The First Michael Jordan: And Before DiMaggio, There Was Christy Mathewson," *Newsweek*, 133, 12 (March 22, 1999): 61. The writer Gilbert Patten, under the name of Burt L. Standish, had created the fictitious character Frank Merriwell, who captured the imagination of millions from 1896 to 1914 as a transcendent, athletic saint whose exploits were chronicled in *Tip Top Weekly*, the most popular five-cent novel of the time. Will writes that "by 1914 Mathewson had become Merriwell." Cf. Robinson, *Matty*, 6–7 and also the fine account with wonderful pictures in Jonathan Yardley, "Pitcher: The Real Frank Merriwell," in *The Ultimate Baseball Book*, eds. Daniel Okrent and Harris Lewine, with Historical Text by David Nemec (Boston: Houghton Mifflin Co., 2000), 65–80.

99. See the essays above by Christopher Evans: "Baseball as Civil Religion: The Genesis of an American Creation Story" and "The Kingdom of Baseball in America: A Chronicle of an American Theology."

100. Honig, *Baseball America*, 153.

101. Cited in Ward and Burns, 175.

102. Honig, *Baseball America*, 153. In nearly five thousand innings of pitching, Mathewson was never ejected from a ball game.

103. As "protector" of baseball, Commissioner Landis once dispatched a scout to retrieve Alex from Lancaster, Pennsylvania, when he was with the House of David. The evening before in Harrisburg he was too inebriated to play and "just lay on the bench drunk." See David Pietrusza, *Judge and Jury: The Life and Times of Judge Kenesaw Mountain Landis* (South Bend, Ind.: Diamond Communications, 1998), 386. When Alex was with the Cubs, he shared the roster with another notorious drinker, Hack Wilson. Manager Joe McCarthy, whom Alexander disliked, required unquestioning obedience to his authority and traded Alexander, believing that he was a bad influence on the younger players. McCarthy also drank, but unlike Alex, who sought the bar room, McCarthy drank in private. See Kavanagh, *Ol' Pete*, chap. 13 and Clifton Blue Parker, *Fouled Away: The Baseball Tragedy of Hack Wilson* (Jefferson, N.C.: McFarland and Co. Publishers, 2000), chap. 3. No one ever claimed that Alex's drinking affected his pitching. He committed his first—and only!—balk in his one-hundredth inning of pitching. He pitched 5,189 innings in his career.

104. In Christian theology, Jesus Christ is seen as the savior, sent by God to live and die and be resurrected from the dead by God's power. Jesus Christ brings forgiveness of human sin and enables a new life of meaning and obedience to emerge in a person's life by the power of the Holy Spirit at work within and among us.

105. Kavanagh, *Ol' Pete*, 109.

106. B. A. Gerrish, *Saving and Secular Faith: An Invitation to Systematic Theology* (Minneapolis: Fortress Press, 1999), 14.

107. Gerrish, *Saving and Secular Faith*, 20. Gerrish had described the work of the historian of religion, Wilfred Cantwell Smith (b. 1916) as seeing faith as "a universally human phenomenon that need not take explicit or conventional religious form. . . . Faith defines the generically human: humans are beings who are open to transcendence and, as such, find meaning in the world and in their own lives, whether they identify themselves with a religious tradition or not. The opposite of faith is then, not disbelief in some proposition or other, but the loss of order, meaning, and purposes—in a word, nihilism." 19.

108. Gerrish, *Saving Faith and Secular Faith*, 21.

109. Ibid., 33.

110. See the story told below by William R. Herzog II in "From Scapegoat to Icon: The Strange Journey of Shoeless Joe Jackson."

111. This accords with a T-shirt sometimes seen: "Life is Baseball. The Rest Is Details."

112. From the baseball side, writer Thomas Boswell makes a remarkably similar point in his delightful essay, "Why Time Begins on Opening Day":

> In contrast to the unwieldy world which we hold in common, baseball offers a kingdom built to human scale. Its problems and

questions are exactly our size. Here we may come when we feel a need for a rooted point of reference. In much the same way, we take a long hike or look for hard work when we suspect what's bothering us is either too foolish or too serious to permit a solution.

Baseball isn't necessarily an escape from reality, though it can be; it's merely one of our many refuges *within* the real where we try to create a sense of order on our own terms. Born to an age where horror has become commonplace, where tragedy has, by its monotonous repetition, become a parody of sorrow, we need to fence off a few parks where humans try to be fair, where skill has some hope of reward, where absurdity has a harder time than usual getting a ticket.

Thomas Boswell, *Why Time Begins on Opening Day* (New York: Penguin Books, 1984), 288. In continuing to blend the language of religion and baseball in this essay, Boswell even provides "a preliminary Ten Commandments of the Dugout," 292–95.

Chapter 4

1. I am indebted to Edwin Mellen Press for permission to reprint this article, which was originally published in an abbreviated form in my book *Hemingway's Debt to Baseball in* The Old Man and the Sea: *A Collection of Critical Readings* (Lewiston: Edwin Mellen Press, 1992).
2. Ernest Hemingway, *The Old Man and the Sea* (New York: Charles Scribner's Sons, 1952), 9. Hereafter referred to as Hemingway.
3. Hemingway, 17–18.
4. Robert N. Broadus, "The New Record Set by Hemingway's Old Man," in *News and Queries* 10 N.S. (April 1963): 153.
5. John Halverson, "Christian Resonance in *The Old Man and the Sea*," in *English Language Notes* (1964): 52.
6. Edward H. Strauch, "*The Old Man and the Sea*: A Numerological View," in *The Aligarth Journal of English Studies* 6.1 (1981): 89–100.
7. Hemingway, 21.
8. Hemingway, 16.
9. Hemingway, 66.
10. Broadus, 153.
11. Ibid.
12. Grey's remarks first appeared in *Tales of Tahitian Waters* in 1931 and were reprinted in 1952 by Ed Zern in *Adventures in Fishing*, "an anthology of sorts, collected from Grey's books about fishing" (Broadus, 153). Zern, noting that many of Grey's records had in fact been broken in recent years, assures the reader that "It's unlikely, though, that anyone has yet surpassed his record of eighty-three straight days without a fish" (Zane Grey, *Adventures in Fishing*. New York: Harper, 1931), 199. Whether or not Hemingway read and remembered Grey's account of 1931, he could not have known Zern's collection of Grey's work.

Adventures in Fishing appeared late in 1952, several months after Hemingway's novel was published.

13. James Hinkle's support of Broadus's claim is misleading (see Hinkle, "Some Unexpected Sources for *The Sun Also Rises*," in *The Hemingway Review* 2.1 [Fall 1982]:26–42). Neither Hemingway's letter to T. Aitken in 1936 stating "I want to best him [Grey] but I don't want any bitterness about it" (see Matthew Bruccoli and C. E. Frazer Clark Jr., *Hemingway at Auction, 1930–1973*, Detroit: Gale Research Co., 1973, 81), nor Dos Passos's statement that Hemingway "wanted to go Zane Grey one better" (see *The Best Times*, New York: The American Library, 1966, 211) refers to Grey's "eighty three days . . . without catching a fish" as Hinkle seems to suggest.

14. Hemingway, 17.

15. William Adair, "Eighty-five as a Lucky Number: A Note on *The Old Man and the Sea*," in *Notes on Contemporary Literature* 8.1 (1978): 9.

16. Joseph Waldmeir, "'Confiteor Hominem:' Ernest Hemingway's Religion of Man." *Papers of the Michigan Academy of Science, Arts and Letters* 42 (1957): 349–56. Included in Carlos Baker, ed., *Ernest Hemingway: Critiques of Four Major Novels*, (New York: Charles Scribner's Sons, 1969), 144–49, quotation from page 145.

17. Halverson, 50.

18. The date of the novel's composition has been debated [see, for example, Darrel Mansell's "When Did Ernest Hemingway Write *The Old Man and the Sea*?" in *Fitzgerald/Hemingway Annual 1974*: (311–24)]. Baker indicates, however, that Hemingway "after the holiday hubbub [of late December 1950 and early January 1951] began to tell the story of the old Cuban fisherman and the giant marlin that Carlos Gutiérrez had told him in 1935." See "On the Blue Water," in *Esquire* 5 (April 1936): 31, 184–85. "By January 17th, his manuscript stood at 6000 words, about a quarter of the whole. . . . Working like a bulldozer, averaging a thousand words a day for sixteen days . . . by February 17th it stood virtually finished" (see *Ernest Hemingway: A Life Story*, New York: Charles Scribner's Sons, 1969, 489–90). Drawn from the recently completed season, many of Hemingway's references to baseball were only several months old. For a detailed account of the novel's historical background, see "The Facts Behind the Fiction: The 1950 American League Pennant Race and *The Old Man and the Sea*" in *Hemingway's Debt to Baseball in* The Old Man and the Sea.

19. Halverson, 50–51.

20. Halverson, 51.

21. Ibid., 52.

22. Strauch, 89.

23. Leo Gurko, "The Heroic Impulse in *The Old Man and the Sea*," in *English Journal* 44 (1955):377–82.

24. Strauch, 96.

25. Ibid.

26. Ibid., 93.
27. Ibid., 97.
28. Ibid., 90–91.
29. Ibid., 97.
30. See, especially, Joseph M. Flora's "Biblical Allusion in *The Old Man and the Sea*," in *Studies in Short Fiction* 10 (1973): 143–47.
31. Strauch, 98.
32. C. Harold Hurley, "The Facts Behind the Fiction: The 1950 American League Pennant Race and *The Old Man and the Sea* in C. Harold Hurley, ed., *Hemingway's Debt to Baseball in* The Old Man and the Sea: *A Collection of Critical Readings*, 77–93.
33. Hemingway at this point alters the facts slightly. Although the Yankees indeed lost to the Indians as Manolin reports, the game was played on the night of Tuesday, September 12, not during the day, as called for in the story.
34. Hemingway, 67–68.
35. Hemingway, 17.
36. The Yankees, with an 84–49 record, began the week of September 10 in second place, one-half game behind the Tigers and one-half game ahead of third-place Boston. The Indians were seven games back. By winning six of eight games during that crucial week, the Yankees finished the span with a slim half-game edge over the Tigers and a two-game lead over the Red Sox. In a week that saw the American League leadership change hands no fewer than five times, Joe DiMaggio hit six home runs, drove in his hundredth run of the season, and raised his batting average from .287 to .297.

    Building on my original findings, Bickford Sylvester, in "The Cuban Context of *The Old Man and the Sea*" (found in Scott Donaldson, ed., *The Cambridge Companion to Ernest Hemingway*, Cambridge: Cambridge University Press, 1966) reveals the magnitude of DiMaggio's outsized accomplishment on his record-breaking day in noting that the Yankees' great outfielder recorded a perfectly statistical game of four at-bats, four hits, four runs, and four runs-batted-in (248).
37. Richard Ben Cramer in *Joe DiMaggio: The Hero's Life* (New York: Simon and Schuster, 2000), 291, wrongly places DiMaggio's three home runs in Griffith Stadium on September 12, 1950.
38. Hemingway, 43.
39. Ibid., 32.
40. Ibid., 13.
41. Ibid., 14.
42. Claire Rosenfield's observation about the old fisherman's regard for the number eighty-five merits note: "To remember the ancient tie in archaic religions between games of chance and divination is to understand this old man's prelogical desire that his disciple 'buy a terminal of the lottery with an eightyfive.'" See "New World, Old Myths" in Katherine T. Jobes, ed., *Twentieth Century Interpretations of "The Old Man and the Sea": A*

Collection of Critical Essays. Englewood Cliffs, N.J.: Prentice-Hall, 1968, 41–55.

43. Hemingway, 64–65.
44. Ibid., 65.
45. Ibid., 103.
46. Ibid., 66.
47. Ibid., 68.
48. Philip Young, *Ernest Hemingway: A Reconsideration* (University Park: Pennsylvania University Press, 1966), 130.
49. Hemingway, 103.
50. In the novel, Hemingway refers directly or indirectly to the following major-league players and managers: Joe DiMaggio (844), Leo Durocher (859), Mike Gonzalez (928), Adolpho Luque (1774-75), John J. McGraw (1138–39), Dick Sisler (1330–31), and George Sisler (1331). For a statistical overview of their careers, see the pages cited parenthetically above after each player's name in *The Baseball Encyclopedia, Bicentennial Edition: The Complete and Official Record of Major League Baseball*. 3rd ed. (New York: Macmillan, 1976).
51. Hemingway, 63.
52. Ibid., 22.
53. Ibid., 21.
54. Ibid., 104.
55. Hemingway, 68. Carlos Baker is mistaken in his belief that even then the great DiMaggio was suffering from a bone spur (*Writer as Artist*, 305, n. 28). George Monteiro, although aware that DiMaggio had recovered from the painful right heel by the middle of the preceding season, is also mistaken in his belief that "it is essential to Hemingway's handling of the theme of endurance that Santiago not know of this [recovery]" ("Santiago," 277). But Santiago, as we have seen, has carefully followed DiMaggio's progress in the newspapers and for reasons of his own purposely sets himself in competition with the ailing ballplayer.
56. Hemingway, 104.
57. Ibid., 126.
58. Michael Reynolds, "Hemingway as American Icon" in Frederick Voss, ed., *Picturing Hemingway: A Writer in His Time* (New Haven, Conn.: Yale University Press, 1999), 9.

Chapter 5

1. If it were proper to dedicate this essay, I would dedicate it to Donald Gropman, whose pioneering work on Joe Jackson made this work, and the work of many others, possible. I owe him a debt of gratitude. This essay is one way of repaying a small portion of it.
2. This summary of Jackson's life is based on two works: Harvey Frommer, *Shoeless Joe and Ragtime Baseball* (Dallas: Taylor Publishing Co., 1992) and Donald Gropman, *Say It Ain't So, Joe: The True Story of Shoeless Joe Jackson*, 2d rev. ed. (Secaucus, N.J.: Citadel Press, 1999).

3. John Thorn, Pete Palmer, and Michael Gershman, eds., *Total Baseball,* 7th edition (Kingston, N.Y.: Total Sports Publishing, 2001), 882.

4. See Eliot Asinof, *Eight Men Out: The Black Sox and the 1919 World Series* (New York: Henry Holt & Co., 1963). The eight men were as follows: Chick Gandil, first baseman; Swede Risberg, shortstop; Oscar "Happy" Felsch, center field; Fred McMullin, utility player; Eddie Cicotte, pitcher; Claude "Lefty" Williams, pitcher; Buck Weaver, third base; and Joe Jackson, left field.

5. Ken Burns and Lynn Novick, producers. "The Third Inning: The Faith of Fifty Million People" in *Baseball: A Film by Ken Burns.* Florentine Films and WETA-TV, 1994.

6. Ken Burns, Prologue to *Baseball: A Film by Ken Burns.* Florentine Films and WETA-TV, 1994.

7. Ken Burns, *Baseball.* "The Third Inning: The Faith of Fifty Million People." Section titled "An Awful Thing to Do." The quotation is from Hugh Fullerton's article in *The New York Evening World,* September 30, 1920.

8. Quoted in Donald Gropman, *Say It Ain't So, Joe! The True Story of Shoeless Joe Jackson,* 2d rev. ed. (Secaucus, N.J.: Citadel Press, 1999), 97.

9. In addition to being found in the film, this remark is found in the companion volume, Geoffrey C. Ward and Ken Burns, *Baseball: An Illustrated History* (New York: Alfred A. Knopf, 1994), 138.

10. Harold Seymour, *Baseball: The Golden Age* (New York: Oxford University Press, 1971), 302–303.

11. *New York Times,* September 29, 1920, 2.

12. Copies of Jackson's Grand Jury testimony can be found in Harvey Frommer, *Shoeless Joe and Ragtime Baseball* (Dallas: Taylor Publishing Co., 1992), 191–215, and in Donald Gropman, *Say It Ain't So, Joe,* 256–76.

13. The 1919 *New York Times* provides a pitch-by-pitch description of the game. I have studied each incident in which Jackson handled a play. There is no hint of his slowing down to let a runner take an extra base or missing a cutoff throw. His arm kept runners from taking an extra base.

14. Though there is no space to report the results in detail, I have studied each instance in which Jackson handled the baseball. There is no hint in the contemporary descriptions of his slowing down or making an odd play in the field. He had opportunities to do so, especially on balls hit down the left-field line, but his arm held runners to singles and did not allow them to take an extra base.

15. Ibid., October 5, 1919.

16. Ibid., October 5, 1919.

17. This point is emphasized by Gropman, op. cit., 193–94.

18. Arnold "Chick" Gandil as told to Melvin Durslag, "This Is My Story of the Black Sox Series," in *Sports Illustrated.* September 7, 1956: 62–68.

19. Shoeless Joe Jackson as told to Furman Bisher, "This Is the Truth." *Sport Magazine.* October 1949: 12–14, 83–84, 14.

20. ESPN.com: Shoeless Joe in the 1919 Series (6.11.99), 5.
21. The alert reader will note the slight discrepancy between my numbers and those cited by the ESPN Web site. I have based my numbers on an at-bat by at-bat analysis of the World Series as printed in *The New York Times* from October 1919.
22. *New York Times,* October 3, 1919.
23. The reason Jackson's five runs and six RBIs account for only ten of the twenty runs that the White Sox scored is that his home run counts as a run scored and an RBI even though it is only one run.
24. See Victor Luhrs, *The Great Baseball Mystery: The 1919 World's Series* (New York: A. S. Barnes and Co., 1966).
25. *New York Times,* September 30, 1919.
26. Joe Jackson as told to Furman Bisher, "This Is the Truth," in *Sport Magazine.* October 1949, 14.
27. Quoted in Burns and Ward, *Baseball,* 143–44.
28. David Pietrusza, *Judge and Jury: The Life and Times of Judge Kenesaw Mountain Landis* (South Bend, Ind.: Diamond Communications, 1998), 187.
29. Burns and Ward, *Baseball,* 145.
30. Ken Burns, *Baseball: A Documentary.* "The Third Inning: An Awful Thing to Do."
31. The information about Comiskey is available in any study of the scandal. See, for example, Asinof, *Eight Men Out,* 20–22.
32. Chick Gandil, "This Is My Story of the Black Sox Series," in *Sports Illustrated.* September 7, 1956, 62.
33. Asinof, *Eight Men Out,* 20.
34. The chronology that follows is my own, based on an analysis of several reconstructions, such as those of Asinof, Gropman, Seymour, Gandil, and Thompson and Boswell, as well as my effort to coordinate these reconstructions with the White Sox actual schedule. It is clear that the proposed reconstructions have not made an adequate effort to correlate events with the White Sox schedule and travels. The Hall of Fame Library was kind enough to furnish me with a 1919 schedule, which I confirmed by following the White Sox in the daily *New York Times* from July 15 through September 28, the final day of the season. My reconstruction assumes that traveling teams left town by train directly after the final game of a series was played. This information is also courtesy of Mr. Eric Enders of the Hall of Fame Library staff.
35. According to *Total Baseball,* 7th edition, 1372, Burns pitched for Washington (AL, 1908–1909), Chicago (AL, 1909–1910), Cincinnati (NL, 1910–1911), Philadelphia (NL, 1911), and Detroit (AL, 1912). His lifetime record was 30–52.
36. Chick Gandil, "This Is My Story," in *Sports Illustrated.* September 7, 1956, 64.
37. See Gropman, *Say It Ain't So, Joe,* 164–65.
38. Ibid., 165.

39. *New York Times,* July 20, 1921, front page.
40. See the excerpt from Williams's testimony in Gropman, *Say It Ain't So, Joe,* 226.
41. Ibid., 169.
42. See Donald Gropman, *Say It Ain't So, Joe,* 169–71, 197–98, who makes the same point.
43. Ibid., 169–70. See also Jackson's comments in Harvey Frommer, *Shoeless Joe and Ragtime Baseball* (Dallas: Taylor Publishing Co., 1992), 96.

    "I never said anything about it until the night before the Series started. I went to Mr. Comiskey and begged him to take me out of the lineup. . . . If there was something going on I knew the bench would be the safest place, but he wouldn't listen to me."

44. Joe Jackson as told to Furman Bisher, "This Is the Truth," in *Sport Magazine.* October 1949, 14.
45. Asinof, *Eight Men Out,* 58–59.
46. Joe Jackson as told to Furman Bisher, "This Is the Truth," in *Sport Magazine.* October 1949, 14.
47. Asinof, *Eight Men Out,* 74–77.
48. Harold Seymour, *Baseball: The Golden Age,* 299.
49. Asinof, *Eight Men Out,* 77.
50. Joe Jackson, "This Is the Truth," in *Sport Magazine.* October 1949, 12.
51. David Pietrusza, *Judge and Jury,* 173.
52. Harold Seymour, *Baseball: The Golden Age,* 323.
53. Donald Gropman, *Say It Ain't So, Joe,* 171–72.
54. Ibid., 192.
55. Ibid., 226–27.
56. Ibid., 172.
57. A note on the $5,000. Neither Joe nor Katie believed the money was theirs. So they put it in savings and let it earn interest. After Katie's death, the money, which had grown through years with interest, was donated to the American Heart Fund and the American Cancer Society.
58. This information about the meeting between Comiskey and Gandil and Felsch is contained in Harry Grabiner's diaries and cited in Gropman.
59. For information on Comiskey's raises, see Robert F. Burk, *Never Just a Game: Players, Owners & American Baseball to 1920* (Chapel Hill: University of North Carolina Press, 1994), 233.
60. Donald Gropman, *Say It Ain't So, Joe,* 174–76.
61. The letters are reprinted in Gropman, *Say It Ain't So, Joe,* Appendix B, 275–84. The misspelled words reflect the original letter. Following Gropman, I have kept the original spellings in these citations.
62. Ibid., 178.
63. Ibid.
64. Chick Gandil, "This Is My Story of the Black Sox Series," in *Sports Illustrated.* September 7, 1956, 62.

65. Alan Dershowitz, "Introduction to the Revised Edition," in Gropman, *Say It Ain't So, Joe,* xx.
66. See Gropman, *Say It Ain't So, Joe,* 185–99.
67. Donald Gropman, *Say It Ain't So, Joe,* 196.
68. Ibid., 189.
69. *New York Times,* September 29, 1920.
70. Ibid.
71. *New York Times,* October 1, 1920.
72. Quoted in Gropman, *Say It Ain't So, Joe,* 201–202.
73. Joe Jackson, "This Is the Truth," in *Sport Magazine.* October 1949, 14.
74. Edward White, *Creating the National Pastime: Baseball Transforms Itself, 1903–1953* (Princeton, N.J.: Princeton University Press, 1996), 103.
75. Austrian was a partner in the predecessor firm, Mayer, Meyer, Austrian & Platt, the name by which the firm was known from 1908 to 1954. Letter of Frank D. Mayer Jr. to the Chicago Historical Society (October 19, 1988).
76. Harold Seymour, *Baseball: The Golden Age,* 307.
77. Ibid.
78. *Cleveland Plain Dealer,* January 10, 1929, and January 12, 1929.
79. Nims was a White Sox fan who had bet on the Sox to win the Series.
80. Harold Seymour, *Baseball: The Golden Age,* 326.
81. Short was appalled at the low salaries of the ballplayers. One of the revelations of the trial was how poorly Comiskey was paying his players.
82. Edward White, *Creating the National Pastime,* 92–93.
83. David Q. Voigt, *American Baseball: From the Commissioners to Continental Expansion* (University Park: Pennsylvania State University Press, 1983), 130.
84. Dom Helder Camara, *The Spiral of Violence* (London: Sheed and Ward, 1971).
85. James C. Scott, *Weapons of the Weak: Everyday Forms of Peasant Resistance* (New Haven, Conn.: Yale University Press), xvi.
86. David Q. Voigt, *American Baseball: From the Commissioners to Continental Expansion,* 130.
87. For a full description of the "blaming the victim" syndrome, see William Ryan, *Blaming the Victim,* revised, updated edition (New York: Vintage Books, 1976).
88. Joe Jackson, "This Is the Truth," in *Sport Magazine.* October 1949, 84.
89. Thomas K. Perry, "'Shoeless' of Mill Hill," in *Sandlapper.* Spring 1993, 35.
90. Joe Williams's column in the *Chicago Tribune.* September 30, 1959.
91. Joe Jackson, "This Is the Truth," in *Sport Magazine.* October 1949, 84.
92. The column is in the Joe Jackson file at the Hall of Fame Library. My copy at least is not dated.
93. Letter of July 20, 1989, to an unspecified fan. Letter found in Gropman, *Say It Ain't So, Joe,* 310 (Appendix J).
94. Letter of April 23, 1980, in Gropman, op. cit., 309.

95. Fay Vincent in the *Philadelphia Inquirer,* January 4, 2000. Article found in the Joe Jackson file at the Hall of Fame Library.
96. James C. Scott, *Weapons of the Weak,* xvii.
97. For an example of Landis's bias against Jackson, see Gropman, *Say It Ain't So, Joe,* 218–19.
98. Dan Foster, "Joe Jackson Case Re-raises Questions," in *Greenville News.* November 3, 1983.
99. Alan Dershowitz article in the *Boston Herald.* September 3, 1984.
100. René Girard, *The Girard Reader,* ed. James Williams (New York: Crossroad Herder, 1996), 76–78.
101. Richard Gaughran, "Saying It Ain't So: The Black Sox in Baseball Fiction," in *Cooperstown Symposium on Baseball and American Culture,* Alvin L. Hall, ed. (Westport, Conn.: Meckler Press with the State University of New York at Oneonta, 1990), 39.
102. Ibid., 45.
103. Williams's and Feller's petition is reprinted in Donald Gropman, *Say It Ain't So, Joe,* Appendix L, 315–30.
104. Alan Dershowitz article in the *Boston Herald.* September 3, 1984.
105. Donald Gropman, *Say It Ain't So, Joe,* 164.
106. W. P. Kinsella, *Shoeless Joe* (New York: Ballantine Books, 1982), 7.
107. Ibid., 6.
108. Ibid., 12.
109. See note 25.
110. James C. Scott, *Weapons of the Weak: Everyday Forms of Peasant Resistance,* 178.

Chapter 6

1. Jules Tygiel, *Baseball's Great Experiment*: *Jackie Robinson and His Legacy* (New York: Oxford University Press, 1983), 9.
2. Ibid., 15.
3. According to Tygiel, "White indifference, rather than fan hostility, posed the principle obstacle to integration." Ibid., 34.
4. Arthur Mann, *Branch Rickey: American in Action* (Boston: Houghton Mifflin, 1957), 214.
5. Major League Committee (Ford Frick, Sam Breadon, Philip Wrigley, William Harridge, L. S. MacPhail, Thomas A. Yawkey), "Report to the National and American Leagues," (27 August, 1946), 18. This document and the discussion that took place were never made available to the press at the time; their existence was denied. The document was discovered among the papers of Commissioner A. B. ("Happy") Chandler. While I discovered this document in the Branch Rickey file at the Baseball Hall of Fame's Research Library in Cooperstown, excerpts are also available in *The Jackie Robinson Reader,* ed. Jules Tygiel (New York: Penguin Books, 1997), 129–33.
6. Ironically, the last club integrated by race was the Boston Red Sox in 1959. The owner of the club, Tom Yawkey, was a member of the

committee who recommended the integration of baseball take a more gradual approach.

7. Jackie Robinson, *I Never Had It Made: An Autobiography as Told to Alfred Duckett* (Hopewell, N.J.: Ecco Press, 1995), xxii.
8. Quoted in Harvey Frommer, *Rickey and Robinson* (New York: Macmillan Publishing, 1982), 115.
9. Quoted in David Falkner, *Great Time Coming: The Life of Jackie Robinson from Baseball to Birmingham* (New York: Simon & Schuster, 1995), 134. Arthur Mann writes later, "No one could question his desire to win, or to make victory paramount, or his right to win with any kind of eligible player. He never spoke of social consequences. He had firm beliefs about the equality of man, but they were never a factor in his decision. The sole issue was a colored player's ability to play organized baseball." Mann, 217. One black newspaper, however, characterized Rickey as "a deeply religious man with the fire of the crusader burning in his breast." Quoted in Bill L. Weaver, "The Black Press and the Assault on Professional Baseball's Color Line, October, 1945–April, 1947," *Phylon*, vol. XL, no. 4 (Winter 1979), 306.
10. Falkner, 107–108.
11. Mann, 2.
12. John C. Chalberg, *Rickey and Robinson: The Preacher, the Player, and America's Game* (Wheeling, Ill.: Harlan Davidson, Inc., 2000), 39. See also, "Interview with Carl Erskine," Jackie Robinson Society, January 2001 (http://www.utexas.edu/students/jackie/robinson/erskine.html).
13. Tygiel, 1983, 49.
14. Arthur Mann notes, "Branch Rickey knew the Bible before he could say the words." Mann, 8.
15. Ibid., 11.
16. Chalberg, 30.
17. Ibid., 25.
18. Tygiel, 1983, 52.
19. Chalberg, 25.
20. Quoted in Tygiel, 1983, 48.
21. Quoted in Falkner, 105.
22. Dan W. Dodson, "The Integration of Negroes in Baseball," in *The Jackie Robinson Reader,* 156.
23. Thorn and Tygiel claim that Rickey's original intent was to integrate baseball with several players at once. However, political forces beyond his control forced Rickey to go with Robinson alone. Yet even had the original plan been successful, Thorn and Tygiel note that Robinson was the central figure in the effort. See John Thorn and Jules Tygiel, "Jackie Robinson's Signing: The Untold Story," in *The Jackie Robinson Reader,* 81–93.
24. Tygiel, 1983, 58.
25. Quoted in Chalberg, 101.
26. Ibid., 102.

27. See Falkner, 24–25.
28. Arnold Ampersand, *Jackie Robinson: A Biography* (New York: Ballantine Publishing, 1997), 25.
29. Robinson, 8–9.
30. Ibid., 23.
31. See Ampersand, 23.
32. Falkner notes one other formative influence on Robinson at Camp Hood, where he was assigned to the 761st Tank Battalion. This was an all-black tank unit whose role it was to provide the training for white antitank units. They were a very proud group and worked hard to ensure that they did their best. They often got the upper hand of the white units, causing many to fail their final test. Falkner notes that, through his leadership role in this unit, Robinson gained strength and pride as a leader. More important, "this brief membership in an all-black fighting unit that had answered prejudice with performance was one of the genuinely formative experiences he had just prior to his breaking baseball's color barrier." Falkner, 76.
33. I have drawn this account of the meeting from three sources noted previously. See Robinson (31–34), Tygiel (1983, 59–67), and Mann (222–23).
34. Giovanni Papini, *Life of Christ*, freely translated from the Italian by Dorothy Canfield Fisher (New York: Harcourt, Brace & Co., 1923), 106.
35. Ibid., 107.
36. Glen Stassen, *Just Peacemaking: Transforming Initiatives for Justice and Peace* (Louisville, Ky.: Westminster/John Knox Press, 1992), 64.
37. Ibid., 70.
38. Dan W. Dodson, "The Integration of Negroes in Baseball," in *The Jackie Robinson Reader*, 164.
39. Tygiel, 1983, 63.
40. Robinson, 33.
41. Many, including Robinson's daughter, contend that holding in his anger contributed to the health problems that would later emerge and lead to an early death for Robinson. See Sharon Robinson, *Stealing Home: An Intimate Family Portrait* (New York: HarperCollins, 1996), 16.
42. Papini, 108, 144.
43. Quoted in Falkner, 169.
44. Quoted in Falkner, 144.
45. Quoted in Mann, 218.
46. Red Barber with Robert Creamer, "He Did Far More for Me . . ." in *The Jackie Robinson Reader,* 53–63.
47. Tygiel, 1983, 103–104.
48. Ibid.
49. Quoted in Robinson, 49.
50. Ibid., 53.
51. Harold Parrott, "The Betrayal of Robinson," in *The Jackie Robinson Reader,* 141–42.
52. Falkner, 148.
53. Robinson, xxi.

54. Quoted in Robinson, 53.
55. Quoted in Falkner, 179.
56. These and other decisions made by Rickey that had potential negative economic effects lead me to conclude that Rickey's motive for integration was not primarily financial.
57. As a result, these towns were crucified by the media and press from the North, which seems to have made an impact on indifferent whites in northern cities and towns. See Tygiel, 1983, 112.
58. Dodson, 165.
59. See story in *Michigan Chronicle*, Saturday, May 17, 1958, 14. I found a copy of this story in the Branch Rickey file at the Research Library of Baseball's Hall of Fame in Cooperstown.
60. These statements come from the Branch Rickey papers at the Library of Congress and are quoted in Stephen Fox, "The Education of Branch Rickey," in *Civilization*, September/October 1995, 52–57. A copy of this essay is available in the Branch Rickey file at the Research Library of Baseball's Hall of Fame in Cooperstown.
61. Robinson, 265.
62. Falkner, 348.
63. Ibid., ix.
64. Tygiel, 1983, 9.
65. Quoted in Jim Armstrong, "A Century of Sport: Oppressed knock down door to success," in *Denver Post*, March 28, 1999, 2.
66. It is ironic that Robinson claimed later in life, "As much as I loved him, I never would have made a good soldier in Martin's army. My reflexes aren't conditioned to accept nonviolence in the face of violence-provoking attacks." Robinson, 211. His own demonstration of such non-violent resistance in the face of verbal and physical abuse was one source of inspiration for King to do the same. King acknowledged his debt to Robinson. When he once came to a point where he wanted to turn back, King told one of his aides that Jackie Robinson was his inspiration to keep going. "Jackie Robinson made it possible for me in the first place," said King. "Without him, I would never have been able to do what I did." Quoted in Falkner, 237.
67. Cornel West in his foreword to Jackie Robinson's autobiography, *I Never Had It Made*, ix.
68. Quoted in Falkner, 263.
69. Tygiel, 1983, 9.
70. Cited in an editorial by Roger Thurow, "Thrown for a Curve," in *Wall Street Journal*, August 28, 1998, A6.
71. Robinson, 259.
72. See Gerald Early, "American Integration, Black Heroism, and the Meaning of Jackie Robinson," in *Chronicle of Higher Education*, May 23, 1997, B4–B5.
73. Thurow, A6.
74. While baseball has changed, we have to note with Robinson that base-

ball, although it "poses as a sacred institution dedicated to the public good," is still a business, "a big, selfish business." Robinson, 259.

75. The baseball coach at Dunbar High School in Baltimore (known for its basketball program) contends that baseball was losing black kids. Many times he would forfeit games because kids were not interested. See story in John Eisenberg, "Baseball losing its grip on the black community," in *The Sunday Observer-Dispatch,* June 23, 1991, 6D.

76. Robinson, 259. Major-league baseball is making some effort to provide baseball opportunities for inner-city black youth. Their RBI (Reviving Baseball in Inner Cities) program that began in 1989 now has 100,000 kids involved, and its World Series is held at Disney World. While National League President Coleman notes that such efforts at reintegrating the baseball fan "takes focus, commitment," it is not clear whether justice or economics is the driving force behind baseball's efforts.

77. Robinson, 265–66.

Chapter 7

1. Recreational sport in the English colonies was not common. Indeed, sport and games were a questionable activity among Puritans. While people did engage in relaxing activities within the colonies, men—perhaps as an extension of their hunting privileges—had more opportunities for play than had women. Refer to Bruce C. Daniels, *Puritans at Play: Leisure and Recreation in Colonial New England* (New York: St. Martin's Griffin, 1995), especially chap. 9, "Men Frolic by Themselves: Sport and Games in Male Culture," 163–84.

2. For a select overview of the early history of baseball, refer to the following works: Peter Bjarkman, ed., *Baseball and the Game of Ideas: Essays for the Serious Fan* (Delhi, N.Y.: Birch Brook Press, 1993); Stephanie L. Twin, *Out of the Bleachers: Writings on Women and Sport* (Old Westbury, N.Y.: Feminist Press and McGraw-Hill, 1979); J. A. Mangan and Roberta J. Park, *From "Fair Sex" to Feminism: Sport and the Socialization of Women in the Industrial and Post-Industrial Eras* (London: Frank Cass and Co., Ltd., 1987); David Q. Voigt, *America Through Baseball* (Chicago: Nelson-Hall, 1976).

3. Steven A. Riess, *Touching Base: Professional Baseball and American Culture in the Progressive Era* (Westport, Conn.: Greenwood Press, 1980) writes that baseball came to be "viewed as an edifying institution which taught traditional nineteenth-century frontier qualities, such as courage, honesty, individualization, patience, and temperance, as well as certain contemporary values, like teamwork" (13). Refer also to Colin Howell, "A Manly Sport: Baseball and the Construction of Masculinity" in *Gender and History in Canada,* Joy Parr and Mark Rosengfeld, eds. (Toronto: Copp Clark Ltd., 1996).

4. Refer to Debra A. Dagavarian, *Saying It Ain't So: American Values as Revealed in Children's Baseball Stories, 1880–1950* (New York: Peter

Lang Publishing, 1987), especially 136. Sheldon's story was originally published in *St. Nicholas,* October 1882.

5. Refer to William T. Ellis, *"Billy" Sunday: The Man and His Message,* (Toronto: McClelland, Goodchild and Steward, 1914), especially chap. 3, "A Base-ball 'Star,'" 33–38, and chap. 18, "Help Those Women," 231–48. For an examination of the relationship of Fundamentalism and manly Christianity to understandings of women refer to Betty A. DeBerg, *Ungodly Women: Gender and the First Wave of American Fundamentalism.* (Minneapolis: Fortress Press, 1990).

6. On women and baseball, refer to Gai Ingham Berlage, *Women in Baseball: The Forgotten History* (Westport, Conn.: Praeger, 1994); Barbara Gregorich, *Women at Play: The Story of Women in Baseball* (San Diego: Harcourt, Brace Javonovich, 1993); and Debra A. Shattuck, "Bats, Balls and Books: Baseball and Higher Education for Women at Three Eastern Women's Colleges, 1866–1891" in *Journal of Sport History,* vol. 19, 2, 1992: 91–109. See also *Baseball Girls,* a video written and directed by Lois Siegal, produced by Silva Basmajian (National Film Board of Canada, 1995, 82 minutes), which utilizes historical and contemporary footage.

7. On physiological arguments regarding women, refer to Carroll Smith-Rosenberg and Charles Roseberg, "The Female Animal: Medical and Biological Views of Women and Their Role in Nineteenth-Century America" in *From "Fair Sex" to Feminism,* Mangan and Park, eds., 13–37. For more general discussion, refer to Carole A. Oglesby, ed., *Women and Sport: From Myth to Reality* (Philadelphia: Lea and Febiger, 1978); and Helen Lenskyj, *Out of Bounds: Women, Sport, and Sexuality* (Toronto: Women's Press, 1986).

8. Berlage, *Women in Baseball,* chap. 3, "Women's Own Semi-Professional and Professional Baseball Teams in the Late 1800s and Early 1900s," 25–44.

9. Refer to Frances Willard's classic treatise, *How I Learned to Ride the Bicycle: Reflections of An Influential 19th Century Woman* (Sunnyvale, Calif.: Fair Oaks Publishing Co., 1991 [1895]), on the liberating effects of cycling for women. Helen Lenskyj, "Physical Activity for Canadian Women, 1890–1930: Media Views," 208–31 in *From "Fair Sex" to Feminism,* Mangan and Park, eds.

10. Barbara Welter, "The Cult of True Womanhood: 1820–1860," 224–50 in *The American Family in Social-Historical Perspective,* Michael Gordono, ed. (New York: St. Martin's Press, 1973); Lenskyj, *Out of Bounds,* 66f.

11. Catherine Rondina and Joseph Romain, *Ladies Day: One Woman's Guide to Pro Baseball* (Toronto: Warwick Publishing, 1997), i.

12. Voigt, *America Through Baseball,* 20f.

13. Berlage, *Women in Baseball,* xiii.

14. Ellen W. Gerber, Jan Felshin, Pearl Berlin, and Waneen Wyrick, *The American Woman in Sport* (Reading, Mass.: Addison-Wesley Publishing Co., 1974), 39f; Lynne Emery, "From Lowell Mills to the Halls of Fame: Industrial League Sport for Women," chap. 7, 107–19 in *Women and*

Sport: Interdisciplinary Perspectives, D. Margaret and Sharon R. Guthrie, eds. (Champaign, Ill.: Human Kinetics, 1994).

15. Berlage, *Women in Baseball,* 134.

16. On the AAGPBL, refer to Mary Pratt, "The All-American Girls' Professional Baseball League," in *Women and Sport: Issues and Controversies,* Greta L. Cohen, ed. (Newbury Park, Calif.: Sage Publications, 1993), 49–58; Susan E. Johnson, When Women Played Hardball (Seattle: Seal Press, 1994); W. C. Madden, *The Women of the All-American Girls' Professional Baseball League: A Biographical Dictionary* (Jefferson, N.C.: McFarland and Co., 1997). Penny Marshall's film, *A League of Their Own,* provides an entertaining and loosely historically accurate depiction of the league.

17. Refer to Berlage, *Women in Baseball,* chap. 7, "Women in the Negro Leagues: Effa Manley, Owner, and Toni Stone, Player," 117–32. Lois Siegel's *Baseball Girls* includes an interview with pitcher Mannie "Peanut" Johnson, who simply wasn't allowed to try out for the AAGPBL. When Toni Stone's contract was sold to the Kansas City Monarchs, the Indianapolis Clowns replaced her with Johnson and infielder Connie Morgen.

18. Quote in Siegel, *Baseball Girls.* The victory song was written by two players, La Vonne "Pepper" Paire-Davis and Nalda "Bird" Phillips. Refer to William Humbar, Appendix B, "Canadian Women in the AAGPBL, 1943–1954," in *Diamonds of the North: A Concise History of Baseball in Canada* (Toronto: Oxford University Press, 1995), 198–200.

19. *The Rules of Conduct and Charm School Guide*—plus numerous articles, player sketches, and overview of the league—are online at http://www.aagpbl.org.

20. Siegel, *Baseball Girls.*

21. Madden, *The AAGPBL: A Biographical Dictionary,* 60f.

22. G. Edward White, *Creating the National Pastime: Baseball Transforms Itself, 1903–1953* (Princeton, N.J.: Princeton University Press, 1996), 349, no. 1.

23. Robert McAfee Brown, "Theology and Baseball" in *Christianity and Crisis* (1958), vol. 18, no. 13: 107.

24. Michael A. Messner, "Ah, Ya Throw Like a Girl!", 28–32 in *Sex, Violence and Power in Sports: Rethinking Masculinity,* Michael A. Messner and Donald F. Sabo, eds. (Freedom, Calif.: The Crossing Press, 1994). Refer also to Merritt Clifton, "Baseball and American Manhood," 139–53 in *Baseball and the Game of Ideas,* Bjarkman, ed.

25. Nancy Shinabargar, "Sexism and Sport: A Feminist Critique," 44–53 in *Sport,* Gregory Baum and John Coleman, eds. (Edinburg: T. & T. Clark, 1989). Shinabargar, for example, writes that "[s]port as a social institution plays a powerful role in the cultural definition of male and female." Refer also to Mangan and Park, *From "Fair Sex" to Feminism,* who write that "sport has had a large part to play in maintaining and sustaining a patriarchal social order in Western society. To overlook this is to fail to recognize the potent influence of sport not only in terms of class but also of gender" (4).

26. Berlage, *Women in Baseball*, 14.
27. Shinabargar, "Sexism and Sport," 45.
28. Shinabargar, "Sexism and Sport," 47.
29. For a philosophical treatment of this topic, refer to Paul Weiss's "Women Athletes," 286–301 in *Sport and Society: An Anthology*, John T. Talamini and Charles H. Page, eds. (Toronto: Little, Brown & Co., 1973), where he writes: "[w]here a man might be proud of his body, [a woman] is proud in her body" (291).
30. Denise Larner Carmody, "Big-Time Spectator Sports: A Feminist Christian Perspective" in *New Catholic World*, July/August 1986, 177.
31. Carmody, "Big-Time Spectator Sports," 173.
32. Shirl J. Hoffman, "The Sanctification of Sport: Can the Mind of Christ coexist with the killer instinct?" in *Christianity Today*, April 4, 1986: 18.
33. George Gmelch, "Magic in Professional Baseball," 128–37 in *Games, Sport and Power*, Gregory P. Stone, ed. (New Brunswick, N.J.: Rutgers University Press, 1972), 129.
34. Shinabargar, "Sexism and Sport," 47.
35. Carol A. Gilligan, *In a Different Voice: Psychological Theory and Women's Development* (Cambridge, Mass.: Harvard University Press, 1982).
36. Carmody, "Big-Time Spectator Sports," 175.
37. Birrell and Richter, "Is a Diamond Forever? Feminist Transformation of Sport," 221–44 in *Women, Sport and Culture*, Susan Birrell and Cheryl L. Cole, eds. (Windsor, Ont.: Human Kinetics, 1994), 231f.
38. Birrel and Richter, "Is a Diamond Forever?", 235.
39. Charles Schulz, *Classic Peanuts Featuring Good ol' Charlie Brown* (United Feature Syndicate, Inc. 1973). See http://www.snoopy.com.
40. See for example M. Ann Hall, *Feminism and Sporting Bodies: Essays on Theory and Practice* (Champaign, Ill.: Human Kinetics, 1996), 90f.

Chapter 8

1. Peter Golenbock, *Fenway: An Unexpurgated History of the Boston Red Sox* (North Attleborough, Mass.: Covered Bridge Press, 1992), 221.
2. Jules Tygiel, *Baseball's Great Experiment: Jackie Robinson and His Legacy* (New York: Oxford University Press, 1984), 43–45. See Golenbock, 220–23.
3. Al Hirshberg, *What's the Matter with the Red Sox?* (New York: Dodd, Mead & Co., 1973), 145–46.
4. Tygiel, 291.
5. Ibid., 299.
6. See David Halberstam, *October 1964* (New York: Villard Books, 1994).
7. Tygiel, 261–64.
8. Hirshberg, 143, who defends Yawkey and lays the blame elsewhere in the organization, 142–53; See also Tygiel, 331.
9. Golenbock, 227.
10. Tygiel, 330–31.

11. On the timing of Higgins's action, see Hirshberg, 143–44.
12. See Tygiel, 330–32.
13. The statistics are my own, based on contemporary newspaper accounts and box scores. The summary of Green's early career as a Red Sox player is based on the same data. In addition, Golenbock's interview with Green in Golenbock, 226–29, has been helpful in providing Green's personal view of matters.
14. Golenbock, 227.
15. Ibid., 228.
16. See John Updike, "Hub Fans Bid Kid Adieu," in Dan Riley, ed., *The Red Sox Reader* (Boston: Houghton Mifflin Co., 1991), 53–72.
17. See Brendan C. Boyd and Fred C. Harris, *The Great American Baseball Card Flipping, Trading and Bubble Gum Book* (New York: Ticknor & Fields, 1973), 79, and for a fuller account, Golenbock, 255–62.
18. Golenbock, 259.

Conclusion

1. For an account of Games Six and Seven in the 1956 World Series, see Peter Golenbock, *Bums: An Oral History of the Brooklyn Dodgers* (Chicago: Contemporary Books, 2000), 457–62.

Selected Bibliography

Introduction: More than a Game

Ashe, Arthur R. Jr. *A Hard Road to Glory: A History of the African-American Athlete, 1919–1945*. New York: Amistad, 1988.

Barzun, Jacques. *God's Country and Mine: A Declaration of Love Spiced with a Few Harsh Words*. Boston: Little, Brown & Co., 1954.

Fitzgerald, F. Scott. *The Great Gatsby*. New York: Charles Scribner's Sons, 1925.

Part I: Baseball and American Religion

Chapter 1: Baseball as Civil Religion

Alexander, Charles C. *Our Game: An American Baseball History*. New York: Henry Holt, 1991.

Chadwick, Henry. *The Game of Baseball: How to Learn It, How to Play It, and How to Teach It*. New York: George Munro & Co., 1868.

Costas, Bob. *Fair Ball: A Fan's Case for Baseball*. New York: Broadway Books, 2000.

Giamatti, A. Bartlett. *Take Time for Paradise: Americans and Their Games*. New York: Summit Books, 1989.

Goldstein, Warren. *Playing for Keeps: A History of Early Baseball*. Ithaca, N.Y.: Cornell University Press, 1989.

Jones, Donald G. and Russell E. Richey, eds. *American Civil Religion*. New York: Harper & Row, 1974.

Levine, Peter. *A. G. Spalding and the Rise of Baseball*. New York: Oxford University Press, 1985.

Rader, Benjamin G. *Baseball: A History of America's Game*. Urbana and Chicago: University of Illinois Press, 1992.

Spalding, Albert G. *America's National Game: Historical Facts Concerning the Beginning, Evolution, Development and Popularity of Base Ball*. With an Introduction by Benjamin G. Rader. Reprint, Lincoln and London: University of Nebraska Press, 1992.

Ward, John Montgomery. *Base-Ball: How to Become a Player*. Philadelphia: Athletic Publishing Co., 1888.

White, G. Edward. *Creating the National Pastime: Baseball Transforms Itself, 1903–1953*. Princeton, N.J.: Princeton University Press, 1996.

Chapter 2: The Kingdom of Baseball in America

Curtis, Susan. *A Consuming Faith: The Social Gospel and Modern American Culture*. Baltimore: Johns Hopkins University Press, 1991.

Goodwin, Doris Kearns. *Wait Till Next Year*. New York: Simon & Schuster, 1998.

Greenberg, Eric Rolfe. *The Celebrant*. Lincoln: University of Nebraska Press, 1983.

Kinsella, W. P. *Shoeless Joe*. New York: Ballantine Books, 1982.

———. *The Iowa Baseball Confederacy*. New York: Ballantine Books, 1986.

Kuklick, Bruce. *To Everything a Season: Shibe Park and Urban Philadelphia, 1909–1976*. Princeton, N.J.: Princeton University Press, 1991.

Niebuhr, H. Richard. *The Kingdom of God in America*. New York: Harper & Row, 1937.

Riess, Steven A. *Touching Base: Professional Baseball and American Culture in the Progressive Era*. Westport, Conn.: Greenwood Press, 1980.

Ward, Geoffrey C. and Ken Burns. *Baseball: An Illustrated History*. New York: Alfred A. Knopf, 1994.

Part II: Saints and Sinners

Chapter 3: "Matty" and "Ol' Pete"

Crepeau, Richard C. *Baseball: America's Diamond Mind*. Lincoln: University of Nebraska Press, 2000.

Gerrish, B. A. *Saving and Secular Faith: An Invitation to Systematic Theology*. Minneapolis: Fortress Press, 1999.

Honig, Donald. *Baseball America: The Heroes of the Game and the Times of Their Glory*. New York: Galahad Books, 1993.

———. *Baseball When the Grass Was Real: Baseball from the Twenties to the Forties Told By the Men Who Played It*. Reprint, Lincoln: University of Nebraska Press, 1993.

Kavanagh, Jack. *Grover Cleveland Alexander. Baseball Legends*. New York: Chelsea House Publishers, 1990.

———. *Ol' Pete: The Grover Cleveland Alexander Story*. South Bend, Ind.: Diamond Communications, 1996.

Lieb, Fred. *Baseball as I Have Known It*. Reprint, Lincoln: University of Nebraska Press, 1996.

Ritter, Lawrence S. *The Glory of Their Times: The Story of the Early Days of Baseball Told by the Men Who Played It*. Reprint, New York: William Morrow, 1985.

Robinson, Ray. *Matty, An American Hero: Christy Mathewson of the New York Giants*. New York: Oxford University Press, 1993.

Chapter 4: The World of Spirit or the World of Sport?

Adair, William. "Eighty-five as a Lucky Number: A Note on *The Old Man and the Sea*." *Notes on Contemporary Literature* 8.1 (1978): 9.

Baker, Carlos., ed. *Ernest Hemingway: Critique of Four Major Novels*. New York: Scribner's, 1962.

——. *Ernest Hemingway: A Life Story.* New York: Scribner's, 1969.

Broadus, Robert N. "The New Record Set by Hemingway's Old Man." *Notes and Queries* 10 N.S. (April 1963): 152–53.

Cramer, Richard Ben. *Joe DiMaggio: The Hero's Life.* Simon & Schuster, 2000.

Dos Passos, John. *The Best Times.* New York: New American Library, 1966.

Gurko, Leo. "The Heroic Impulse in *The Old Man and the Sea.*" *English Journal* 44 (1955): 377–82.

Halverson, John. "Christian Resonance in *The Old Man and the Sea.*" *English Language Notes* (1964): 50–54.

Hemingway, Ernest. *The Old Man and the Sea.* New York: Scribner's, 1952.

——. "On the Blue Water: A Gulf Stream Letter." Esquire 5 (April 1936): 31, 184–85.

Hinkle, James. "Some Unexpected Sources for *The Sun Also Rises.*" *The Hemingway Review* 2.1 (Fall 1982): 26–42.

Hurley, C. Harold. *Hemingway's Debt to Baseball in* The Old Man and the Sea: *A Collection of Critical Readings.* Lewiston, N.Y.: Edwin Mellen Press, 1992.

Jobes, Katherine T., ed. *Twentieth Century Interpretations of "The Old Man and the Sea": A Collection of Critical Essays.* Englewood Cliffs, N.J.: Prentice-Hall, 1968.

Mansell, Darrel. "When Did Ernest Hemingway Write *The Old Man and the Sea?*" *Fitzgerald/Hemingway Annual* 1974: 311–24.

Reynolds, Michael. "Hemingway as American Icon." In Voss, Frederick, *Picturing Hemingway: A Writer in His Time.* New Haven, Conn.: Yale University Press, 1999.

Rosenfield, Claire. "New World, Old Myths." In Jobes, Katherine T., ed. *Twentieth Century Interpretations of "The Old Man and the Sea": A Collection of Critical Essays,* Englewood Cliffs, N.J.: Prentice-Hall, 1968, 41–55.

Sylvester, Bickford. "The Cuban Context of *The Old Man and the Sea.*" In Donaldson, Scott, ed. *The Cambridge Companion to Ernest Hemingway.* Cambridge: Cambridge University Press, 1996.

Waldmeir, Joseph. "'Confiteor Hominem': Ernest Hemingway's Religion of Man." Papers of the Michigan Academy of Science, Arts, and Letters 42 (1957): 349–56. Reprint in Carlos Baker, ed. *Ernest Hemingway: Critiques of Four Major Novels.* New York: Scribner's, 1962, 144–49.

Young, Philip. *Ernest Hemingway: A Reconsideration.* University Park: Pennsylvania State University Press, 1966.

Chapter 5: From Scapegoat to Icon

Asinof, Eliot. *Eight Men Out: The Black Sox and the 1919 World Series.* New York: Henry Holt, 1963.

Burk, Robert F. *Never Just a Game: Players, Owners & American Baseball to 1920.* Chapel Hill: University of North Carolina Press, 1994.

Burns, Ken. *Baseball: A Film by Ken Burns.* Florentine Films and WETA-TV, 1994.

Camara, Dom Helder. *The Spiral of Violence.* London: Sheed & Ward, 1971.

Frommer, Harvey. *Shoeless Joe and Ragtime Baseball.* Dallas: Taylor Publishing Co., 1992.

Gandil, Arnold "Chick" (as told to Melvin Durslag). "This Is My Story of the Black Sox Series." *Sports Illustrated,* September 7, 1956: 62–68.

Girard, René. *The Girard Reader.* James Williams, ed. New York: Crossroad Herder, 1996.

Gropman, Donald. *Say It Ain't So, Joe! The True Story of Shoeless Joe Jackson.* Revised 2d edition. Secaucus, N.J.: Citadel Press, 1999.

Jackson, Joseph J. (as told to Furman Bisher). "This Is the Truth." *Sport Magazine,* October 1949: 12–14, 83–84.

Luhrs, Victor. *The Great Baseball Mystery: The 1919 World Series.* New York: A. S. Barnes and Co., 1966.

Pietrusza, David. *Judge and Jury: The Life and Times of Kenesaw Mountain Landis.* South Bend, Ind.: Diamond Communications, 1998.

Scott, James C. *Weapons of the Weak: Everyday Forms of Peasant Resistance.* New Haven, Conn.: Yale University Press, 1985.

Seymour, Harold. *Baseball: The Golden Age.* New York: Oxford University Press, 1971.

Voigt, David Q. *American Baseball: From the Commissioners to Continental Expansion.* University Park: Pennsylvania State University Press, 1983.

Part III: Baseball and the Search for "the American Dream"

Chapter 6: Baseball's Surprising Moral Example

Chalberg, John C. *Rickey and Robinson: The Preacher, the Player, and America's Game.* Wheeling: Oxford University Press, 1983.

Falkner, David. *Great Time Coming: The Life of Jackie Robinson from Baseball to Birmingham.* New York: Simon & Schuster, 1995.

Mann, Arthur. *Branch Rickey: American in Action.* Boston: Houghton Mifflin, 1957.

Papini, Giovanni. *Life of Christ,* freely translated from the Italian by Dorothy Canfield Fisher. New York: Harcourt, Brace and Co., 1923.

Robinson, Jackie. *I Never Had It Made: An Autobiography as Told to Alfred Duckett.* Hopewell, N.J.: Ecco Press, 1995.

Stassen, Glen. *Just Peacemaking: Transforming Initiatives for Justice and Peace.* Louisville, Ky.: Westminster/John Knox Press, 1992.

Tygiel, Jules. *Baseball's Great Experiment: Jackie Robinson and His Legacy.* New York: Oxford University Press, 1983.

———., ed. *The Jackie Robinson Reader.* New York: Penguin Books, 1997.

Chapter 7: A Diamond Is Forever?

Berlage, Gai Ingham. *Women in Baseball: The Forgotten History.* Westport, Conn.: Praeger, 1994.

Cohen, Greta L., ed. *Women and Sport: Issues and Controversies.* Newbury Park, Calif.: Sage Publications, 1993.

Gregorich, Barbara. *Women at Play: The Story of Women in Baseball.* San Diego: Harcourt Brace Jovanovich, 1993.

Humbar, William. *Diamonds of the North: A Concise History of Baseball in Canada*. Toronto: Oxford University Press, 1995.

Johnson, Susan E. *When Women Played Hardball*. Seattle: Seal Press, 1994.

Madden, W. C. *The Women of the All-American Girls Professional Baseball League: A Biographical Dictionary*. Jefferson, N.C.: McFarland and Co., 1997.

Shinabargar, Nancy. "Sexism and Sport: A Feminist Critique," 44–53 in *Sport*, Gregory Baum and John Coleman, eds. Edinburg: T. & T. Clark, 1989.

Part IV: The Lure of the Elysian Fields

Chapter 8: The Coming of Elijah

Boyd, Brendan C. and Fred C. Harris. *The Great American Baseball Card Flipping, Trading and Bubble Gum Book*. New York: Ticknor and Fields, 1973.

Golenbock, Peter. *Fenway: An Unexpurgated History of the Boston Red Sox*. New York: G. P. Putnam's Sons, 1992.

Halberstam, David. *October 1964*. New York: Villard Books, 1994.

Hirshberg, Al. *What's the Matter with the Red Sox?* New York: Dodd, Mead & Co., 1973.

Riley, Dan. *The Red Sox Reader*. Boston: Houghton Mifflin Co., 1991.

Tygiel, Jules. *Baseball's Great Experiment: Jackie Robinson and His Legacy*. New York: Oxford University Press, 1983.

Chapter 9: Baseball

Augustine. *The City of God* (Books XIV and XIX).

Creamer, Robert. *Babe*. New York: Penguin Books, 1974.

Duncan, David James. *The Brothers K*. New York: Bantam Books, 1992.

Kahn, Roger. *The Boys of Summer*. New York: Signet Books, 1971.

Milbank, John. *Theology and Social Theory*. Cambridge: Basil Blackwell Ltd., 1990.

Pickstock, Catherine. *After Writing*. Malden, Mass.: Blackwell Publishers, 1998.

Conclusion: The Faith of Fifty Million

Golenbock, Peter. *Bums: An Oral History of the Brooklyn Dodgers*. Chicago: Contemporary Books, 2000.

Contributors

Stanley M. Hauerwas is Gilbert T. Rowe Professor of Theological Ethics, Duke University Divinity School, Durham, North Carolina.

Christopher H. Evans is Associate Professor of Church History at Colgate Rochester Crozer Divinity School, Rochester, New York.

William R. Herzog II is Crozer Professor of New Testament Interpretation at Colgate Rochester Crozer Divinity School, Rochester, New York.

Donald K. McKim is Academic and Reference Editor of Westminster John Knox Press, Louisville, Kentucky.

C. Harold Hurley is Professor of English at Roberts Wesleyan College, Rochester, New York.

Fred Glennon is Professor of Social Ethics in the Department of Religious Studies, Le Moyne College, Syracuse, New York.

Eleanor J. Stebner is Associate Professor of Theology and Church History at the University of Winnipeg, Winnipeg, Manitoba.

Tracy J. Trothen is Assistant Professor of Ethics and Pastoral Theology at the University of Winnipeg, Winnipeg, Manitoba.

Tex Sample is Professor Emeritus of Church and Society at Saint Paul School of Theology, Kansas City, Missouri, and Coordinator of the Network for the Study of U.S. Lifestyles.

Permissions Acknowledgments

Every effort has been made to determine the ownership of all photos. The publisher regrets any error or oversight that may have occurred and will readily make proper acknowledgment in future editions if such omission is made known.

Grateful acknowledgment is made to the National Baseball Hall of Fame Library, Cooperstown, New York, for permission to reprint the following photos:

Photos of Albert Goodwill Spalding, star pitcher for the Boston Red Stockings in the 1870s

Photo of Philadelphia's Shibe Park, opening on April 12, 1909 and photo of outside Shibe Park for the opening game of the World Series on October 9, 1914

Photo of Franklin D. Roosevelt, throwing out the first pitch on opening day

Photos of Christy Mathewson

Photos of Grover Cleveland Alexander

Photos of Joseph Jefferson "Shoeless Joe" Jackson

Photo of Charles "Old Roman" Comiskey

Photo of Joe DiMggio, the "Yankee Clipper"

Photo of Toni Stone

Courtesy of the National Baseball Hall of Fame Library, Cooperstown, New York:

Photo of young women baseball players

Photo of Julie Croteau

Grateful acknowledgment is made to Corbis Images for permission to reprint the following photos:

Photo of Jackie Robinson signing a contract with Branch Rickey
©Corbis

Photo of Elijah "Pumpsie" Green with manager Billy Jurges ©Corbis
Photo of Pumpsie Green sliding into second ©Corbis

Grateful acknowledgment is made to the Library of Congress for permission to reprint the following photos:

Photo of Woodrow Wilson throwing out the first ball on opening day
Photo of Branch Rickey in his office.

Grateful acknowledgment is made to the Associated Press for permission to reprint the following photos:

Photo of Dwight Eisenhower throwing out the first pitch on opening day
Photo of John F. Kennedy throwing out the first pitch on opening day

Permission granted by the All-American Girls' Professional Baseball League (AAGPBL) Players' Association for permission to quote lyric excerpt from the "Victory Song"

Index of Names

Weaver, Buck, 107, 109, 112, 128, 136
Weber, Max, 3
Welter, Barbara, 172
Wertz, Vic, 189, 198, 201
Wesley, John, 150
  and Wesleyan, 149
West, Cornel, 163-164
White, G. Edward, 14-15, 38, 128, 137, 175-176

Will, George, 106
Williams, Claude, "Lefty," 109-110, 112, 115-118, 120-123, 126
Williams, Joe, 132
Williams, Marvin, 195
Williams, Roger, 4
Williams, Ted, 137, 188-191, 200-201, 206, 214
Wilson, Earl, 204

Winchell, Walter, 158
Wolfsheim, Meyer, 1
Woodall, Larry, 196
Wrigley, Philip, K., 174

Yastrzemski, Carl, xii
Yawkey, Tom, 189, 197
Yoder, John Howard, xii
Young, Cy, 51
Young, Philip, 91

Index of Subjects

The Faith of Fifty Million